SHARON & TRACY
& THE REST

SHARON & TRACY & THE REST

The Best of Keith Waterhouse in the *Daily Mail*

Hodder & Stoughton
LONDON SYDNEY AUCKLAND

British Library Cataloguing in Publication Data

Waterhouse, Keith
  Sharon and Tracy and the Rest: Best of
  Keith Waterhouse in the "Daily Mail"
  I. Title
  828.91407

  ISBN 0-340-57065-2

Published by Hodder and Stoughton,
a division of Hodder and Stoughton Ltd,
Mill Road, Dunton Green, Sevenoaks, Kent TN13 2YA.
Editorial Office: 47 Bedford Square, London WC1B 3DP.

Photoset by Rowland Phototypesetting Ltd,
Bury St Edmunds, Suffolk

Printed in Great Britain by Biddles Ltd,
Guildford and King's Lynn

Contents

New columns begin here

Who, me? I'm a columnist, actually. And what do you do? Really? That's fascinating.

It must be very interesting, being a *Daily Mail* reader.

Was it always an ambition of yours, then, or was it something you kind of drifted into?

What – so you just walked into a newsagent's one morning and the whole thing took off from there? That's amazing. So luck was on your side, really. I mean, if they'd chanced to have run out of the *Mail* on that particular day, who knows where you might have finished up? You could have been on the scrapheap at forty, doing *Sun* bingo.

And did you need any special training to become a *Daily Mail* reader or did you just pick it up as you went along?

That's fantastic. You must have a talent for it.

Oh well, if your father's always started the day on Peanuts and Nigel Dempster, that explains it. It runs in the family. It's an inherited gift, like playing the piano.

Even so, it must have been difficult at first. I expect you started with the Quick Crossword and worked your way up to the leader page. No? So you just sort of plunged in. Best way, I suppose, like throwing the kids in at the deep end when they're learning to swim.

You know, I've often toyed with the idea of being a *Daily Mail* reader myself. I think I've got the knack for it. I have a cousin who's one and he says I should definitely take it up.

Is there a course I could go on, do you know? And is it easy to get taken on these days, or do you have to know someone?

Look – I don't suppose you'd like to put a word in for me, would you?

Monday, June 2, 1986

Blackberry special

I t was a sultry late afternoon when British Rail's get-you-there-in-your-own-lifetime Brighton train slumped to a halt at a Beeching-forsaken abandoned station somewhere between East Croydon and Gatwick.

The name of the station was now DO NOT ALIGHT HERE and it had been closed so long that Platform One where we had come to rest was covered in brambles, and tall weeds grew out of the cracked tarmac.

The guard came down the train telling us that there was an embankment fire further down the track and that our guess was as good as his as to when we would start moving again.

The passengers were hot and restless in the August fug and first windows were lowered and then carriage doors were opened to let in what little breeze there was. A woman asked timidly of no one in particular: 'Are we allowed to get out, do you think?'

A man of legal appearance considered the question and said judiciously: 'I should think so, in the circumstances.' One by one, with varying degrees of diffidence, the passengers on the 16.35 from Victoria began to alight at DO NOT ALIGHT HERE. Soon Platform One under its bramble carpet was as busy as it had ever been since the golden age of steam.

The woman who had asked if we were allowed to get out now noticed that the brambles were thick with big fat juicy blackberries, the biggest and fattest and juiciest that anyone can have seen for many a season. She asked: 'Are we allowed to pick the blackberries, do you think?'

'Property of British Rail I imagine, but I don't suppose they'd mind,' counselled the legal brain. The timid one still hesitated, but then she saw that a fellow-passenger had already filled a zip-up make-up bag with enough succulent black-berries to bake a pie. She began picking with a will, and soon there was a whole blackberrying task force at work among the brambles, filling plastic bags, crisp packets, anything to hand.

2

Meanwhile a few young blades had not only alighted at DO NOT ALIGHT HERE but had committed a further breach of the regulations by hopping over a wall and sprinting down to the village store for fizzy drinks. As they returned, about half-a-dozen children aged between three to ten had come on to the platform. Although they were standing among the brambles they showed no interest in the luscious fruit growing at their feet. Instead they stared longingly at the fruity canned drinks the young blades had brought back with them.

Then the mother of one of them said: 'Ooh, look, blackberries!' and stooped to pick a handful. Like pre-war East End urchins who had never seen a cow, the children had probably never seen blackberries growing and they looked down uncomprehendingly. The mother encouraged them to join in. 'Come on, then – just the big black ones, not the red ones and not the green ones.'

First one and then another of the children gingerly plucked a blackberry and then they were all picking away diligently, the occasional yelp betraying the discovery that brambles have thorns and the occasional gasp of pleasure revealing that one or other of them had stumbled upon that abiding gift of serendipity, the clump of ripe and glistening fruit hidden under leaves.

There, on that dusty abandoned railway platform on an unscheduled break in services due to unforeseen conditions, they were learning the art of blackberrying.

Then, after 50 minutes, the red signal turned to green. The timid lady, who had been keeping an anxious eye on it, was the first to see it. 'I think we'd better get back on,' she advised all and sundry.

The blackberry-laden passengers, including several happy tots with purple juice around their mouths, trooped back on the train, resumed their seats and, the summer diversion over, opened their newspapers and magazines and became strangers again. And the Blackberry Special pulled out from DO NOT ALIGHT HERE.

Monday, August 7, 1989

It's your line, Shar & Tray

That delectable duo Sharon and Tracy, as all who have been trying to make business calls during the summer know to their cost, are currently working as switchboard temps.

During a slack period, when only six potential customers at most were trying to get through, and no more than the same number of irate executives were trying to make calls out, the pouting pair's conversation turned to 1992 and the Single Market.

'Did you see where this lady reporter's been ringing up firms speaking in foreign to see if they knew what she was rabbiting on about, and none of them did?' asked Sharon.

'Silly cat,' said Tracy. 'Pity she hasn't nothing better to do. I only wish she'd rung us up – she'd have got a right earful.'

There was an interlude while Sharon dealt with a persistent caller: 'Mr Who? What department's he in? Well if you don't have an extension number I can't help you, can I?' As Sharon pulled the plug on her nuisance call, Tracy continued: 'What was it in aid of, Shar, anyway?'

'Sunnink to do with joining the Common Market, Tray,' hazarded Sharon. 'I only read it over somebody's shoulder in the bus queue style of thing, so I didn't take it all in, but it was sunnink to do with exports and that – how all these Europeans are missing out on buying British goods because they can't speak English.'

'They'll just have to learn, then, won't they?' said Tracy, summarily dealing with three outstanding calls by disconnecting them.

'That's what I say,' Sharon agreed. 'Besides, they can understand it when they want to – because when me and Shane went to Torremolinos two months ago, they could speak even better English nor what we could.'

With mild interest Tracy regarded an urgently blinking light on her switchboard. 'Whoever this is can't have much to do,' she observed. 'He's been trying to get through for a good fifteen minutes.'

'They've no patience, some people,' said Sharon, as Tracy's caller finally gave up the ghost. 'It's a pity that lady reporter couldn't spend a day on a switchboard, putting up with what we've got to put up – then she'd see the other side of the story style of thing.'

'Too right,' said Tracy. 'Like that Sir Somebody ranting and raving just because I accidentally gave him four wrong numbers in a row.'

'You mean the company chairman? He's going to have a heart attack one of these days. I had to keep him waiting yesterday while I was talking to my Mum, and by the time he got through he was in such a state I thought he was a heavy-breather. So of course, I did no more, I cut him off.'

By coincidence, a peremptory buzz indicated that the chairman once again wished to make contact with the outside world. Tracy had responded to the call before realising what she was doing. 'Yes sir? How are you spelling that, sir? I – C – I. What is it, a company? And do you have the number? Hold on then, sir, I'll put you through to Directory Inquiries.'

Meanwhile deep corrugations on Sharon's fair brow indicated that she had been thinking. 'No, only getting back to this Common Market style of thing,' said Sharon. 'If it does come to pass, what will you do if somebody rings up and starts banging on in French?'

A flurry of powder from Tracy's blemishless forehead showed that she too was engaged in the cerebral process, while the lights on her switchboard continued to twinkle like the fairy lights on a Christmas tree.

'It couldn't happen,' announced Tracy at last.

'How do you mean, it couldn't happen?'

'Well, I mean to say, I wouldn't know whether they was speaking French, Italian or Double Dutch, now would I? So before I knew they was speaking French, they'd have to tell me in English what language it was. So if they can speak English, no problem.'

'I bet that lady reporter never thought of that,' said Sharon.

'Silly cat,' said Tracy again. As if selecting the winner in a raffle, she attended to one of her waiting calls at random.

'Yes, can I help yooooou? Sorreee, I'm afraid he's dead at the moment . . .'

Thursday, July 28, 1988

Off with the show

Clogthorpe District Council's Parks, Recreation Grounds and Amenities Committee, under the chairmanship of Cllr Enoch Bulge, yesterday considered the question of inviting superstar musician Jean-Michel Jarre's two-hour laser and fireworks extravaganza to the town's Nelson Mandela Leisure Centre.

Explaining the situation, Cllr Bulge said the show had been booked to be put on in Newham, down in London, but the council had given backword. There had been fears of a safety hazard, also that it would create traffic congestion and frighten the horses. The entertainment was now up for grabs and feelers had been put out in the direction of Clogthorpe.

Cllr Parkin asked if this Mr Jarre was foreign in any way.

Cllr Bulge said he was believed to be French, but looking at it in the context of 1992 and the Single Market when Clogthorpe tomato sausages would be freely available in Paris and frogs' legs in Clogthorpe covered market, the committee should not hold that against him.

Remarking that he would not be seen dead eating frogs' legs, Cllr Hopcraft asked if this Jarre chap had ever been to South Africa.

Cllr Bulge said that could be checked up on when the appli-

6

cation was lodged. Mr Jarre would be made fully cognisant with council policy appertaining to South Africa. It would also be made plain that Clogthorpe was a nuclear-free zone and an equal opportunities employer, and that smoking was not allowed anywhere in the leisure centre complex.

Cllr Nepworth asked what guarantee was there that this so-called extravaganza would appeal to the people of Clogthorpe. That time the Pontefract Girls' Accordion Band had come to the town, the leisure centre had been half-empty.

Cllr Bulge said that all he could say was that when Mr Jarre had put on his show in Houston or wherever it was, down in Texas, it had attracted an audience of a million-and-a-half.

Cllr Tweedyman said that by the left, they would never get that number of people into the hall.

Commenting that some mothers did have them, Cllr Bulge pointed out that the show was an open-air do. The leisure centre would be pressed into service only for its bogs and changing facilities, and for bouncing images off its walls.

Cllr Parkin asked what images.

Cllr Bulge said how the thump did he know what images. He had not seen a programme. However, it must be summat worth watching to attract a million-and-a-half folk.

Cllr Parkin asked what if it rained.

Cllr Bulge retorted that they'd all get bloody wet, then, wouldn't they?

Cllr Hopcraft stated that a million-and-a-half people milling around the town centre would present certain problems. Extra buses would have to be laid on. The St John Ambulance Brigade would have to stand by. It was to be doubted whether the shopping precinct car stack amenity would be able to cope.

Cllr Tweedyman said and another thing, there was the hooligan element to be considered. There was a risk of beer cans being chucked about. The occasion would be a bonanza for pick-pockets. Women and kiddies might get their feet trampled on. There would be insufficient toilet facilities. This Mr Jarre might not turn up. All manner of things might go wrong.

Cllr Bulge said that while he understood the need for caution, he would ask his colleagues if they were not being a bit pessimistic. Looking on the other side of the coin, the show

7

would be a feather in Clogthorpe's cap. It would be summat new for the town. It would be summat different.

Cllr Parkin said that in that case he had no hesitation in declaring it should be banned.

The motion, that this committee do tell Mr Jarre where he can put his laser beams, was carried unanimously.

Thursday, September 15, 1988

Apostrophe Apocalypse

L adies and gentlemen, welcome to the first working breakfast of the Association for the Annihilation of the Aberrant Apostrophe – the AAAA as it is known to our myriad town and country members – to be held in its commodious new headquarters here at Carmelite House.

As Life President of the Association, I should like to extend an especially cordial welcome to the many new faces I can see from the platform. Since not a few of them are looking distinctly puzzled – perhaps some of our friends strayed accidentally into the meeting in search of the stock exchange prices or television listings – I will explain the aims and objects of the AAAA.

The AAAA has two simple goals. Its first is to round up and confiscate superfluous apostrophes – from, for example, fruit and vegetable stalls where potato's, tomato's and apple's are openly on sale.

Its second is to redistribute as many as possible of these impounded apostrophes, restoring missing apostrophes where they have been lost, mislaid or deliberately hijacked – as for instance by British Rail, which as part of its refurbishment programme is dismantling the apostrophes from such stations as King's Cross and shunting them off at dead of night to a secret apostrophe siding at Crewe.

Ladies and gentlemen, examples of the misuse of apostrophes abound. In the AAAA's Black Apostrophe Museum in the basement, which you are welcome to visit (no children or persons of nervous disposition, please), you will find an advertisement from the *Guardian* for Technical Author's; a circular from the National Council for the Training of Journalists, if you please, containing the phrase 'as some editor's will know'; an announcement from Austin Rover about the new Maestro's; a leaflet from Hereford and Worcester County Council called 'How the Council Spends It's Money'; and many other apostrophic atrocities too gruesome to describe while you are eating your Danish pastries.

How has this pestilence come about? The AAAA's laboratories have identified it as a virus, probably introduced into the country in a bunch of bananas and spread initially by greengrocers, or greengrocer's as they usually style themselves.

Apostrophe Interpolation, Displacement and Suppression – AID'S, as the affliction is known – recognises no frontiers. It afflicts the highest and the lowest of the land alike, the educated along with the sub-literate. *The Times* (shortly to be renamed *The Times's*) as well as the *Sun*. Why, even the *Daily M**l* itself, it has to be confessed between those four walls, is not immune. I hold in my hand a misprinting of who's for whose which was detected in its pages only a short while ago.

Ladies and gentlemen, when we find ourselves in a world where a newsagent's placard can read GLENY'S KINNOCK LEAD'S TEACHERS STRIKE, the Apocalypse is near and something must be done.

Apostrophic anarchists, deliberately disrupting the apostrophe's function as part of their wider plan to destroy English grammar, must be weeded out root and branch. Innocent misusers of the apostrophe – for instance the Darlington bus company promising Shopping Trips to Leed's – must be hustled off to night-school in plain vans for a crash-course in punctuation. If necessary, children must be stopped outside the classroom and frisked for aberrant apostrophes, and the pushers identified.

But what can we, as individuals, do to stop the rot, bearing in mind that your Association will have no truck with the proscribed militant Apostrophe Abolition Army, whose declared aim is to stamp out the now universal use of 'it's' for the possessive 'its' by blowing up offending printing-plants?

What we can do, ladies and gentlemen, is to be vigilant and relentless in our pursuit of the aberrant apostrophe.

We must write to each and every publication that transgresses in this respect. When they write back pleading that it was a regrettable printers error, we must reply by return of post that no it wasn't, it was a regrettable printer's error, or even more accurately, the error of a regrettable printer. We must boycott shops selling Co's lettuce, bean's, and suchlike contaminated produce.

Members of the AAAA are invited to forward examples of misplaced apostrophes to the Association for possible use in our touring exhibitions, provided that these do not infringe the Post Office regulations on the sending of obnoxious matter through the mails.

The AAAA regrets that its hard-working staff will be unable to acknowledge contributions individually but assures members that every apostrophe submitted will be scrutinised keenly and considered on its demerits.

The AAAA has no membership cards and no subscription. Members are, however, asked to donate at least one aberrant apostrophe when attending our meetings, rallies and conferences.

I have to point out that we are considerably overstocked on their's, it's and who's, and can consider no further examples until those we have accumulated have been ploughed into the Association's apostrophe dump at Devizes.

You are now asked to place the aberrant apostrophes you have brought with you in the offertory bags being passed among you by the ushers. During the collection we will all rise and sing the AAAA's battle anthem, 'Sister Susie's Sewing

Shirts For Soldiers.' Anyone singing a misplaced apostrophe will be instantly ejected from the hall.

Monday, June 30, 1986

Egg on their faces

The good news is that when trains start running through the Channel Tunnel, and assuming that the restaurant-car isn't closed owing to operational difficulties (ie, the staff haven't turned up), you will be able to while away the journey with the Great British Breakfast.

British Rail have done battle with the French and the Belgians – foreigners of the worst sort, the kind who would put a stopper on oak-smoked salmon as soon as look at you – and wrung the concession out of them. Earlybird cross-Channel passengers will not, after all, be confined to a croissant and a bit of cake dipped in hot chocolate.

Why BR should have to go peaked-cap-in-hand to their confrères in Paris and Brussels to establish what British travellers are to be allowed for breakfast on their own trains is not explained. No matter: let us proceed.

The bad news, the extraordinary news, the almost unbelievable news, is that the Great British Breakfast will consist of (a) sausage, (b) bacon, (c) tomatoes and (d) mushrooms. Name the missing ingredient. You are right. There is no fried egg.

No fried egg! A cooked breakfast without fried egg is like afternoon tea without thinly-sliced cucumber sandwiches or Sunday dinner without the Yorkshire pudding. But there we

11

are – British Rail have blown it again. No fried egg. The Channel Tunnel trains, we are told, will not be equipped with the hot plates needed to mass-produce them.

It is incredible, is it not? We scrape together a sum equivalent to the gross national product of Kuwait to finance this great lark of driving a tunnel under the sea from Folkestone to France. We develop giant boring machines, 500-tonne mechanical moles with a maximum speed of 0.003mph and the capacity to swallow and regurgitate a semi-detached house. We recruit teams of geologists, squads of engineers, an army of construction workers. The railways draw up a plan to spend £500 million on new high-speed trains. We propose, in the process, to dig up half of Kent. The dream has been 20 years in the making and in all this time it has occurred to no one to ask how they are going to fry the bloody eggs.

Didn't anyone think? Didn't British Rail consult its brother-in-law Arnold in the matter? How on earth could they embark on so mighty an adventure without having solved this simplest of technological problems? And what kind of super system is it anyway – the railway equivalent of Concorde, we were led to believe – that cannot produce a fried egg?

For heaven's sake, fried eggs have been served on trains for as long as trains have been serving breakfast. Before, even. The firemen on the original Stockton and Darlington Railway are on record as frying eggs on their shovels.

There must now be a full-scale inquiry, presided over by a High Court judge, into why the rolling stock of the future will lack the capacity for egg-frying, why technology in this regard seems to have taken a giant step backwards since the days when the Flying Scotsman used to thunder northwards to the sound of cracking eggshells and the sizzle of the frying-pan. There must be recommendations: all Chunnel trains to be recalled and refitted with hot plates capable of handling a complete British breakfast and not a British breakfast with its key component missing. And heads must roll.

No fried egg, indeed! I have heard nothing like it since they knocked off the kippers on the Brighton Belle.

Thursday, July 11, 1991

12

A children's garden

The saffron crocus: pink lily of the valley. Variegated asparagus. Clematis and columbine, bell-flowers, wall-flowers, peonies, pansies and primrose, and sweet violets. Let us sing of them, but in muted tones, for they wilt in the shadow of the Grim Reaper.

Hundreds of garden plants face extinction. Some, like old varieties of cottage tulips and tea-roses, are gone forever. Other varieties, once as common as buttercups, are now as rare as four-leafed clover. Conservationists have drawn up a black-bordered catalogue of familiar flowers threatened with oblivion.

They are falling prey to the decline of the large private garden, the closure of many old-fashioned nurseries of the rambling, pottering kind where there was always a cat asleep on a sack of John Innes No 1, and to the commercial plant-growers concentrating on the easy-to-grow, sell-like-hot-carnations horticultural equivalent of sliced bread.

While I am no gardening columnist, I would suggest that there may be yet another contributory factor. On a recent visit to the street where I grew up I noticed that a particular strain of the iris which once flourished there has now all but vanished. I am not sure of its Latin name but I believe it is what botanists would call council house purple. When the irises were in bloom, our street's back gardens rivalled the tulip fields of Holland for spectacular colour.

Old bicycle wheels and rotting cardboard boxes grow there now. The back gardens, for the most part, are hip-high in weeds and the front gardens are concreted over for carports. Saddest of all, the children's gardens where *iris domicilum senatum* blossomed in all its garish purple glory, are all gone.

Let me tell you about this institution of the children's garden. Our council estate, the oldest in the city, was laid out on the principle of garden city pioneer Ebenezer Howard – namely, that if you build your houses in the ratio of twelve to the acre you will fool townsfolk into believing they are living in the country, not to mention ensuring that if they are handy with a spade they will never have to buy another potato.

The enormous tracts of garden thus created being far beyond the capacity of most individual householders to husband, there grew up a tradition of fathers parcelling out bits of garden for their offspring to tend, rather as feudal barons would allow their serfs a strip of land to grow lentils for their soup.

These gardens within a garden, usually separated from the parent plot by a border of half-bricks, were put to a variety of uses. Some children cultivated flowers, others cultivated rabbits. Some developed pocket-handkerchief kitchen gardens, growing the ingredients for Sunday tea from seeds. The lad next door, affecting indifference towards his allotted patch, was secretly growing deadly nightshade. He was seen watering it under cover of dusk.

The Waterhouse estates were so vast that they could effortlessly accommodate children's gardens measuring about ten feet by six for the whole brood of us, five in number, and still have a rolling acre to spare for the ubiquitous iris, a display of lupins, and enough rhubarb to feed a constipated army. For one no higher than a Michaelmas daisy, I perhaps initially overstretched myself when formally endowed with my own garden. Eschewing the conservative efforts of my brothers and sister who planted nothing more challenging than lettuce, spring onions and pansies, I determined to raise a bijou prairie of wheat from cuttings obtained from a nearby field. The crop failure was total.

Next, inspired by a floral clock which had fascinated me in a municipal park, I embarked upon constructing one of my own, using an old alarm clock with two tulips secured to the hands with rubber bands. Embedding this in the earth in a surrounding circle of assorted seeds with sunken potted-meat jars of dandelions marking out the hours, I awaited results.

I had reckoned without having to dig up the clock again to wind it up. Soil got into the works and it stopped. Both the big hand and the little hand lost their petals. The dandelions wilted. The seeds did not come up. Experiment not an unqualified success.

Of my proposal to cover the entire surface of my children's garden with bluebells, snowdrops and poppies in the form of a Union Jack I shall say nothing, except that it looked good on the crayoned blueprint and how was I to know that the flags of St George, St Andrew and St Patrick did not all flower at the same time?

As my green fingers grew, so I became more orthodox and settled for the street's standard arrangement of a lozenge-shaped flower bed enclosed in a mini-lawn of grass sods curling at the edges like railway sandwiches. I surveyed my little principality daily, as did everyone else, except the deadly nightshade fanatic who surveyed his nightly. Gardening was a highly satisfactory pursuit and if you got bored with weeding you could always try your hand at digging your way to Australia.

Well now, I don't suppose we did much to preserve the saffron crocus from extinction but we did feed and water and watch over our crop of hardy Woolworth seed packets, and there must have been many a clump of irises and host of daffodils, not to mention a nest of deadly nightshade, that was grateful for our attention.

Who knows – had more children's gardens survived, perhaps fewer garden flowers would be in danger.

Monday, August 25, 1986

As whine wheezes go

There's an idea born every minute. Here's one that's lately flashed into the corporate mind of the TUC: High Street centres where the public can go to complain about State-owned enterprises such as the Post Office, the railways, and the gas and electricity boards.

These grievance parlours would be part of an 'aggressive public relations campaign' which the TUC bosses want to launch to convince us all that nationalisation is better than privatisation.

A good wheeze as wheezes go, the only snag being that the place where you go to whinge and whine about the sloth and ineptitude of State-run bodies would itself be State-run. You can imagine the scene.

'Next.'

'Good morning. I'd like to complain about a very rude ticket-collector on the 4.55 from . . .'

'Can't you read?'

'Pardon?'

'There's a notice up there informing complainants quite plainly that owing to staff shortages and refusal by management to negotiate on manning levels, transport complaints cannot be dealt with after 11 a.m.'

'But it's only just turned half past ten.'

'Don't take it up with me, take it up with head office. The agreed procedure lays it down that fifteen minutes must be allowed for registering each complaint, so that takes us to past 10.45 which happens to be the start of my tea-break. Next.'

'Wait a minute – if I can't make a complaint about the railways, will you allow me to make one against the gas board?'

'Name?'

'My name's Smith.'

'Not your name, squire – the name of the gas board official.'

'I don't know – he never turned up. That's what I want to complain about.'

'Had the gas board given you a specific time?'

'Yes. July.'

'You've got this in writing, have you?'

'No, this was on the phone.'

'So it's your word against theirs. How do I know this isn't a malicious complaint? We get a lot of your sort around here, you know.'

'How do you mean, my sort?'

'People with a chip on their shoulder, coming in here moaning and groaning about hard-working, underpaid employees of the nationalised industries. Next.'

'Hang on – I've got one more complaint.'

'All right, sunshine, who is it this time? If it's the Post Office, you'll have to join the queue at the next counter.'

'It's not the Post Office, it's this office. It's you.'

'What is the nature of your complaint?'

'Rudeness, unhelpfulness and obstructiveness.'

'Name?'

'I've already told you my name – Smith.'

'Not your name – my name.'

'How the hell do I know your name?'

'Would you mind not cursing and swearing? If you can't furnish the name of the person complained against, I'm afraid I'm unable to process your complaint.'

'All right then, tell me your name.'

'For security reasons, staff are not allowed to divulge personal details. Next.'

Thursday, August 14, 1986

Case for the Eurocrisp

Proceedings of the European Community Regulatory Body on artificial colouring and sweetening agents in foodstuffs. Three hundred and nineteenth day.

Mr Bratwurst (Germany) said let him see now. The commission had stipulated that Yorkshire hotpot and Lancashire pudding must take their brand names from the place of origin.

What else could it do to make life difficult for food manufacturers?

Mr Mortadella (Italy) said how about having a go at potato crisps? The one thing he could not stand about potato crisps was that you opened a bag of them and they were all in different shapes, like snowflakes. It really got up his nostrils.

Mr Fruitcake (UK) said the Italian delegate was being unfair. You could get square potato crisps these days.

Mr Bratwurst said right, the commission would issue a directive that all potato crisps had to be square. But as well as coming in different shapes they came in different flavours. What was the thinking behind some of them tasting of prawn and others of crispy bacon or barbecued beef? It did not make sense.

Mr Pommefrite (France) said the commission had not heard the half of it. Not only were some crisps vinegar flavoured, but the vinegar employed was malt vinegar and not wine vinegar.

Mr Taramasalata (Greece) said he was under the impression that the commission had outlawed malt vinegar.

Mr Bratwurst said only on fish and chips.

Mr Mortadella said he was under the impression that the commission had outlawed fish and chips.

Mr Fruitcake said that the British public would never stand for its fish and chips being regulated from Brussels. The British public would only stand for its fish and chips being partially regulated from Brussels. It would agree to the standardisation of chip size, the harmonisation of cooking fats, and the gradual phasing out of white fish, and that was as far as it would go. He was fairly firm on that point.

Mr Waffle (Belgium) said he would tell the commission what had always puzzled him and that was British seaside rock. Some of it had Blackpool stamped all the way through it and some of it had Brighton all the way through. Some of it was pink and some of it was yellow. It was a complete shambles.

Mr Bratwurst said that the commission would be turning its attention to seaside rock just as soon as it had settled the hash of the peppermint humbug manufacturers. Peppermint humbugs were being turned out with stripes of varying widths. It was not good enough.

Mr Tapas (Spain) said talking of sub-standard striping, what about striped toothpaste?

Mr Fruitcake said surely striped toothpaste was not a food.

Mr Tapas said it was if you ate it. Let the toothpaste barons get away with it and the next thing you knew they would be producing tomato ketchup-flavoured toothpaste.

Mr Bratwurst said in a pig's eye they would. Had not Mr Tapas forgotten the commission's recent directive putting a complete ban on anything flavoured with tomato, including ketchup?

Mr Fruitcake asked what Mr Bratwurst had got against tomatoes.

Mr Bratwurst said he had once been hit in the eye with one during an election campaign. But look at the time. It was nearly the lunch-hour and speaking personally he could murder a lobster thermidor. He would tell the commission what it could do. It could ban one more food item and then he would call it a day.

Mr Mortadella said all right then, how about stopping the Brits from putting mincemeat labels on jars which had no meat content whatever?

Mr Pommefrite said why not a ban on Pontefract cakes? Even if it could be proved that they came from Pontefract, they were certainly not cakes and the practice of calling them such should be stopped off.

Mr Bratwurst said they would toss up for it. Heads they would ban mincemeat and tails they would ban Pontefract cakes.

The Ecu having come down heads, the commission framed a directive that mincemeat should henceforth be called suet with added raisins, sultanas and chopped orange peel, and adjourned for lunch.

Thursday, May 2, 1991

Unbrick the Bricklayers

Ordering the brewers to sell their pubs is like ordering the banks to give away their money at street corners. While they will make billions on the dissolution of the Dog and Pullet – that, after all, is what being a brewer is all about – the break-up will not come easily to a trade used to owning everything in sight.

(I thought that's how we came by the phrase 'lock, stock and barrel', but it turns out to mean the lock, stock and barrel of a gun. Not a lot of people know that.)

I admire the breathtaking impudence of the Brewers' Society spokesman who said: 'Cutting the tied house system will be a leap in the dark and we believe it means the death knell for the traditional British pub.' This is on a level with a spokesman for Sainsbury's saying: 'Forcing us to sell our supermarkets will mean the end of the corner shop as we know it.'

But if it does not sound a death knell the Monopolies and Mergers Commission report cannot be said to ring joybells for the traditional British pub, and that is because it lacks a vital recommendation – namely, that every pub released from the maw of the mighty beer barons should be compelled to restore its bricked-up corner doorway.

It is not watering the workers' beer that the brewers will be accused of when they answer in heaven for their sins. The charges, of course, will be numerous: of converting the Ratcatchers' Arms into a 'theme pub' resembling the promenade deck of the QEII; of conspiring with the Crosseyed Ferret to introduce a Happy Hour complete with reggae tapes at 120 decibels; of aiding and abetting the Jolly Rivetters in the sale of hamburgers and fried onions.

But above all they will stand arraigned on the misfeasance of knowingly and wilfully bricking up the corner doorway of the Limping Cockroach. This will be a specimen charge: 15,698 similar offences will be taken into consideration when sentence of being dangled headfirst in a keg of their own lager is passed.

We all know what is physically behind that bricked-up doorway: it is the blasted space invaders game or the blasted electronic fruit machine or the blasted video juke box. But behind it, psychologically, is an attitude. When Bumpkin's Brewery or the landlord of the Snivelling Coalman bricks up that corner doorway he is making an announcement that could not be clearer if he spelled it out in neon (which, incidentally, he is quite capable of doing).

This is to the effect that the customer can go and hang himself. In future the whole point and purpose of the pub will not be merely to make a decent profit (which is reasonable enough), but to screw every last penny out of the dispensation to sell ales, porter and spirits on the premises.

If there is money in noise, then there will be noise. If there is money in discomfort, then there will be discomfort. If there is money in purple strobe lights, then purple strobe lights there will be. If there is money in stinking the place out with the smell of hot dogs, then switch on the microwave. If there is money in clearing out the regulars because they spend the evening nursing a pint and taking up valuable space, then good riddance to 'em.

It may be, of course, that I am making a cruel misjudgment about the brewing interests and that they are motivated not by greed but by madness. There is a strong case for believing that all concerned with pubs are collectively insane. Just as the Romans are supposed to have gone mad from drinking water drawn through lead pipes, so brewers, publicans and, indeed, many of their customers may prove to be not quite twelve pence to the shilling as a result of drinking lager out of cans.

Why else, come to think of it, would the brewers gut a genuine Victorian pub and refurbish it as a mock Edwardian pub? Why else would they get rid of marble and iron tables designed to last another century and replace them with rickety plastic ones designed to last six months? Why else, indeed, would they make the expensive mistake of disguising their pubs as galleons or medieval castles and then have to spend even more money making them look like pubs again? People have been taken away by men in white coats for less.

It may be that Brewers' Madness, like Hatters' Madness, is terminal and that, with a little help from the Monopolies and Mergers Commission there will emerge a new generation of sane, intelligent, competent and unavaricious brewers who will run pubs as pubs and not as licensed amusement arcades. It will be a hard life for them, down to their last 2,000 tied houses apiece, but I can promise them at least one new customer if they make a start by unbricking the corner doorway of the Bricklayers Arms.

Thursday, March 23, 1989

Shar & Tray & Charlotte

Despite the clamour of would-be customers on the first day of the sales, Perfumes and Toiletries was an oasis of calm, thanks to Sharon's and Tracy's knack of keeping their big blue eyes fixed on the middle distance.

The topic of conversation was names. Sharon was cock-a-hoop to discover that the top first name for daughters of top people was Charlotte.

''Cos don't you see, Tray?' crowed Sharon. 'It means that everyone what's christened Charlotte's got to be called Shar, same as me!'

'Fancee!' cried Tracy enviously. 'Does it say anyfink about Tray being a poplar name?'

Sharon consulted the list. 'Sorree! The next most poplar girl's name's Sophie.'

'Sofe,' corrected Tracy.

'Then there's Lucy, Emily, Alexandra, Alice and Emma.'

Tracy translated. 'That's Luce, Em, Alley, another Alley and another Em.'

'Pretty names, ain't they, Tray?' sighed Sharon.

'Lovelee. What about blokes' names? I bet Wayne and Shane's in the first ten, ain't they?'

''Fraid not,' said Sharon, frowning in concentration as she ran down the list of top boys' first names. 'The winner is James, apparentlee.'

'That's a funny name for a boy,' giggled Tracy. 'Still, I spose everyone'll call him Robbo.'

'Robbo?' echoed Sharon, baffled even more than usual when discussing the intelligence of the day with Tracy. 'Why should he be called Robbo?'

'That's if his second name's Robinson,' explained Tracy. 'I mean you can't go round calling a bloke James, can you? Everyone'd think he was a wally.'

Sharon was still puzzled. 'What if his second name's Smiff?'

'Then he'd be called Smiffy, wouldn't he? And if his second name's Thompson he'll be called Tommo.'

'That's the second name on the list,' Sharon pointed out.

'What – Thompson? That's not a first name, Shar.'

'Not Thompson, sillee. Thomas.'

'Oh I see,' said Tracy. 'Tommo. What other names have they got?'

'Alexander, William, Oliver, Charles and Edward comes next.'

'Al, Wills, Olly, Chas and Eddy,' construed Tracy.

'Do you know what I fink the top boys' name should be, if it was left to me?' said Sharon, popping a post-Christmas chocolate into her rosebud mouth. 'Gazza.'

'Yeh, but that's not a first name, is it?' Tracy pointed out. 'I mean to say, when he got christened the vicar didn't say, "I name this nipper Gazza", did he?'

'He'd of got a right moufful if he had,' said Sharon. 'But you know what I mean, Tray – no one gets called by the names they was christened with no more, do they? I mean to say, look at Paul McCartney. Everyone used to call him Paul but these days you've got to call him Macca.'

'I wonder why?' mused Tracy.

''Cos it's shorter.'

A twitching of crimson fingernails indicated that Tracy was doing some mental arithmetic. After a while she objected, 'No it ain't.'

'It is if you say it quick,' said Sharon.

'So what's the next name on the list?' asked Tracy, conceding defeat.

'George.'

Tracy thought for a moment and translated. 'Besty.'

Thursday, January 3, 1991

Think of a number . . .

The National Union Of Statistics Massagers, Fact Benders And Graph Manipulators has called a 23.9-hour strike in protest against the amount of overtime demanded of its members by the Department Of Guesswork.

Union officials claim that average adjusters and percentage inflaters at Guesswork House are having to work up to three times more overtime than at any period since the invention of passive smoking, when they had to slave round the clock to churn out dubious statistics for the Health Education Authority.

A convener said: 'It is flipping ridiculous. The lads are 29 per cent more whacked than at any time since records began. It is ruining our home life, putting eight out of ten marriages at risk. Take me, for instance – I have 2.7 kids at home but I never get to see them. As for the physical side of my marriage, the wife is complaining that it is up to 50 per cent under the national average.'

The crisis arises from a twin rush demand by Health Secretary William Waldegrave and Shadow Health Minister Robin Cook for alarming figures to back up their respective 'healthier Britain' programmes. A workforce already overstretched by the constant need for more and more horrendous statistics on AIDS, alcohol-related road deaths, rabies, smoke-induced lung diseases, the disturbingly high ratio of prospective heirs to the throne now being swiped with golf clubs, and the likelihood that two million pit bull terriers will be roaming the country by the year 2000 unless something is done about it, found itself unable to cope.

A spokesman for the Department of Guesswork said: 'We have every sympathy with the men. The demands put on them by Government and Opposition alike have become intolerable in recent years. At one time we only had to find statistics for things that had already happened – births and deaths, road accidents, rainfall, that sort of thing. But nowadays 89.45 per cent of our work consists of looking into the future and projecting and extrapolating the worst that can happen if new laws are not passed or there is a failure to provide 74.5 per cent more resources.

'Take yesterday, for instance. The Home Secretary waltzes in without so much as a by-your-leave and says: "All right, stop whatever you're doing and tell me how many lives it will save if we make all back-seat passengers wear safety belts". He seems to think we can pluck figures like that out of thin air. Well, we do actually, but it's very hard work, and you've got to check, check, check, to make sure that you're not claiming to save more lives than were actually being lost in the first place. Statistics show that we now make 27 per cent fewer mistakes of this sort than formerly, but the strain on the workforce is enormous.'

The union convener confirmed this, adding: 'It is too flipping much of a good thing. The general public doesn't realise that it takes an average of fourteen man-hours just to make a simple prediction such as how many are going to die of AIDS by next Tuesday if present trends continue. We had a bloke working on that yesterday and he came up with the answer 23,614,948. He was just 97.5 per cent knackered, poor devil – he'd added in the population of Yugoslavia by mistake. I kid you not, the pace is killing. We have 2,000 men off sick with stress-related illnesses.'

Two thousand? Surely not.

'Well, eleven, if you want to quibble. But if we weren't kept 500 per cent understaffed, and reported cases continued to rise at only 20 percentage points above present averages, stress-related absenteeism would be approaching the 2,000-mark by the end of the next century.'

The Department Of Guesswork's last statistic before yesterday's shutdown was an estimate that a bomb hoaxer's telephone call had 'cost' £25million. The figure bears a remarkable resemblance to the population of Canada.

Thursday, June 6, 1991

The Mee generations

When I was a child, I spake as a child, I understood as a child, I thought as a child: but when I became a man, I put away childish things – including, clot that I was, my ten-volume set of Arthur Mee's *Children's Encyclopedia*.

I don't know how many of you remember this golden treasury of all the knowledge in the world with its colour plates of snakes and butterflies and airships and man-eating tigers and the seven wonders of the world and the flags of all nations. At one time it was to be found in every school and every public library, as well as in hundreds of thousands of ordinary homes.

My own set, much read and much cherished, was acquired for a few bob from a secondhand bookshop. Alas, when I reached man's estate, or at any rate when I started shaving twice a week, I let it go for even fewer bob, to raise capital for my new obsession of taking girls to the pictures.

All that was a very long time ago and I now have more reference works in my shelves than the British Library; but I guess I must have been muttering the name of Arthur Mee in my sleep, for what should be in my Christmas stocking this year – what, indeed, should be my star present – but a battered old edition, all 7,340 pages of it, of Mr Mee's *Enquire Within* about cannibals, battleships, brontosauruses, poisonous spiders and the secrets of the Pyramids?

It is everything I remember it to be, from the story of the Willow-pattern Plate and the colour cross-section of a volcano in volume one to the potted version of the *Pilgrim's Progress* and *350 Abbreviations In Everyday Use* (I had forgotten that DLO stands for Dead Letter Office, which I always imagined as a Gothic crypt in the bowels of Postal HQ at St Martin's-le-Grand) in volume ten.

There had been children's encyclopedias before Arthur Mee's masterwork and there have been children's encyclopedias since – indeed, I am told that a hefty addition to the genre has just been published. But there had never been and has never been and never will be anything remotely like the ten-volume cornucopia that now adorns my shelves – or that will adorn my shelves once I can tear myself away from the engrossing story of *The Plants That Clothe Us* with especial reference to *The Little Insect That Changed the Face of the Cotton World*.

Nowhere else will you find the rules of rounders cheek by jowl with the life of Isaac Newton, tricks with matches next to an account of what you might expect to find at the North Pole (and the South Pole too, for that matter), instructions for making a Foucault's Pendulum and directions on how you can watch the Unfolding of Life in an ordinary jam-jar wedged in with *The Story of the Boundless Universe and All Its Wondrous Worlds* and *Imperishable Thoughts of Men Enshrined in the Books of the World*.

Not so much an encyclopedia, more a jumble sale of knowledge, with poems and legends and picture puzzles and handy hints and experiments in chemistry (To make chalk, find a piece of glass tubing and some lime water . . . To make lime water, see p. 6,424) all bundled together with history and geography and geology and zoology and all the other ologies in a series of bumper fun books. You will have gathered that the arrangement is not alphabetical. In the wise words of its editor, who should be required reading in today's teacher training colleges: 'The alphabet is for those who know; the *Children's Encyclopedia* is for those who do not know.'

Arthur Mee, who also founded the legendary *Children's Newspaper* (and incidentally was, for a time, literary editor of the *Daily Mail*) was a self-educated man who left school at fourteen and had the knack of writing in the plain doorstep English of the people. An even greater talent was that he understood the minds of children. When his encyclopedia first began to appear in fifty fortnightly parts in Edwardian times, it was an instant sensation. He enchanted a whole generation – and went on to enchant their children and their children's children.

One of the features which gave the work its vast popularity was a section in each part called Wonder, which set out to give 'Plain Answers to the Questions of the Children of the World'. It reveals Mee's genius at winkling out the things children want to know as distinct from what we think they ought to know. What is smoke made of? Why are negroes black? Why does the sun fade carpets and not flowers? Where does the wind go when it doesn't blow? Why can we see ourselves in a mirror? Is it true that people rise three times to the surface before they drown? What makes us hungry? Why is it the sea never gets any bigger? What makes water gurgle when it comes out of a bottle?

Alas, I have no space for the Plain Answers to these fascinating questions, although I think that the chore of working them out could well have provided a short sharp answer to the question Why does hair turn grey? Indeed, I have room left only for Arthur Mee's moving words at the conclusion of his monumental opus:

'. . . Yet with a book as with a friend, it is surely not the

28

sadness of farewell, for the spirit of a book grows into our lives and will not die . . . It will go on in your own life, as long as you see with these eyes and feel with these hands; and when these eyes no longer see, and these hands no longer feel, all that this book has meant to you will go on working in the lives of those who remember you. And after them, for ages after them, whatever is good in this book will live . . .'

Never was a truer word spoken. And now that's enough columnising for the time being – I have some reading to catch up on.

Monday, December 30, 1991

Three wise social workers

A nd it came to pass in those days, that there went out a decree from Caesar Augustus that all the world should be poll-taxed.

And all went to be poll-taxed, every one unto his own city, that he might not be taxed as if he had an second home.

And Joseph also went up from Galilee, out of the city of Nazareth, unto the city of David which is called the borough of Bethlehem, to be taxed with Mary his wife, being great with child.

And she brought forth her first-born son, and wrapped him in swaddling clothes, and hid him in an cardboard box, because there was no room for them in the hostel for homeless people.

And there were in that same borough three social workers

named Ros, Kev and Glo, keeping watch over their cases by night.

And lo, their Co-ordinator came upon them saying, I want you to get down to this address and sus out what is going on, for we have had a tip-off from one of our field backup team that there may be an child at risk living in an cardboard box.

And it came to pass, as the Co-ordinator was gone away from them back to the office, that the three social workers said one to another, Let us get our skates on and see this thing which is come to pass, which our Co-ordinator hath made known to us.

And they came with haste, and found Mary, and Joseph, and the babe, lying in an cardboard box.

And that social worker which was named Ros spake unto Mary, saying, All right, love, we are taking this babe into care.

And Mary, being sore afraid, asked of the social workers wherefore they wouldst take the child of her loins into care.

And that social worker which was named Kev said, We do not have to give a reason, but just look at the poor little mite, it is blue with cold.

But Joseph protested unto the social workers, beating his breast and saying, Is it our fault there was no room in the hostel? If we hadst not been forced to journey unto Bethlehem, this babe would be tucked up in his crib in Nazareth.

And that social worker which was named Glo said, So you do not even live in the borough? There's a care order out for the kid in Nazareth, right, so you thought you'd do a runner?

Then did Mary tell the social workers how she with her husband Joseph had been commanded to come unto Bethlehem to pay their poll tax.

And the three social workers looked one upon the other and tapped their noses. And that social worker which was named Ros said unto Joseph, You're not telling us you've been living in these squalid conditions yet you've never had the nous to apply for poll tax relief.

And that social worker which was named Kev said, Pull the other one. And that social worker which was named Glo said, Surely your social worker told you the score, about your benefit entitlements and that?

And Joseph shrugged saying, We have not a social worker.

And Ros gasped in wonder saying, I do not believe it. You have not a social worker? Who then looketh after you?

And Mary said, Just an Angel of the Lord.

Then came unto Bethlehem from the east to Jerusalem three wise men bearing gifts for the young child with Mary his mother of gold, and frankincense, and myrrh.

And Ros looked upon Glo and Glo looked upon Kev and Kev spake unto himself saying, This is getting fishier by the minute.

And Ros took out her note tablet and began to inscribe words upon it, saying to the three wise men who had come bearing gifts, Excuse me, but what are you lot on precisely?

And the three wise men replied, saying, We saw a star in the east which went before us and led us here.

Then went the three social workers into an huddle. And that social worker which was named Ros said, What do you reckon? Satanists? And that social worker which was named Kev said, Some kind of evil ring, believe you me. And that social worker which was named Glo said, If they are into myrrh-sniffing, we have cometh not an moment too soon.

Then seized they the babe, and took away its swaddling clothes, and clad it in an romper suit.

And Mary wept saying, Where are you taking him?

And Ros said, We do not have to tell you that, love, but since you ask we will probably foster him out to a very nice family named Herod which art longing for a toddler.

And Joseph said, Can we come and visit him?

And Kev said, Not unless you get a court order, mate.

And the three wise men said, Can we not give the child his gifts?

And Glo said, I should cocoa. He will get an black doll to play with from the women activists' toy bank.

Then asked Kev of Joseph, Hath this child an name?

And Joseph said, Not yet, no.

And Glo said, We will call him Rory after my bloke. Now we had better be legging it, gang.

Then leggeth it the three social workers, with the babe.

And the three wise men returned from whence they came, shaking their heads and asking one unto another. What was that all about, then?

Monday, December 24, 1990

Greenboring for Britain

It was by no mere coincidence, I fancy, that the more furrow-browed among us began to worry about the ozone layer just as they were starting to ease off worrying about the bomb going off.

Some people need an Armageddon in the offing as a kind of insecurity blanket, and the greenhouse effect is an excellent substitute for Greenham Common, the melting ice cap a good trade-in for the Cold War.

The difference between these two great causes is that where unilateralism is a well-defined wedge in the political spectrum, when it comes to Green issues it is difficult to see where serious, informed concern leaves off and the open-toed sandals begin.

It is fine when Mrs Thatcher agrees at the Green Summit to take no further economic decisions without first considering their environmental consequences (it would be finer still if she actually meant it). But what are we to make of, say, the dramatic warning that 'civilisation is hanging on by its fingernails to the cliff'?

A touch of the Ben Eltons there, you might think – but think again, for this end-of-the-world-is-nigh message comes to us from the chairman of the Tory-dominated energy select committee, Sir Ian Lloyd, who with his technical and scientific track record knows a good deal more about energy than your average coalman – or your average Cecil Parkinson, come to that.

MPs of all sides have made suitable clucking noises and we may be sure that henceforth many a debate, like many a White Paper, will have Green edges. We will hear the environment dragged into every conceivable piece of business from the White Fishbone Authority (Enabling Powers) Bill to the Question in the House as to whether the Prime Minister has any plans for visiting Jimmy Knapp. Conservation-conscious backbenchers will be careful to recycle their best quips in order to preserve what is left of Commons wit.

But how many of them will actually know what they are talking about? When Nicholas Ridley took one more step towards recycling his own career by denouncing the Greens, in effect, as a gang of scientific ignoramuses, he might as well have gone the whole hog and told his Parliamentary colleagues that most of them too, ecologically speaking, are Green only behind the ears. A survey would show that the majority of Tory MPs believe the sun revolves around Mrs Thatcher.

There is a Tosh Layer in the making where a build-up of half-digested theories about global warming, rain forests, carbon-dioxide emissions and all the rest of it will be seeping out of Westminster and Whitehall into the saloon bars, killing all intelligent conversation about cricket or the exploits of Florida Phil and spreading alarm and despondency.

Already, in a restaurant the other day, I overheard someone declaring that chemical waste dumped into the River Humber had put four million lives at risk. What he meant was that if poison flushed into the Humber over a fourteen-month period had been concentrated into London's drinking water, it could have wiped out four million people. But it wasn't put in London's drinking water, it was put in the River Humber. Reprehensible no doubt, and a good time not to be a North Sea cod, but this is the kind of misinformation we are going to be up against.

As well as the Tosh Layer we have the dangerously rising Puritan Level. This is that end of the Green market cornered by unilateralists and the like who, with the coming of glasnost, have switched their enthusiasm from banning the bomb to banning everything else. Ban economic growth, ban cars, ban aerosols, ban ozone-unfriendly, energy-consuming hair driers and electric razors. We are about to move into an era where not only cigarettes but just about everything you buy will have a label on it warning what your purchase can do to the atmosphere.

How is the ordinary citizen, who can see very clearly that the world is turning into a great revolving dustbin yet does not entirely believe that his great-grandchildren will be barbecued by the sun's unfiltered rays if he doesn't stop using his deodorant spray, supposed to separate the organic wheat from the pesticide-polluted chaff?

My own rule of thumb is never to take on trust a single fact or figure quoted by anyone who talks about Planet Earth. Show me a person who talks about Planet Earth and I will show you a person whose idea of a watertight case is as follows: 'Acid rain is a Bad Thing. Nuclear power is a Bad Thing. Therefore nuclear power causes acid rain.'

I am also pretty wary of people who preface their forecasts that all the capitals of the world will be under water by the year 2050 with the words, 'Unless something is done now' (which usually means unless this or that lobby is given a lot of money now).

But just as none of us can escape the Greenhouse Effect, neither can we escape the Greenbore Effect. We are already into an era where bossy teenagers are haranguing their mothers for making holes in the ozone layer with their furniture polish sprays, where nosy neighbours deliver lectures over the backyard fence upon the environmental folly of garden bonfires, where office Prodnoses, fresh from their triumph in getting smoking banned in the typing pool, turn their reforming zeal towards the compulsory return for recycling of all aluminium soft drink cans.

I cannot see Planet Earth surviving the Greenbore Effect . . . unless something is done now.

Thursday, July 20, 1989

34

British Rail's brother-in-law

I used to be very fond of a small, family-run New York
hotel that was discreet, old-fashioned, shabbily comfort-
able and, for the area, secure. Then, on one of my visits,
I got a shock.

The sturdy old mortice-lock keys on their brass number tags
had been replaced by those electronically-controlled plastic
cards which you punch into a slot to gain access to your room.
This being the place it was, no one could work the system so
that half the guests were permanently locked out while the
other half were permanently locked in.

The extra security supposedly afforded by this upheaval was
totally negated by the fact that the master key was left hanging
on a piece of string in the lift. So how had this conservative
establishment allowed itself to be so traumatically seared by
the white heat of the new technology?

The explanation was disarmingly simple. The system had
been sold to the hotel by the manager's brother-in-law who
was in the electronics racket.

Ever since, when I have come across this or that enterprise
lumbered by unnecessary gadgetry which nobody knows how
to operate, I have blamed the manager's brother-in-law for the
innovation.

For instance, while enjoying a few days in the south of Italy
last week I dropped into a modest back street pizza joint I
remembered from years ago. Then, the arrangements for one's
ablutions had been a modest tap jutting out of the wall. Now,
the tap had been replaced by a battery of gleaming devices
bearing the legend: 'For the use, place one's hands under each
appliance.'

To wash your hands you were supposed to put them under
one chrome fixture and the water would come on automatically. Nothing happened. To dry them, you put them under

another chrome fixture which would dispense hot air. Nothing happened. All was clear. The manager's brother-in-law had been round.

Then again, in a Naples supermarket I encountered a speaking cash register obviously flogged to the store by the manager's brother-in-law. You plonked down your purchases and a disembodied female voice, possibly that of the manager's sister-in-law, pronounced 'That will be five thousand seven hundred lire. Four thousand three hundred lire change. Thank you for your custom.' Miraculous. Trouble was, she gave the wrong change.

I was musing on the phenomenon of the manager's brother-in-law last week on a train that was taking longer to get me from Gatwick to Victoria than British Airways had taken to get me from Naples to Gatwick. The papers were laughing themselves silly at British Rail's claim that its cancellations and delays were caused by the wrong type of snow falling. My *Daily Mail* carried the news that BR's flashy new rolling stock was as vulnerable to the weather as the old Puffing Billies.

Suddenly, as we groaned to one more incomprehensible stop in the middle of nowhere, it came to me in a blinding flash. The whole of British Rail's multi-million pound modernisation programme, from its computerised destination boards that are always on the blink to its sophisticated electric trains whose motors burn out when afflicted by the wrong type of snow, was sold to it by the management's brother-in-law.

There can be no other explanation for the great blanket of inefficiency, thicker and more impenetrable than the snow itself, which enveloped wretched commuters when 'adverse weather conditions' came fluttering down from the winter sky.

It was as totally unexpected by British Rail as fog in November or April showers but you can imagine the slightly agitated phone call as brother-in-law called to brother-in-law across the snowy wastes.

'Hello, Arnold? Barry here. How's Moira and the kids?'

'Moira's fine, Barry. Young Kevin's got a bad case of the sniffles but you've got to expect that at this time of the year. How's Elaine?'

'Still on her blue pills, Arnold, but as well as she'll ever be.

Listen, I'll tell you why I'm ringing. You remember those railway engines you sold us?'

'Railway engines, yes, Barry. Would you like us to do you another dozen? Only we've our winter sale on at present, so now's the time to buy.'

'No, it's not that, Arnold. The thing is, they don't go.'

'How do you mean, they don't go, Barry? Every one of those engines was tested before it left the factory, plus which, they all carry our twelve-month guarantee.'

'I'm relieved to hear that, Arnold, because at the first fall of snow they all conked out.'

'Ah, well that's because you must have let Type A snow into the engines, Barry. See, these engines should only be taken out in adverse weather conditions if it's Type B snow. I'm afraid they're not guaranteed against Type A. It's all in the sales leaflet.'

'Oh dear, so we don't get our money back?'

'I'm afraid not, Barry, but I'll tell you what – I'm glad you rang because I've been meaning to give you a bell about a new ticket barrier we're just perfecting. If one of your passengers . . .'

'Customers, Arnold, customers!'

'Sorry. If one of your customers tries to get through it without having paid his fare, everyone is automatically locked in the station and all the trains stop running until the culprit owns up.'

'Sounds fantastic, Arnold. Put us down for two gross. And listen – why don't you come down for a game of golf this weekend?'

'Love to, Barry, but the bloody trains aren't running.'

'Of course, I was forgetting. Cheerio, Arnold.'

'All the best, Barry.'

Monday, February 18, 1991

Clogthorpe in the red

Clogthorpe District Council's Finance Committee has been meeting in the upstairs room of the Snivelling Coalman public house to discuss matters arising out of the loan of £14 million, the borough's entire liquid assets, to the now defunct Bank of Fun.

The reason the meeting was held in the Snivelling Coalman and not in the council chamber was that the Town Hall is now in the hands of the bailiffs.

Opening the discussion Cllr Bulge (Chair) said he had always known there would be tears before bedtime. If the District Treasurer had taken his advice the money would still be safely in the Post Office. But no, the District Treasurer had big ideas. He had to be greedy. He was lured by the siren of 27 per cent interest from the Bank of Fun.

On a point of information, Cllr Potter asked what had put this daft, dozy, doolally idea into the silly beggar's head.

Cllr Nepworth, through the Chair, said the District Treasurer had read an advert in the *Whippet Fancier's Telegraph & Greyhound Argus*. It said, '££££s! Double Your Money!!! Simply fill in this coupon and we will do the rest!!! Thousands of satisfied punters!!!' It had seemed a sound scheme to him so he sent off a cheque for £14 million.

Cllr Elland asked if the District Treasurer was not in any way put off by the fact that the Bank of Fun's only known address was c/o a newsagent's shop in Abattoir Street.

Cllr Tweedyman said not now it wasn't. The Bank of Fun's only known address was c/o Armley Jail, Leeds. As for the council's £14 million, the lot had been blown on an elaborate roulette system at the Clogthorpe Starlight Room Casino and Karaoke Centre.

Cllr Nepworth said he held no brief for the District Treasurer, even if he did happen to be married to his (Cllr Nepworth's) eldest niece Kimberley. He would just point out that if zero had come up twelve times in a row the council would

38

have got its money back twice over. The District Treasurer had behaved in no way improperly. He had got an authorised official receipt and while he had accepted an Introductory Free Gift of a rolled gold pen and pencil set, he had made no effort to retain this for his personal use. It was now with the mayoral regalia.

Cllr Parkin said in that case it was in the bloody pawnshop.

Cllr Potter asked where the Bank of England stood in all this.

The Chair said that the Bank of England had in effect told Clogthorpe to get stuffed. The Chair had personally rung Sir Robin Leigh-Whatsisname only that morning from a public call box, being as how the council's phones had been cut off. Sir Robin had not been able to come to the blower personally but the young flibbertigibbet who took the call had said: 'I'm ever so sorree, but I'm afraid you're on your own, sunshine, hee hee hee.'

Cllr Tweedyman asked what about the Department of the Environment.

The Chair said the Department of the Environment had been most helpful. They had given him an almost surefire tip for the 3.30 at Lingfield. Unfortunately, the Chief Executive had been unable to act on this information owing to the Exigency Fund having been cleaned out to pay the dustbinmen's wages.

Cllr Elland said that talking about financial commitments, the cost of the upstairs room at the Snivelling Coalman was £15 an hour plus breakages. Since there was damn-all in the kitty the Finance Committee would have to have a personal whip-round to pay it. Was it not time to get down to the nitty-gritty?

The Chair said he could not agree more. Thanks to the District Treasurer, who would have found himself suspended on full pay if there had been anything to pay him with, the Council found itself unable to meet its statutory obligations. Cash would have to be borrowed, probably from that bloke who ran the amusement arcade in Corporation Street who had kindly offered to help, but the interest would have to come out of the pockets of poll tax payers and the Council would have to look to its priorities. The immediate question was, pending said loan, how were councillors to be paid their attendance allowances?

Cllr Potter said what about a cut-back on social services?

Cllr Elland said it wasn't a question of cutting back, it was a question of raising revenue. It was a question of beer money. What about flogging the council cemetery?

Cllr Tweedyman said the wife's mother wouldn't like that.

The Chair said he thought Cllr Tweedyman's wife's mother was dead.

Cllr Tweedyman said she was. She was buried in the council cemetery under a stone Gabriel with his wings outstretched.

The Chair said in that case she would know nowt about it. The council could flog the cemetery and Cllr Tweedyman could have the stone Gabriel to put in his garden.

There being no further business, the Finance Committee adjourned to meet a property developer in the back bar of the Snivelling Coalman.

Monday, July 15, 1991

The street's final over

If, as market researchers tell us, only three in every hundred Englishmen now play our national game of cricket, then what can have happened to street cricket? Gone the way of hop-scotch, I shouldn't wonder.

A kindergarten teacher, by way of assurance that hop-scotch was alive and well in her school, once sent me a photograph of a neatly-painted playground hop-scotch grid, complete with plastic tiles. She missed the point that half the joy of playing hop-scotch is marking out your own grid with chalk (preferably brown quarry chalk) and finding your own personal sliver of shiny slate or stone. God, they'll be giving the little monsters plastic conkers next. (If they already are, I don't want to hear about it.)

Doubtless in those few remaining boroughs where cricket is not regarded as elitist (I can only assume most council play co-ordinators have never heard of Ian Botham), youngsters may be able to get a game at the leisure centre or adventure playground with equipment provided by the local authority. But that is a far cry from street cricket.

Street cricket is a do-it-yourself sport played to make-up-yourself rules on a find-it-yourself ground with get-it-yourself gear. Any number can play.

The equipment consists of one bat, one ball and one stump, top weight. The wicket is more usually chalked on a wall or it consists of a plank supported by two bricks, or it is a lamp post. The bat itself may also take the form of a short plank, paling or segment of orange box. The ball is either a shapeless lump of cork that looks as if someone has been eating it, or it is a worn tennis ball. Pads will not be worn.

The ground is ideally a traffic-free terrace (where the cambered cobbles make every delivery a googly), but street cricket can also be played on any yard, alley, stretch of asphalt or piece of waste ground – even on a flat roof. Just so long as it's not played on grass, that's all.

As for the rules of street cricket, there are as many variations as there are – or were – streets to play it in. Some games split the players into sides, others pit the entire field against the batsman (there are rarely two batsmen, for the reason that there are rarely two bats) who plays until he is run out – or, in some versions, rugby-tackled. The batsman can hardly ever be clean bowled, since he flatly refuses to believe that he has been, and there is no umpire. An over consists of as many balls as the bowler can get away with before someone else demands a turn. A broken window counts as a six. Stumps shall be deemed to have been drawn when the player owning the bat goes home for his tea.

And then of course there is French cricket, played only with a hard ball, where the aim is solely to maim the batsman, who shall then be declared out.

I cannot remember when I last retrieved a street cricket ball from the main road in response to an urchin's shout. (Total strangers proceeding about their business are expected, of course, to man the outfield.) Insofar as street games are played at all these days, it seems to be year-round street soccer.

A pity, for it was great fun, and as I said about hop-scotch, half the fun was in getting the game together. I shall never forget the excitement in my own street cricket XI – well, more of a street cricket IV, really – when one of our number had the idea of fashioning pads out of corrugated cardboard. By the time we had got the things made, we had lost the light.

Still, better that the game should wither away than that the council leisure co-ordinator should get hold of it and start painting wickets up in properly-supervised play streets.

Monday, March 21, 1988

Apostrophe agenda

The hordes of correspondents, commentators, cameramen and other media folk seen heading north this weekend were presumably making for Lytham St Anne's where the annual conference of the Association for the Annihilation of the Aberrant Apostrophe – the AAAA – starts today.

In a crowded agenda 1,000 delegates will debate the apostrophe and the economy, the apostrophe and defence, the apostrophe and agriculture, the apostrophe and the NHS and, time permitting, the role of the apostrophe in education.

In his keynote speech which will be a stinging indictment of the rise and rise of the misplaced apostrophe, the Life President of the AAAA is expected to put all the blame on Mrs Thatcher.

As with every other conference this autumn, green issues will be very much to the fore, with a robust attack from the platform on greengrocers who persist in poisoning the atmosphere with apostrophised cabbage's, cucumber's and carrot's. The Life President will introduce a crusading pamphlet, 'Towards an apostrophe-free neuter possessive pronoun' which calls for swingeing fines for apostrophe pollution.

There will be a six-minute period just before lunch on Friday when paid-up members of this democratic institution who have been lucky enough to win a place in the ballot will be allowed to put motions from the floor.

These are some of the resolutions that may be debated:

Oxford branch: This conference condemns Buckinghamshire County Council for advertising in the *Oxford Times* for two teacher's.

Middlesex branch: While congratulating Fregg Approved Free Range Eggs upon its honest slogan, 'Our hen's food contains no antibiotics or hormones', this conference wonders whether it is humane to ask one poor hen to do all the work.

Kent branch: This conference urges fraternal delegates to let their hair grow rather than patronise the Kent barber who advertises 'Cut's for men's style's'.

London (West End) branch: This conference calls upon student members to boycott the Charing Cross Road bookshop where, in the grammar section, one shelf is labelled 'Beginner's'.

High Wycombe branch, while condemning violence, recommends that a local travel agent advertising 'See Rome in all it's glory' be pushed off the top of the Colosseum.

Westminster branch: This conference calls for the abolition of the British Tourist Authority for its part in publishing a picture postcard of the House's of Parliament.

Lewisham branch cordially invites any fraternal delegates who chance to be passing through the borough to heave a brick through the town hall windows in reprisal for the council's advertisement for secretary's and treasurer's.

An emergency resolution from Nottingham branch draws attention to an internal document from the City of Nottingham Housing Stores Department which lists door's, window's, tile's, eye bolt's and basin tap's, and calls for immediate suspension of the city's housing grant pending a full enquiry.

Bath and Wilts branch asks conference to send fraternal greetings to the International Freedom Foundation but to advise it that it would carry more clout with the general public if in an open letter to the African National Congress it did not invite the ANC to 'prove it's democratic nature by allowing any of it's members who wish to leave to do so of their own free will'. Conference calls upon the IFF to release all imprisoned apostrophes forthwith.

South London branch, while in no way condoning the burning down of places of entertainment, urges conference to recognise the need to do something drastic about cinemas which persistently announce attractions such as *Lord of the Fly's*, *Look Whose Talking* and *War of the Rose's*.

Hampshire branch: This conference instructs Head Office to send a bouquet of dead rats to the school admin officer who, having posted up a notice giving the venue for a 'Governors Meeting' and been advised that it required an apostrophe, altered it to 'Governor's Meeting'. An amendment from Bristol branch proposes a further rodent bouquet to Filton College which has been advertising that it opens it's doors on it's Open Day.

So many delegates wish to draw attention to the practice of their local restaurants of bespattering their menus – or menu's as they usually style themselves – with surplus apostrophes that this aberration has been made the subject of a composite resolution: This conference calls upon statutory health authorities to regard aberrant apostrophes in restaurants and cafés on a level with cockroaches and mouse droppings, and to close down any premises infested with hot and cold drink's, soup's, sandwich's, hot pie's, homemade sweet's and other pests.

Another composite resolution urges a complete boycott of the many ladie's hairdressers up and down the country where appointment's are not alway's necessary.

The most surprising resolution at this year's AAAA Conference will be a motion from the Signwriting Monitoring Committee calling for solidarity with the Lord's Day Observance Society in its campaign against Sunday trading, on the grounds that the moment the law is relaxed there will be a rash of signs in shop windows all over the land reading *Now open Sunday's*.

Monday, October 1, 1990

The Pudding Lane Plan

I n one of those quaint English ceremonies which are a boon to the 'And finally' slot on the Nine O'clock News, the Worshipful Company of Bakers has formally, if belatedly, apologised to the Lord Mayor of London for 'the great damage caused by one of their number 320 years ago.'

Next month, according to my social diary, will see a similar ceremony involving the Worshipful Company of Town and Country Planners which became all-powerful following the Pudding Lane disaster and has remained so ever since.

But instead of giving the Lord Mayor their apologies, they will demand one from him for parking his coach on a double yellow line and wearing funny clothes which clash with the modern environment of the City.

Few of the planning applications for rebuilding London after the Great Fire survive. I do have to hand, however, a copy of the planning committee report on an application by one Sir Christopher Wren to build a cathedral. It recommended rejecting the proposal in favour of a traffic roundabout.

The committee's main objection was that the cathedral's unsightly dome would obscure the views of Hackney Marshes to the east and the Fleet ditch to the west, and that hovel-dwellers across the river could not avoid seeing it.

Furthermore, like Sir Christopher's grandiose scheme for a whole new City of avenues and piazzas – already rejected out of hand – the cathedral was foreign in appearance and not in keeping with the Pudding Lane Master Plan. The architect already had commissions for fifty-one new churches and had failed to prove the public demand for an additional place of worship.

The proposed cathedral had no underground sedan-chair park, no crutch ramp for the stumpishly disadvantaged, and no adequate fire-exit out of the crypt. The so-called Great West Door was an encouragement for crowds of worshippers to enter or leave the premises at once, with a resultant danger of being trampled underfoot. The bells would wake people up. The whispering gallery would encourage pick-pockets, for whom there was insufficient gallows accommodation.

Finally, the horse-traffic attracted to the area would impede the whipping of vagrants through the streets towards the proposed new Tyburn slip-road. The Wren scheme was therefore rejected.

On appeal to Mr Seckretary for the Environment, however, the planning committee's decision was reversed on condition that the architect scaled his cathedral down a bit and incorporated a tablet inscribed with the motto of the Worshipful Company of Town and Country Planners.

Looking out from St Paul's over the vista of stunted, rust-streaked office blocks reminiscent of Slough, visitors can read that tablet to this day: 'If you seek a monument, look around you.'

Thursday, June 12, 1986

46

Thank you for nothing, Jeeves

Ask anyone at The Drones, and they will tell you that Bertram Wooster is an easy-going cove who does not stand on ceremony. Nevertheless, it was with a certain lack of gruntlement that I received a most astonishing request from Jeeves as he shimmered in with the restoring cup of tea and the morning paper.

'Do my ears deceive me, Jeeves? Am I to understand that you are asking me to run my own bath?'

'It would be advisable, sir, in the present climate.'

'What has the climate to do with it, Jeeves? It is as perfect a summer's morn as one is likely to encounter in a day's march. Or was, until you introduced a cloud to an otherwise blemishless horizon with this absurd suggestion of sprigs of the nobility and gentry running their own baths. Good Lord, Jeeves, you'll be asking me to tie my own dashed shoelaces next!'

'In the climate to which I allude, sir, namely the political climate as it pertains to local government, that also would be a judicious concession on your part. Perhaps you have not read the paper, sir.'

'You know dashed well I haven't, Jeeves, since you have yet to polish my monocle. Acquaint me with the intelligence of the day in not more than one sentence.'

'A certain local council, sir, Lewisham by name, has instructed its librarians through its women's committee that in selecting books for library use, stereotypes should be avoided; that for example, in descriptions of men in a domestic context, references to a general ineptness should be eschewed.'

'I say! Rather below the belt, what?'

'I would emphatically agree that it is gratuitously offensive, sir. What is more to the point, if I may say so, sir, is that this iniquitous instruction could threaten your very existence in the borough of Lewisham.'

'Does one wish to exist in Lewisham, Jeeves?'

'It is the thin end of the wedge, sir. What Lewisham thinks today, other boroughs may well be thinking tomorrow.'

'And you think a spot of bath-running and shoelace-tying on my part should curb this unhealthy tendency?'

'Not entirely, sir. If I may venture to say so, it would be as well to persuade the council that you are capable of supporting yourself in other directions. To that end, I have taken the liberty of sending off a number of job applications in your name.'

I was astounded. 'Job applications, Jeeves? You mean to stand there and tell me that those birds one sees walking about in dungarees actually *apply* to go down drains and so forth?'

'So I am given to understand, sir. However, there is no question of your wearing dungarees – they would not suit you. The job applications which I have presumed to despatch are directed at Lewisham Council itself. They are for such posts as project leader, co-ordinator and liaison officer.'

'And what may they be when they are at home?'

'I have no idea, sir, but it would enable the various chronicles of your escapades to be rewritten with titles such as "No Problem, Jeeves," "Cheers, Jeeves," and "You Must Be Joking, Jeeves." It is my considered view that we should then be in the clear.'

I was aggrieved, I don't mind telling you. I felt like that cove in the Book of Thingummy when he was smitten under the fifth rib. 'This is all very well, Jeeves,' I protested, 'but why should the last of the Woosters be the scapegoat for this crackbrained council's bally witch-hunt? What about Bulldog Drummond, to name only one?'

'I fear you would not find Capt Drummond in many public libraries in this day and age, sir,' said Jeeves gravely. 'However, you are far from being the only victim. The Misses Bennet from *Pride and Prejudice*, for example, also implicitly come under the council's lash. Librarians are clearly advised that "women should be shown as pursuing a variety of career goals, and both deserving of and receiving public attention".'

'Good lord! And how have the Bennet fillies taken the bad news?'

'I understand they are taking posts as teachers and raffiawork instructresses with the Leicestershire Education Authority, sir. As for Miss Jane Eyre –'

'You mean the one who wrote *Wuthering Heights?*'

'No, sir, the one who is a novel by Charlotte Brontë. Miss Eyre regrettably fails the requirement that stereotypes of the emotional female are to be avoided. The book will have to be completely rewritten.'

I mopped the weary brow. 'Spare me the gory details, Jeeves. This Lewisham Council of which you speak. Are you sure it was entirely sober when issuing these hare-brained guidelines?'

'So far as is known, sir.'

'Then say no more, Jeeves. Lead me to the bathroom, and point out the taps.'

'Very good, sir.'

Thursday, September 17, 1987

Shar & Tray in clover

Sharon and Tracy, taking advantage of a lull in Perfumes and Toiletries caused by their neglecting to catch the eye of a customer waiting to be served, were discussing the case of the Woolworth girl who has won the right not to work on the tobacco counter.

'I fink it's a breakfroo,' said Sharon, absently dabbing Chanel No 5 behind one ear, Joy by Patou behind the other, and the last of the sample bottle of Youth Dew to her wrists.

'Fancy them freatening to sack her just for not doing what she was told.'

'Worse than living in Nazi Russia,' agreed Tracy, applying a liberal coating of the store's Yves St Laurent lip gloss to her rosebud mouth. 'So does that mean if Mr Wotherspoon tells us we've got to go work in a particlar department and we don't want to, we can tell him where to stick it?'

'Too right,' said Sharon. 'So long as we've got a good reason, that is. Same as if he tries to make us go back to Linens and Drapery, all we've got to say is Sorree, Mr Wotherspoon, only we don't want to work down there cos it's boring.'

'And if he has the cheek to say All right then girls, off you go to Lampshades and Light Fittings, we can say Sorree, Mr Wotherspoon, that's even more boring,' said Tracy with one of her delightful titters.

'We've got him over a barrel, Tray,' said Sharon. 'Just wait till the next time he tries to make me do holiday relief in Dining Room Furniture. Sorree, Mr Wotherspoon, I shall say, but it just so happens I don't agree with Dining Room Furniture.'

'You never told me you didn't agree with Dining Room Furniture, Shar,' said Tracy in surprise. 'Is that cos you believe in eating off your knees so you can watch telly at the same time?'

'No, it's cos it's made of wood,' said Sharon.

Tracy's forehead furrowed in concentration as she tried valiantly to follow Sharon's drift.

'What have you got against wood, Shar?'

'It comes off trees,' Sharon said, 'and they're getting reely scarce, trees are. Wayne says Planet Earth's running out of its sources.'

'I've never noticed no shortage of trees, Shar. I mean to say last time me and Shane went to Epping Forest it was full of them.'

'Not them kind of trees,' said Sharon knowledgeably. 'These are special kinds of trees what I'm talking about, what they make dining room furniture out of. Trees what grow in rain forests.'

'Rain forests? I didn't know rain came out of forests, Shar. I fought it came out of clouds, like.'

'Yeh, it does – after it's been blown up into the sky out of these rain forests. So if we go on chopping down the rain forests to make dining room furniture, we won't have no more rain.'

'Suits me,' said Tracy carelessly. 'I've lost my umbrella.' She added, her pretty brow creased in thought again, 'Are you sure they make dining room furniture out of rain forests, Shar? I mean to say in that case, why ain't it all wet?'

'I spect they dry the wood out before they turn it into tables and chairs,' said Sharon. 'And talking of your umbrella, Tray, that's another department I'm not going to work in no more, not if Mr Wotherspoon goes down on his bended knees – Umbrellas and Rainwear.'

'I fought you liked working in Umbrellas and Rainwear, Shar.'

'Only during that long hot summer when we didn't have no rain.'

'Cos of the rain forests being turned into dining room furniture,' chipped in Tracy.

'That's right. Only now that it's bucketing down every day, Umbrellas and Rainwear is worked off their feet.'

It crossed Tracy's seething mind to ask where, if all the rain forests had been turned into dining room furniture, the rain was coming from; but then she decided that these would be deep waters she was getting into. Instead she volunteered, with a sweet smile at the by now impatient customer who was rapping on the counter with her credit card: 'Know what department you won't catch me working in no more, now that they can't force us to, Shar? The sweeties counter.'

'But you love sweeties, Tray.'

'That's just it. Last time they put me on the sweeties counter I gained six pounds.'

Thursday, March 1, 1990

Europe in a lather

The European Community Protocol Commission met over a jolly good lobster dinner in Brussels yesterday to hammer out the final agenda for December's summit talks at Maastricht.

Mr Bratwurst (Germany) said that while monetary and political union, defence, foreign policy and so on had been penned in as urgent items for discussion, there were still many equally important issues jostling for position. For example, the standardisation of soap throughout the Community.

Mr Pommefrite (France) said the standardisation of soap was of the first priority, and there would never be a better opportunity to raise the anomaly of soap being manufactured in different shapes and sizes. The EC had had a great success with abolishing round cheeses, so that there was no longer any danger of them rolling off the back of a lorry and injuring innocent Europeans. Now was the time to abolish round soaps.

Mr Mortadella (Italy) said there was far more to soap standardisation than shape, although he agreed that was of paramount importance. Moving extensively about Europe as he did, he had occasion to wash a lot, and he was amazed at the different kinds of soap he had encountered in different countries. Not only was there round soap and oblong soap but there was soap in different wrappings. There was opaque soap and there was transparent soap, coal tar soap and soap with bits of oatmeal in it. There was soap which floated and soap which sank. There was soap in the shape of fruit, which if eaten by children would cause them to froth at the mouth. It was outrageous.

Mr Fruitcake (UK) said that Mr Mortadella had not mentioned soap on a rope. Mr Fruitcake had a nephew who had given him soap on a rope every Christmas since 1979. He would fervently support any motion to outlaw the stuff.

Mr Gateau (Luxembourg) said he had a dream. He had a dream that one day, wherever Europeans washed, from the

Mediterranean to the Atlantic, whether in the tiled bathrooms of great mansions or under the cold water pumps of dusty village squares, they would all be using the same type of standardised Eurosoap, oblong with sharp corners so that it did not slip out of one's hands. That was what being European was all about.

Mr Sardine (Portugal) said this was excellent lobster, by the way.

Mr Smorgasbord (Denmark) said it was all right, but all the claws were of different lengths. He would take it up with the EC Regulatory Body (Fisheries).

Mr Poteen (Ireland) said that getting back to soap, he had often wondered why they bothered to manufacture it in different colours. You could get green soaps and red soaps and white soaps and yellow soaps and he did not know what all. They were like liquorice allsorts.

Mr Taramasalata (Greece) asked what were liquorice allsorts?

Mr Fruitcake said they were what they name implied. They were all sorts of liquorice sweets – little liquorice rolls, little liquorice sandwiches, little liquorice pancakes covered in hundreds and thousands, little liquorice cachous and so on – sold in the same packet with a picture of Bertie Bassett on the front.

Mr Taramasalata said and this was allowed, was it?

Mr Fruitcake asked what Mr Taramasalata was driving at.

Mr Taramasalata said that when he bought a packet of sweets he expected them to be all the same sweet. If he bought a packet of jelly babies, then jelly babies he would expect to find, not jelly babies, aniseed balls, fruit pastilles and the odd mint imperial.

Mr Fruitcake said surely, if all the sweets in the packet were the same, they could hardly pass themselves off as liquorice allsorts.

Mr Bratwurst said in that case, to conform with EC regulations, this Bertie Bassett, whoever he was, would have to think of a new name. He would have to call his confection liquorice similarities or something of the kind.

Mr Waffle (Belgium) said the Protocol Commission was straying far from the subject in hand. Who was having pudding?

Mr Mortadella said he would see what was on the trolley.

Mr Fruitcake said he would have the profiteroles.

Mr Bratwurst said he would have the crème brûlée.

Mr Gateau said he had a vision. He had a vision that one day everyone in Europe would have the same pudding after finishing their Lobster Thermidor . . .

Thursday, October 31, 1991

Our cigarette card war

I'll tell you one thing about that World War II we've all been banging on about – whatever else was rationed, there was no shortage of education. We were never better informed.

We are going back to a time when I could draw you a map of Crete before I was out of short trousers. Every schoolboy knew the difference between a Messerschmitt and a Heinkel and there were eggheads among us who knew the difference between a Messerschmitt Bf 109E-1 and a Messerschmitt Bf 110C-4.

Looking back from an age when nobody knows anything about anything it seems incredible that ten-year-olds could then name all the members of Hitler's kitchen cabinet and imitate most of them. If you were unaware of the supposed anatomical difference between Hitler and Goebbels you were dubbed an ignoramus.

We knew where the Balkans were and what they were and we could have gone on Mastermind with our specialised knowledge of the principal hotspots of North Africa from Mersa Matruh and Sidi Barrani to Tobruk and Benghazi.

Fifty years ago I could have named just about every ship in the Navy. Now I couldn't even tell you whether we've got one or not. I knew the names of more generals, of all nations, than you could get in a full set of cigarette cards on Famous Fighters. Nowadays it would be a good day for my memory bank if I could scrape together the names of three chief constables.

There were kids who could not even spell cat who could converse about the two-prong German advance on Stalingrad from Kachalinskaya and Proletarskaya. Children who didn't know their ABC could trot off every wartime acronym in the book including the Home Guard's precursor the LDV which any mite of three could tell you stood for Look, Duck and Vanish.

But while I can still clearly recall that blitz is short for blitzkrieg and that Rommel was known as the Desert Fox and that Hitler's real name was Schickelgruber, I cannot properly recollect who told me. We weren't taught anything about the war at school (they must have been practising for Kenneth Baker's core curriculum), we never read anything more enlightening than the *Beano*, and the wireless news was merely a drab interval between Garrison Theatre and Sandy Macpherson at the theatre organ.

I guess some of it must have filtered into our craniums subliminally since the only other source of information was the British Movietone News, of which my sole memory is of chirpy Tommies giving the thumbs-up sign as they embarked for Somewhere In Western Waters. The playground, I do recall, was our great war news nerve centre. It was there that we jigsawed together our barely-digested, fragmentary snippets about Dunkirk or the bombing of Coventry or the Russian counter-offensive, into some overall and reasonably comprehensive picture of what was going on.

Why were we so well-informed? Children have ever been fascinated by war, of course, as anyone knows who has tried to persuade them to play Pacifists and United Nations Observers or to market a conscientious objector's outfit mounted on a card. But there is more to it than that. As I have often maintained in this column, children have an unquench-able thirst for information, which if only it could be tapped instead of sternly turned off like one of 'the ten water and sewage businesses of England and Wales' banning a garden hosepipe, could transform their education overnight.

We knew the names of generals and battles and ships and types of aeroplane for the same reason that we knew the names of cricketers and motor cars and the Seven Wonders of the World – because we loved to cram our heads with lists. That's why those cigarette cards were so popular.

I hesitate to suggest this to the new Education Secretary Mr MacGregor, but if he's as seriously worried about the stan-dards of history teaching as we know the eccentric lodger of No 10 is, has he thought of persuading her to declare war on Germany?

Thursday, August 31, 1989

Found wanting

Among Harold Macmillan's private papers, released under the thirty-year rule, is a pre-Budget note to the Con-servative Research Department: 'I am always hearing about the Middle Classes. What is it they really want? Can you put it down on a sheet of notepaper, and then I will see whether we can give it to them.'

I do not appear to have the reply to hand. Perhaps it is still classified information. Perhaps if the Russians knew what the British Middle Classes really want they could use the information to foster discontent and thus threaten our national security.

Mrs Thatcher, need I say, would never have to ask what the Middle Classes want (although it will be fascinating, thirty years hence, to see if she has ever sent her research people a memo requesting: 'I am always hearing about the Working Classes. What is it they really want? Can you put it down on half a sheet of notepaper, and then I will tell them they can't have it'). Unlike Supermac, Superthatch is middle class through and through. When she is finally laid to rest they will find Dunroamin engraved on her heart.

It is all the more remarkable, then, that as middle-class Maggie becomes the longest-running Prime Minister this century, the middle classes who keep her in the job should be getting far less of what they want than back in 1957.

In material terms, of course, they were never so well off. If they never had it so good with Macmillan, they have never had it better with Maggie. They have traded up the Morris 1000 for a Volvo, terrazzo-tiled the patio, double-glazed the greenhouse and installed a Jacuzzi en suite with the centrally-heated master bedroom. There is a chicken in every middle-class pot and the pot comes from Habitat.

But what is it, after all, that the middle classes really want? What is the answer to Macmillan's question? It is surely that the middle classes want what they already have – and to hang on to it. By definition the middle classes wish to be what they have become. Belonging to the middle classes is all about attainment – and it is this attainment which they now see threatened.

The year 1987 ended with disturbing scenes of violence at new year celebrations up and down the country. Some of them were par for the course, with 139 arrests in and around Trafalgar Square and Greater Manchester announcing itself as 'relatively quiet' with 100 arrests and six stabbings.

But what are we to make of High Wycombe on the fringe of Betjeman's Metroland, with shots, petrol bombs, looting and a full-scale riot in the town centre? What of disturbances, including a knifing or two, in the commuter belt of Kent, street fights in Ipswich, police dogs restoring order in Hereford, police vehicles damaged in Weymouth?

This was not inner-city violence. It was outer-city violence. It was violence brought to the suburbs and market towns where in Macmillan's day a girl from Acacia Avenue could safely attend the revels in the High Street then walk back home with reasonable confidence of getting there intact.

What the middle classes want, apart from a nice home and the car and all the trappings, is a pleasant secure neighbourhood to live in, and this is manifestly harder to find now than in 1957. And then they want good schools, clean streets, well-run hospitals and sound local government, and these too are commodities with an increasing rarity value.

They want, above all, decent standards of behaviour. For a Prime Minister anxious to keep in with the middle classes, that is a far more difficult one to crack these days. Macmillan, after all, did not have the plague of yobbism to contend with. Nor did Somerset mothers fret lest their children be given freedom of choice for their pocket money between the sweet shop and the school condom machine.

What has happened to this country since the Macmillan era is that our bouts of economic buoyancy, being no longer universally enjoyed, are no longer universally endowed, with a resultant drop in what used to be called the quality of life (whatever happened to that phrase?). It's become a case of never mind the quality, feel the wallet.

Thus the middle classes come up to Town on a filthy Underground system barely distinguishable from the main drain, to do their shopping in Harrods and Liberty. They ferry their second cars on the school run for children who if they have ever heard of the Battle of Hastings think it has an apostrophe. The common is a no-go area and they are looking for a Black and Decker attachment to flush the lager cans out of the privet hedge.

When the rich get rich while the poor get poorer it is understandable if reprehensible that concern for those who have drawn the short straw should rest mainly with their own kind and those who seek to represent them. But when the rich get rich while nearly all they behold gets poorer, when the streets grow shabbier and the suburbs are dangerous to walk through at night, when the hospitals are run down and the schools are citadels of bigotry and ignorance, then where is the benefit, and for whom?

That is what the middle classes emphatically do not want. We shall see how their anxieties show up in the Cabinet papers thirty years from now.

Monday, January 4, 1988

Picking up Pelicans

Two tears, no more, at the news that Pelicans are being plucked off their perch. Pelican books that is, the lesser known brothers of Penguins. There will be no new Pelican titles after March.

A spokespenguin for the publishers says that the imprint is losing its market and that it has a 1940s feel with an air of 'This book is a bit worthy, a bit hard going.'

It always did. That was the attraction. Back in those 1940s I was never seen in public without a dog-eared Pelican stuffed into the pocket of my leather-patched sports jacket and I always made sure the title – Freud's *Psychopathology of Everyday Life*, as it might be – was visible. You did not want anyone running away with the idea that you were squandering your time on detective stories.

Pelicans, along with Puffins, Ptarmigans and other ornithological titles, were brought into the world back in 1937 by the publishing genius Allen Lane, who after successfully launching Penguins, the first sixpenny paperback, was looking for another profitable venture beginning with P. One day he heard

59

a woman at the St Pancras station bookstall asking, 'Have you got any Pelican books?' He knew there was no such series and that she must mean Penguins – 'but I knew if somebody else started the word Pelican they'd be stealing some of my thunder.'

With the mystic expertise of a water diviner locating an underground spring Lane identified a great popular thirst for knowledge and found a mass market for the likes of Shaw, Huxley, J. B. S. Haldane and other leading thinkers of the day.

Pelicans were aimed at 'the intelligent layman' – a term now thought to be patronising, although it never seemed so at the time. Puffing my pipe as I browsed through a shelf of those familiar blue and white volumes in Miles's second-hand book-shop in Leeds, it always rather pleased me to imagine that passers-by glancing through the window must be thinking, 'Hello, wonder what that young intelligent layman is swotting up this time.'

It could be anything that took my fancy, from the *Inequality of Man* to an *Outline of European Architecture* or a simple expla-nation, in intelligent layman's terms of course, of the mysteries of the universe. The deciding factor, I confess, was would it impress girls? A well-chosen Pelican in the pocket among the set that hung around the steps of the public library, could be as effective an ice-breaker as a box of Black Magic. Threepence cheaper too.

I will confess something else. With my cigarette card men-tality I rarely read a Pelican book all through. There was only so much a young man could take about politics or philosophy before his mind turned to other things. But Pelicans made a fine cheap home reference library and indeed I still have some of the later ones on my shelves – for instance, the sevenvolume *Guide to English Literature* and the two-volume *History of Music* (actually that should be a three-volume *History of Music*, but I never got round to buying volume three).

Along with Penguin New Writing, the Left Book Club, Picture Post and the Third Programme, Pelican books in their heyday found a good slice of their audience among people of very little formal education. Their readers weren't swotting for exams or planning to become career nuclear physicists – they just wanted to add to their understanding of how things worked. That instinct for knowledge for its own sake is still there, of course – but nowadays it seems to need a BBC 2 series in living colour to kick it off.

I cannot honestly claim that I will miss the old Pelican – serious titles will henceforth continue under the imprint of brother Penguin – but in the course of a ramshackle self-education I couldn't have done without it. Even if I never did get to the end of G. D. H. Cole's *Practical Economics*, I knew a good six-pennorth when I saw one.

Monday, December 18, 1989

Ask a silly question

QUESTION 1. Lolling on the beach with your news-paper, you come face to face with this zonking great Bumper Bank Holiday Quiz. Do you (a) groan and turn over the page; (b) put it aside to do later; (c) start on it right away?

2. Embarking on the quiz, you find you have nothing to write with. Do you (a) forget the whole thing; (b) try to do it in your head; (c) go back to the hotel for a pencil?

3. You establish that the point of the quiz is to decide how good a lover you are. Do you (a) give up in disgust; (b) falsify the answers; (c) do it as conscientiously as you can?

4. At this stage your spouse joins you in the adjoining deck-chair. Do you (a) pretend to be reading the sports pages; (b)

ask her/him how you should answer question four; (c) tell him/her to stop looking over your shoulder?

5. Having assisted you in answering question four, your spouse has somehow managed to commandeer the newspaper. Do you (a) wander off to see what time it is by the floral clock; (b) say 'Do you mind, I was reading that!'; (c) go and buy another copy of the paper?

6. The point of your pencil breaks. Do you (a) toss the pencil into the sea, put your hat over your eyes and settle down for a snooze; (b) ask your spouse for the loan of a pen; (c) go back to your hotel for a pencil sharpener?

7. Round about question seven you become aware of a distraction – a punch-up on the beach, perhaps, or a helicopter rescuing a family of five stranded on a rock. Do you (a) discard the quiz and go and watch the fun; (b) fold up your newspaper and leave it on your deckchair with a pebble on top of it to stop it blowing away; (c) carry on with the quiz despite the fact that the punch-up is now developing into a full-scale riot and the helicopter has crashed into the sea?

8. Resuming or pressing on with the quiz as the case may be, you are nudged by your spouse who says: 'If you've nothing better to do than sprawl in that deckchair answering silly questions, you can go and fetch me an ice cream.' Do you say (a) 'Actually I was just waiting for the pub to open – I'll fetch you an ice cream on the way back'; (b) 'In a minute, as soon as I've finished this quiz'; (c) 'They're not silly questions and you've had four ice creams already'?

9. Your spouse having gone off to buy another ice cream, or to be sick, or both, you are approached by a young and attractive member of the opposite sex who proposes taking you for a walk. Do you say (a) 'Your place or mine?'; (b) 'Only if you help me finish this quiz'; (c) 'Sorry – I'm busy'?

10. Two thirds of your way through the quiz it dawns on you that there is a very simple marking system and that all the a's obviously rate the lowest score while the c's rate the highest. Do you (a) tell yourself you don't know why you're bothering with the thing; (b) go back over your answers and alter all your a's and b's into c's; (c) plod on scoring c's with a self-satisfied smirk on your face?

11. Having as you thought cracked the code, you come to

a question where you suspect that the compiler may be cheating and craftily switching round the scoring order. Do you (a) not give a toss because you're not writing down the answers anyway; (b) take a peek at the scores and adjust your ticked box accordingly; (c) press on regardless?

12. Returning with a strawberry cone in one hand and a vanilla wafer in the other, your spouse finds you being chatted up by the member of the opposite sex featured in question nine and demands a divorce. Do you say (a) 'I'm innocent – look, I haven't answered a single question'; (b) 'Who gets custody of the quiz?'; (c) 'How can I concentrate when people keep interrupting?'

13. Having completed the quiz and being advised to turn to page thirty-five to see how you rated, you find to your intense annoyance that your spouse has used page thirty-five to wipe a bit of oil slick off a pair of beach shoes, and it is now in the bin. Do you (a) completely forget what it was you were looking for anyway; (b) retrieve the oil-stained page and try to decipher the answers; (c) push your spouse off the pier?

14. Locating the answers at last, you find that you are the world's greatest lover, most dynamic personality, most generous, understanding partner or whatever. Do you (a) dismiss these findings as utter twaddle; (b) take them with just a pinch of salt; (c) believe every word?

15. On the other hand, you've got it all wrong about the very simple marking system and it turns out that you are the world's greatest wimp. Do you (a) dismiss this as even more utter twaddle; (b) say with a light laugh: 'Oh, well, one mustn't take these things too seriously'; (c) follow your spouse off the end of the pier?

And now, as they say in all the best quizzes, how do you rate? For each question, score 0 for a, 2 for b and 10 for c.

0–10. You don't like quizzes, in fact you loathe them. You operate on a short fuse and are in the habit of picking quarrels with waiters and taxi drivers. Why don't you calm down and have a go at the crossword?

11–64. You can take quizzes or you can leave them alone. You are a normal, irritatingly average human being who can always see the other fellow's point of view. It is highly possible, indeed, that you are Mr or Mrs John Major.

65–150. Let's face it, you're hooked on quizzes, aren't you? When you finish a quiz you get such serious withdrawal symptoms that you have to rub out the answers and start again. You put great faith in popular psychology and as likely as not you are about to read out the horoscopes.

Monday, August 26, 1991

This way to the North

For sale, M25, as new. Used only once by old lady out for Sunday drive. Suit racing or skateboard enthusiast. Try any offer for quick sale, or would exchange for pair of bicycle clips.

No, I don't think so. The Government's bold, not to say mad, scheme for privatising the road programme will not find me among the bidders, much as I would like to install a porter in a top hat at the wrought iron entrance gates to what looks like a private gravel drive but which turns out to be a 200-mile stretch of motorway.

I have only ever wanted to own one road, and that is long gone. Well, not so much gone as forgotten. I refer to the old A1. A road of that name still exists, of course, but it is now a kind of sub-motorway with three-lane dual carriageways and it goes round Grantham instead of slap bang through the middle.

I am going back to the days when only the AA, the RAC and that class of motorist which used to be known as roadhogs (whatever happened to roadhogs? I know – they all became juggernaut drivers) ever called it the A1. To the rest of us, tootling along in our Austin Sevens and Ford Populars, it went by its proper name of the Great North Road.

This classic route from London to Edinburgh was supposed to have been laid down by the Romans, but I have never believed that, unless the Romans couldn't see straight. It was the original rolling English road made by the original rolling English drunkard.

You have heard of going from A to B? The Great North Road went via Z. If there was a Norman church or something equally pretty to look at, the Great North Road took a hairpin detour to accommodate it. If there was a bottleneck, the Great North Road headed for it.

The hours we A1 tootlers spent crawling through Stamford and Newark would make your present-day Bank Holiday traffic jam seem like a slight pause while the lights turned green.

In those tootling days you still got a salute from the jodhpured AA scout on his motorbike and sidecar, and owners of MGs and suchlike swanky cars flashed their lights at one another in superior acknowledgement.

In every layby there would be a steaming, clapped-out jalopy cooling off, and on what would now be called the hard shoulder but was then a grass verge there would be families picnicking.

With a bar of Motoring chocolate in the glove compartment, that was motoring, that was.

What I liked about the Great North Road was that you really did have a sense of going north (or south, of course, should you be going the other way). I am not anti-motorway, indeed I regard their intersections and spaghetti junctions as astonishing feats of engineering as awesome as the great viaducts of the golden age of railways; but you never have a sense of going anywhere on a motorway except towards the next service area. With the Great North Road, you were keenly aware, as you plunged your wheezing four-seater into second gear, that the north is uphill.

Sad to say, the A1 was abandoned by its friends when they built the M1; but then they straightened it and widened it and guided it round its favourite bottlenecks, and even rechristened stretches of it the A1(M). And once again it became a busy trunk road. But it was no longer the Great North Road.

So thanks for the offer, Mr Channon; but no thanks. But if the traffic cone concession on the M1 is up for grabs, maybe we can do business.

PS. I hope that when we do have privatised roads they will be given names rather than numbers, as the great American freeways are with names like the Roy Rogers Highway and Jimmy Carter Expressway. How about the Great North Motorway?

Thursday, October 4, 1990

And it's your cross line . . .

Good morning, and today's phone-in is to British Telecom. And our first call is from Mr Nerks of Croydon. Are you there, Mr Nerks? No, it appears we don't have Mr Nerks of Croydon in person, because it seems his telephone is out of order, but we do have a postcard from Mr Nerks in which he tells us he is a first-time caller, and his question to British Telecom is: 'Are there any small ways in which your superlative service which we all recognise is the envy of the civilised world bar none could conceivably be improved?'

Let's hear what British Telecom has to say about that.

Hello? Are you there, British Telecom?

Hello? No this is not Marks and Spencer, madam, you have a crossed line. Please replace your receiver and dial again.

Hello, British Telecom, we seem to have a very bad line.

There's good deal of crackling but I think I can hear a very faint voice assuring us that on the contrary, if they could get the parts and didn't have three men off with bad backs, this would be a very good line indeed. Hello?

And I'm afraid we've just been cut off there. We're trying to ring British Telecom back but no, I've just been told the number's unobtainable.

We're just ringing the operator now and while we're waiting for her reply let's have a record. Wagner's *Ring* with Sir Georg Solti conducting the Vienna Philharmonic Orchestra . . .

And we're having to leave that fascinating opera cycle just there in the last hour where Brunnhilde finally submits to Siegfried because the operator's just told us there's a fault on the line and no one has the faintest idea when it can be repaired, but now we've got through to Directory Inquiries to ask if there's another number we can ring.

And Directory Inquiries is asking how we're spelling British Telecom.

And I'm sorry, but Directory Inquiries seem to have hung up on us. Perhaps we were a little hasty in exclaiming 'Oh, come on!' when they said they could find no one of that name listed.

Let's see if we can find British Telecom in the phone book that someone's just brought into the studio – and yes, we do have that number and it's engaged.

We do now have another caller on the line – well not so much on the line as hanging about in the corridor outside having found fifteen phone kiosks vandalised or out of order. And the question Mrs Smirks of Tottenham has handed in to our commissionaire is: 'Does it hurt British Telecom's feelings when ignorant people who do not know the full facts claim that the telephone service is occasionally not 100 per cent totally perfect?'

And there are a lot of clicks and whirring noises on the line but yes, we're succeeding at last in getting reconnected to British Telecom.

Hello? Hello? Hello! Is there anyone there?

Monday, July 13, 1987

67

Look back with Daisy

At a book fair the other day I picked up for a song – well, nearer the libretto of a complete light opera, if the truth be known – the autograph album of a young Edwardian lady.

It belonged to a certain Miss Daisy who appears to have lived in Croydon, and it was a present to her from her Auntie Maude, who has the first entry. Dated 1907, it is a supplication to Daisy's numerous relatives and friends: 'Write your name within this book, for though we may sever, True friendship is a heritage that will last for ever.'

Daisy's autograph album, leather bound and the size and thickness of one of the uplifting books of the period, is altogether a more substantial affair than the puny little autograph books of my own childhood, with their stock couplets such as 'By hook or by crook I'll be last in this book' and their familiar variations on 'Roses are red, violets are blue . . .'

To be sure, there are plenty of examples from what must have been the standard autograph repertoire of the day, and quite charming they are: 'Tulips on two lips, Which are the best? Two lips are sweetest, must be confessed. Tulips are pretty and gay to the eye. But two lips when pressed, electrify.' And 'Man is Creation's masterpiece – but who says this? Man!' And a folded page with the warning FOR MEN ONLY, which when you open it out reads 'Now aren't women inquisitive?'

But Daisy's friends in the main are far more painstaking in their contributions to her album. Every tenth page is a skilfully executed watercolour or chalk or pen-and-ink drawing of a church or a ship or Worthing pier or an Edwardian belle or an arrangement of flowers; there are cartoons, some original, some evidently copied from the comic papers; there is an heroic pencil sketch of a bird of prey signed 'Your affect. Syd.' Daisy's talented circle perhaps may not have been able to earn a living as artists but they would never have starved as pavement artists.

Where they cannot sketch or draw (or more likely choose not to, for this was an accomplished age), some of them compose. Daisy's music tutor – I imagine she was proficient on the pianoforte – signs in with a few staves of music. Cousin Dolly contributes: 'I am anxious to concoct, A verse or two of rhyme. But all the words seem locked. So I think it waste of time.' Someone called Adolf contributes, in 1912, a mini-essay on feminist politics beginning: 'While it may be right that women do not deserve the vote because they have not the same qualities and gifts as men, this does not decide the issue . . .'

Evidently Daisy did some voluntary hospital work during World War I, for there are a few pages of pencilled autographs from wounded Tommies: 'Rifleman Hester, London Irish, wounded Xmas Day 1915 at that famous health resort of the Western Front, the Hohenzollern Redoubt.'

The rest of the volume is made up of favourite poems and passages, most likely quoted from memory, such as the Quality of Mercy speech from *The Merchant of Venice*, Ode To A Frog from the *Pickwick Papers*, snatches of Omar Khayyam and Sir Walter Scott, popular monologues of the day such as 'Laugh and the world laughs with you' and 'How roses came red', and a comic bicycling poem beginning: 'Three young men and three nice girls, All lovers true as steel, Decided in a friendly way, To spend the day awheel . . .'

There are still many blank pages left in Daisy's autograph album. Why she gave it up is anybody's guess. Maybe, reaching woman's estate, she thought such things too frivolous. Or maybe she ran out of potential contributors. Auntie Maude has the last word in 1920: 'Remember well and bear in mind, A faithful friend is hard to find, And when you find a friend that's true, Don't change the old one for the new.'

It is, of course, a different world we are looking at when we browse through Daisy's autograph album. It is, at least in the middle-class suburb of Croydon and all its equivalents up and down the land, an age of leisure and accomplishment. But it is more than that – it is an age of decent education. How many young people today, asked to write a few lines in an autograph book, could draw on their own memorised anthology of verse?

A retired headmaster wrote to me the other day about the terrible bias against knowing things in schools today – 'We do not believe in the acquisition of knowledge for its own sake,' as the Berkshire History Report put it. The Edwardians, though, did believe in exactly that. Daisy and her friends – shock horror – would have learned all that stuff in her album by rote, by sheer application. Yet contrary to modern educational theory, they thrived on it. Daisy's album is a peep into a happy, lively and confident society.

We cannot go back to an era when every young lady could play the piano and every young man could sing a clutch of comic ditties and Cousin Ethel took her watercolours on holiday. But it has come to something when the modest requirement that every child should be able to recite a poem has to become a matter of passionate intervention by the Secretary of State for Education.

By the way, in all the scores of entries in Daisy's autograph album – most of them creditable examples of penmanship – there is not a word misspelled, and not a comma or apostrophe misplaced.

Monday, March 27, 1989

Caught out in Clogthorpe

Under the umbrella of Any Other Business at yesterday's meeting of Clogthorpe District Council's Standing Affairs Committee, Councillor Bulge (Chair) announced that Councillor Parkin would like to make a personal statement.

Committee members would have seen last week's issue of

the scandalmongering *Clogthorpe Free Advertiser*. Cllr Parkin
had done his best to keep the sordid details out of the Press.
He had bought the editor a drink. He had threatened to knock
his teeth down his throat. All to no avail – the *Clogthorpe Free
Advertiser* was interested in one thing and one thing only, and
that was in titillating its readers to put on sales.

On a point of information, Cllr Nepworth said he might be
a bit thick, but he failed to see how a free newspaper could
put on sales.

Advising Cllr Nepworth to get on home as his mother
needed his boots for loaf tins, Chair called on Cllr Parkin to
make his statement.

Cllr Parkin said the world now knew that in the long and
distant past, he had had a brief ding-dong with that red-haired
barmaid at the Snivelling Coalman. The affair had only lasted
eleven years and it had now been over for weeks. He had been
drunk at the time and could not remember much about it, but
he wanted to put an end to the ugly rumours and tittle-tattle
that had been sweeping through the borough. It was a private
matter between himself, the red-haired barmaid, the red-
haired barmaid's bloke, Mrs Parkin, and Mrs Parkin's mother,
and he would not be adding to his statement.

Cllr Elland, after saying that he would go to the foot of their
(Cllr and Mrs Elland's) stairs, added that he had only just got
back from Brazil on that Transport Committee fact-finding
mission to look at the Rio de Janeiro Corporation tramways
system, and so Cllr Parkin's leg-over situation came as a complete revelation. Was this bit of stuff the same red-haired bint
who used to work in the disco bar of the Squint-eyed Poacher
on the Clement Attlee Overspill Conurbation, who had been
found stark bare in the still room with the Recreational Facilities Co-ordinator?

Cllr Parkin conceded that while he failed to see the relevance
of Cllr Elland's question, it was one and the same lady.

Cllr Elland said that she didn't half put herself about, and
that he wished he were ten years younger.

Cllr Hopcraft said that Cllr Elland had not heard nothing
yet. The redhead in question had got through more blokes
than Cllr Elland had had hot dinners.

Ruling these observations out of order as extraneous, Chair

asked Cllr Parkin how Mrs Parkin had taken the news.

Cllr Parkin said she had gone doolally. She had gone spare. She had thrown the dinner at him. She had cut the trouser legs off his best suit. She had poured most of a pint pot of dandelion and burdock over his head. But it was all right – touch wood, she was standing by him.

Cllr Nepworth said thank God for that. With the council elections coming up in May, if Mrs Parkin had packed her bags and gone home to her mother, it would have been a serious blow to British democracy.

Through the Chair, Cllr Hopcraft asked if he could ask what Cllr Nepworth was blathering on about.

Cllr Nepworth said the so-called leak had been planted on the *Clogthorpe Free Advertiser* with the object of discrediting Cllr Parkin in the run-up to the council election. If Mrs Parkin had gone home to mum it could have been goodbye Cllr Parkin, hello Monster Raving Loony Party. But the smear tactics brigade reckoned without the sense of fair play of the British public. The British public would never turn against a man simply because he was behaving like an over-sexed stoat on heat in his private life.

Cllr Elland said that Cllr Nepworth was talking out of the back of his neck. Either what Cllr Parkin had been getting up to in the Snivelling Coalman car park would affect his electoral chances or it would not. Cllr Nepworth could not have it both ways.

Chair said that any road up, Cllr Parkin had now made a clean breast of it and wiped the slate clean. He had the assurance of the Opposition party, if you could call those three senile old fools the Opposition, that Cllr Parkin having been found with his trousers round his ankles did not matter two shakes of a pig's bottom so far as they were concerned, and there Chair thought the Standing Affairs Committee ought to leave it.

Cllr Tweedyman asked what if the red-haired barmaid sold her story to the *News of the World*.

Cllr Hopcraft said in that case half the men in Clogthorpe would be emigrating.

Cllr Parkin said that as regards the gutter Press approaching the red-haired barmaid, the Committee could safely leave matters in the hands of the red-haired barmaid's bloke, who was by way of being a chucker-out at the Pink Coconut night club on Nelson Mandela Boulevard. Committee members would no doubt have observed that he (Cllr Parkin) was on crutches and had his arm in a sling, and that he had a split lip and a patch over his left eye. This was nothing to what the red-haired barmaid's bloke would do to any representative of the gutter Press seen hanging around the Snivelling Coalman.

Congratulating Cllr Parkin on his honour and integrity, Chair said that his handling of a tricky situation had been impeccable, and that he was model of decency and rectitude and an example to all.

Saying that he would drink to that, Cllr Elland enquired through the Chair whether he could have the red-haired bird's phone number.

Monday, February 10, 1992

Coming down to earth

The Soviet cosmonauts Alexander Serebov and Alexander Viktorenko came out of orbit this week after a 166-day trip in space. They immediately repaired to the Commissars' Arms to catch up on the gossip.

'So what's new, Comrade Landlord?' asked Serebov after ordering double vodkas all round.

'Not a lot,' said the landlord. 'They've opened a McDonald's in Pushkin Street.'

Serebov winked at Viktorenko. 'Oh yes?' he said, deadpan.

'And I suppose Gorbachev's running a Pizza Hut outside the Kremlin?'

'No, he's been too busy calling for free elections and handling calls for independence among the Baltic states,' said the landlord. 'Oh, yes, and there was a big demo in Red Square.'

'Against Gorbachev?' inquired Viktorenko.

'Against Communism.'

'Of course,' said Serebov, with another wink at Viktorenko. 'It's the way you tell them, Comrade Landlord. You should go in for one of these talent contests.'

'I suppose you've heard about the Berlin Wall coming down?' said the landlord.

'Mice?' asked Viktorenko.

'Popular uprising.'

'Go on, I'll buy it,' said Serebov, with an anticipatory smile. 'And what's Honecker got to say about that, eh?'

'Not much, seeing as how they're putting him on trial for treason,' the landlord said.

'The neighbours won't like that,' said Viktorenko, still playing along with the landlord. 'How did the Czechs take it?'

'Well, since you ask, President Vaclav Havel seems to think Honecker's going to get what's coming to him.'

'Vaclav Havel?' echoed Serebov blankly.

'The dissident playwright!' chortled Viktorenko, digging the landlord in the ribs. 'And when they made him President I suppose Mr and Mrs Ceausescu of Rumania sent him a greetings telegram!'

'Maybe they would have done,' said the landlord, 'but they were too busy being executed by a firing squad.'

'You don't say,' said Viktorenko.

'Pull the other one,' said Serebov.

Viktorenko ordered another round. 'So what's happening in the rest of the world, Comrade Landlord?' he asked as they clinked glasses.

'Well, there's South Africa,' began the landlord.

'Don't tell me,' said Serebov. 'Nelson Mandela comes out of jail then goes on South African television to urge the ANC to keep up the armed struggle.'

'You're been reading *Pravda*,' said the landlord.

'Come on, Comrade Landlord, stop mucking about,' said

Viktorenko. 'What's really been going on while we've been up there in Soyuz TM-9?'

'The wife slipped on some ice in Gorky Street and sprained her wrist,' said the landlord. 'And the parrot's escaped.'

Serebov shook his head in sympathy, Viktorenko clicked his tongue.

'You can't turn your back for five minutes,' said Alexander Serebov.

Thursday, February 22, 1990

Dark marks for teacher

Race Officer Potts reporting to Education Committee. As instructed, kept Nelson Mandela (formerly Bog Lane) Comprehensive under surveillance for signs of racism. Found whole school rife with same.

Elitist teachers found to be using white chalk on chalkboard despite availability of green ditto. Pupils forced to write on white paper. Demeaning words beginning with black (blacksmith, blackmail, blackball, etc) not crossed out of dictionaries. Racist books such as *Black Beauty* still in school library. Common room pack of cards still contains ace of spades.

Headmaster made racist comment immediately upon my arrival, to wit, 'Oh God'. Pointed out that said remark was offensive to those who may worship different deity.

Ms Dibbs, English teacher, found to be openly teaching English. Reminded her that this language is not mother tongue of many pupils, to which Ms Dibbs made racist reply, 'So what do you want me to teach the little perishers – Double Dutch?'

In staff coffee break, heard dinner lady ask, 'Black or white?' several times. Instructed her to say 'Milk or plain?' in future. Dinner lady used offensive, sexist word.

Mr Dobbs, woodwork teacher, observed showing Form 4C how to make coffee tables without pointing out that much wood grows in Africa and that coffee is produced by perspired Brazilian labour. Reminded Mr Dobbs that coffee tables are elitist and suggested he switch production to mug-of-tea and sausage-sarnie tables.

In break, playground supervisor heard abusing small ethnic boy with offensively-worded instruction, viz, 'Hoy, you, get down off that roof'.

Found Ms Timpkins, who was flaunting wedding ring despite warning that same is insulting to children of one-parent families, teaching children racist song, namely 'God Save The Queen'. Asked to substitute constructive song, 'We shall not be moved', Ms Timpkins made unhelpful remark, 'Go and take a running jump at yourself'.

In sports period, observed racist race, in which ethnic pupil was put to humiliation of coming in second. Suggested that pupils should in future run round in circles to avoid risk of anyone losing.

In common room, Mr Simpkins, geography teacher, made racist observation as follows: 'Sod this for a game of candles, I'm bloody emigrating'. Under cross-examination, Mr Simpkins agreed that country to which he was contemplating emigrating was Australia, notwithstanding that as geography teacher he must be aware of said country's record on aborigines.

Cannot find reference to game of candles in school sports manual but suspect it is elitist.

Thursday, October 23, 1986

When eggs were eggs

I may have left it a bit late in the day for this year, but I am thinking of mounting a campaign for Real Easter Eggs.

A real Easter egg is characterised by its chocolatey chasteness. It is a simple ovoid, either milk or plain – preferably plain, for my taste – somewhat resembling, with its functional criss-cross indentations, a hand grenade.

It does not have 'Happy Easter' fluted across its surface in yellow icing sugar, nor is it encrusted with fluffy chickens, nor is it tied up with ribbon, nor, particularly, is it encased in cardboard.

We will come back to the cardboard in a minute.

The real Easter egg, when opened – but hang on here a moment. Real Easter eggs have to be cracked open like any other egg. Present-day Easter eggs, when separated from their cardboard moorings (we are coming to the cardboard) simply fall apart in two separately-wrapped segments. What, pray, has happened to the art of Easter egg welding, when the two halves were riveted together with a stream of hot chocolate, doubtless by men wearing protective visors and asbestos suits?

But as I was saying: the real Easter egg, when opened, contains nothing but God's air. You peer into the hole you have punctured in it to extract your first bite and it is like squinting into a miniaturised chocolate Grand Canyon. You are not confronted by a hoard of Smarties, a cache of mini-Crunchie bars, or a cellophane-wrapped selection of hard and soft centres.

Nor does the real Easter egg come with any accompanying crockery such as an egg-cup or commemorative mug. Nor is it harnessed to any plastic novelty, board game, or set of cardboard cut-out cartoon characters (we will get to the cardboard). Nor does it play a tune.

An egg devoid of all such encumbrances, as purists will have found to their cost (ie, their purse) this Easter, is hard to find.

To show you a truly real or really true Easter egg I should

have to transport you by Tardis to my third or fourth Easter Sunday on this planet when I first became aware of the very agreeable tradition of smearing oneself from head to foot in chocolate on this particular day.

The eggs I remember from that sticky era were the size of rugby footballs but they were simplistic in their conception to the point of utilitarianism. They were clad in silver paper and nothing else. You tore away the wrapping and there was the dark, daunting face of a chocolate Eiger, which you ate because it was there. You were not looking for contraband Maltesers or for a game of snakes and ladders. There was your unadorned egg (or if you were lucky enough to have indulgent aunties, two or three unadorned eggs) and that was that.

Then came the war and even the flimsy silver paper wrapping disappeared, to be followed a year or so later by the chocolate egg itself, and children grew accustomed to celebrating their Easter with a slice off the family Mars bar. But peace returned, and with it the Easter egg in all its glory – and all its new-fangled packaging.

We have come to the cardboard.

The *Daily Mail* told us on Saturday that we will be chomping our way through more than 17,000 tons of chocolate egg this Easter. Sales, I read yesterday, are expected to touch £300 million. That is a lot of egg.

But it is even more of a lot of cardboard. Think of this bonanza in terms of wrapping – the cardboard, the tissue paper, the cellophane, the aluminium foil – and you are in a dustbinman's nightmare. The cardboard alone, fashioned into every conceivable type of novelty presentation box from a spacecraft to a Dick Whittington's coach, must be enough to build a cardboard cosmopolis, let alone a cardboard city.

And the fillings! Marketing men put the great chocolate egg boom down to the universal taste for eggs containing Mars bars, Double Deckers and suchlike confectionery which cuts across all age groups. What hope is there for the real Easter egg when manufacturers regard their eggs merely as chocolate packaging for half a dozen bite-size Twix bars?

It is time, clearly, for some enterprising rival to Rowntree or Cadbury to launch a new line in novelty eggs. The gimmick is that it will be completely hollow, will not be encased in a cardboard representation of Old Mother Hubbard's cupboard, and will not be accompanied by a plastic bunny rabbit. It will be a perfectly plain egg, the size of a rugby football, wrapped in silver paper.

Of course, I could go even further back into basics and take the Easter egg tradition back to its origins when it was an everyday hen's egg (symbolical of creation at the start of spring, according to Dr Brewer) which you hard-boiled, painted in pretty colours and rolled down a hill for some reason.

But you know what would happen. Some clown would market hard-boiled eggs with a set of non-toxic paints thrown in, and some other clown would go one better and start packaging them by the half dozen in a cardboard hen.

Monday, April 16, 1990

Moving addresses

Among the augurs indicating that there have been rosier periods of history to live in than the last quarter of the 20th century is the fact that everywhere these days is somewhere else.

You may have noticed this. Say you fall off your bicycle and hobble round to your local hospital. You may depend upon it that you will find a big sign advising that there is no casualty department and recommending that you try another hospital on the other side of town.

Check before you do this. It is probably now an old people's home, to accommodate the folk who were in the almshouses until they were pulled down to make way for a new super-market which replaces the one that used to be in the High Street before it became a home computer centre.

The library is in the old town hall. The town hall staff are in the new civic centre, except for the planning department which is in the old library.

Do not look for the vicar in the vicarage. The vicarage, now known as the Old Vicarage, houses only a retired civil servant who writes letters to *The Times*. The vicar is in the new vicarage which is on the site of the old police station. The new police station is on the site of the old brewery.

Few things are certain in this age of anxiety, but of one thing you may be absolutely sure. If you pass an old building that looks like a school, and which has the legend 'School' hewn into the stone, you may take it that it is no longer a school but a used furniture depository.

You think I exaggerate? Then look over my shoulder at the newspaper clipping on my desk. It announces that the Greenwich Observatory is to be moved from Herstmonceux Castle in West Sussex to Cambridge University (which at the moment of writing remains in Cambridge).

These cannot be good times to be a postman.

Everywhere being somewhere else seems exclusively a British convention. If you go to France or Italy or even to America, with its not entirely deserved reputation for demol-ishing buildings almost before they are finished, you will find, by and large, that the school is in the schoolhouse, the fire brigade in the fire station and the mayor in his parlour, and that even if all's not well with the world, at least you know where it is.

Labour councils, with a few allegedly go-ahead Tory ones thrown in, are mainly responsible for turning the country into a gigantic game of chess, where every institution, as well as much of the population, has to keep moving to another square. In the great municipal boom of the Sixties and early Seventies, they nurtured the extravagant belief that any old building must have outlived its use, that only spanking new premises custom-built to contain the white heat of technology were good enough.

This thought process, if that's what you want to call it, is now ingrained. And so even though the money earmarked to pull England down and start again has now run out, there is still this constant urge to re-locate everyone from the 'unsuitable' accommodation they have endured for a hundred or two hundred years usually to somewhere nastier.

I've half a mind to write to the Prime Minister about it. Is she still at No. 10 Downing Street, does anyone happen to know?

Monday, November 17, 1986

Doing a bobby's job

While I have never seen any serious danger of our becoming a police state – the midnight knock, in this country, is more likely to come from the VAT inspector or the TV licence detector van – we do seem well on our way to becoming a Bobby State.

I am talking about the avuncular power exercised by the sensible, mind-how-you-go, move-along-there British bobby as distinct from the baton wielded by the visored, shield-clutching, Martian-looking riot cop.

He was once typified by Dixon of Dock Green. Now he's been promoted and finished up as Chief Constable.

An increasing number of our chief constables and other senior officers have, over the years, been slowly evolving a kind of Bobby's Law by which they strive, not always successfully, to maintain public order by means not necessarily disapproved of by Parliament but certainly not always down there in black and white in the Statute Book.

Bobby's Law has always been with us to some extent. In less troubled days it permitted the village constable to clip youngsters' ears for scrumping apples – a form of rough justice still much hankered after by nostalgic senior citizens. Now it permits him to stop youngsters entering the village at all if he thinks they mean to cause trouble.

Bobby's Law, during the miners' strike, allowed the police to turn cars back at county borders if their occupants looked as if their purpose in travelling was to do something illegal. This particular example of Bobby's Law was tested in the courts and, to my surprise, turned out not to be in default of the laws of the land.

But then, in its well-meaning but often devious way, it rarely is. Bobby's Law provides for the arrest of ticket touts at Wimbledon. But touting tickets happens not to be an offence – indeed, centre court seats are widely advertised in the newspapers. Obstruction, however, is an offence – and it is on this technicality that the touts are hauled in to court, even though the only real obstruction is caused by police getting in the way of those who want to buy tickets.

Random breath-testing for drivers has never been sanctioned by Parliament. It is, however, sanctioned by Bobby's Law. Thus there are now areas where you may be required to stop your car and blow into a bag even though you are a lifelong teetotaller. Challenge Bobby's Law, however, and it will prove that the police have the right to stop any driver who *may* – their italics – have been drinking.

I don't suppose anyone is going to stand up for the rights of soccer hooligans but they – and the mass of decent supporters with them – have long been subject to Bobby's Law in the way their movements have been restricted. Away supporters, for example, are barred from Luton, even though (to the best of my knowledge) it is not a statutory offence to visit that town of hats and girl choristers.

And now Bobby's Law, again with the best of intentions, turns to the problems of juvenile drinking. In Coventry, Bobby's Law forbids drinking in public in the city centre. In Brighton, Bobby's Law allows (as does, to be fair, common or garden law) the constabulary to patrol the pubs looking for potential trouble. In the Somerset town of Chard, Bobby's Law requires young drinkers to carry an identity card – for all that the Home Office has announced that there are no plans to introduce a national identity card scheme. At Henley, in consultation with the appropriate authorities (there is always consultation with the appropriate authorities) Bobby's Law proposes severe restrictions on the sale of drink during the Regatta.

Now what pretty well all these examples have in common (there are plenty more where they came from) is that you would have to be a fanatical libertarian to make a song and dance about them. After all, we are all concerned about juvenile drunks, about soccer hooligans, about drinking drivers, about law 'n' order in general.

And Bobby's Law reflects that concern. That is how the Chief Constable of Dock Green gets away with it.

I am not saying that this state of affairs is necessarily reprehensible – maybe it's what most people want. But I've always rather stuck with the idea that there should be only one law of the land. If we want Bobby's Law, shouldn't they get it down in writing so it can be quoted in court?

Thursday, June 30, 1988

Apostrophe Olympics

The Winter Apostrophe Olympic Games, sponsored by the AAAA (Association for the Annihilation of the Aberrant Apostrophe) opened at St Andrew's last week. Despite gloomy forecasts of adverse conditions, the venue was literally snowed under with surplus apostrophes and no events had to be cancelled.

After the moving torch ceremony, when the Life President of the AAAA set light to a barrel of examples of the misuse of 'it's' as a possessive pronoun, the Apostrophe Olympics got underway with the spectacular Apostrophe Hurling event.

Gold medallist in this class was S. M. Watkins from Oxford, who hurled a greetings card emblazoned 'Congratulations – you've passed you're exams' as far as he could throw it. Silver medal: Mrs Rosemary Styles, Welshpool, Powys, who tossed another greetings card proclaiming 'Christmas greeting's' a record distance of 100 metres. Bronze: A. B. Billany, Hull, who refused medical treatment after hurling a 4ft by 80ft sign from his local supermarket reading 'Gateway Foodmarkets – alway's more for your money.'

In the difficult Apostrophic Slalom, where competitors are required to negotiate both a misplaced apostrophe and a missing apostrophe in the same sentence, the Gold went to Mr P. A. Stapleton of Chelmsford, Essex, for a dating service ad in his local *Advertiser*: 'You're dates the one with the sack on its head – mines the good looker who I chose from First Impressions.' Silver: Mrs I. J. Rycroft, Loughborough, with an estate agent's slogan boasting 'Its house's that we sell.' Bronze: S. Marsden, Fulham, for an unidentified newspaper reference to the rival Games in Canada – 'Its the start of the 88 Winter Olympic's.'

In the Celebrity Figure Skating Event, where well-known personalities have to reproduce on the ice a misplaced apostrophe encountered on their travels, the Gold went to the brilliant duo Richard West and Mary Kenny for a virtuoso rendering of 'Yeat's Country' from a picture postcard. Kingsley Amis took the Silver for the almost impossible-to-execute 'Jones'ys Wine Bar', while the Bronze went to Willis Hall for a plucky reproduction of an official sign seen in Leeds – 'To St Jame's Hospital.'

The gruelling Decathlon, requiring contestants to produce ten misplaced apostrophes in a single document or poster, was won by exporter Colin Lambourne of London NW10 with a letter from a cargo company addressed to 'R.H.M. Export's

Ltd', proposing to visit 'your office's' with the offer of 'vehicle's to suit your need's for example tilt's, boxe's and fridge's' and signed 'Your's faithfully.' Silver: Mrs M. Lowrey, Gillingham, Kent – a sign at Butlin's, Skegness, offering 'beachball's, postcard's, trainer's, ice cream's, can's of coke' etc.

No Bronze was awarded in this section, all the other entries being greengrocers' signs which have been banned from the Apostrophe Olympics on the grounds that they must have been chalked up under the influence of hallucinatory drugs.

Other results:

Downhill grammar: Gold – John Holmes of the Cathedral Shop, Derby, for a parcel label boasting 'Another consignment of hymn book's from Canterbury Press, Norwich.' Silver – Mrs P. M. Foster, Leighton Buzzard, Beds, with an ad in the *Beds and Bucks Observer*, 'Private Tutors – free list in all area's'. Bronze – J. D. Bell, Leeds, for a letter from a Tory councillor referring to 'the season of Christmas party's.'

Cross-country signwriting: Gold – Mrs M. Franklin, Louth, Lincs, for 'Sign's made to order' in London's Abbey Wood. Silver – Mrs Beryl Donnelly, Broadstairs, Kent: sign in a Broadstairs High Street flower shop offering 'cactu's plants'. Bronze: a masked competitor from Harrow with a variety of local signs reading 'St Ann's Road' and 'St Anns Road' respectively.

Lip-curling event: Gold to L. Orage, Birmingham, for a full-page *Daily Mail* ad offering '£2.00 off all boy's football boots.' Silver: B. Thomas, Petersfield, Hants, with the AAAA's first video entry – A 'Blankety Blank' programme where four out of the five of a team asked to give the plural of 'glass' wrote 'glass's.' Bronze: Mrs D. M. Newman, Wigan, for the slogan on carrier bags issued by the council to commemorate the new market hall – 'Hat's Off to Wigan's New Market Hall.'

Absent Apostrophe Hockey (where contestants have to hit a missing apostrophe into place): Gold to R. Ditchburn, London EC1, for a sign-writer's attempt to render the slogan 'Prudential – we're here to help you' as 'Prudential – were here to help you.' Silver: F. Fawcett, Lincoln, for 'St Peters Church.'

Bronze: Helen Albie, London N1, for 'Heres Where Its At' on a junk mail circular.

The Apostrophe Olympics will end tomorrow with the death-defying Bobsleigh event, when crash-helmeted competitors will hurtle down a terrifying 800-metre course with their bobsleighs crammed with unwanted apostrophes. As out-of-control bobsleighs hit corners and overturn, the crisp winter air will be filled with a confetti of ticket's, cut flower's, free-range egg's, fresh'ly cut sandwich'es, roll's, gateaux's, cig's, ice-cold drink's, gents shoe's, lady's wear, paper's-n-mag's, and a veritable hailstorm of potatoe's, tomatoe's, banana's, apple's, orange's, and bru's'sel's s'prout's. Truly a spectacular finale to the Winter Apostrophe Olympic Games.

Monday, February 22, 1988

Facing the front

Around the corner from where I live there has sprung up one of those redbrick Toytown complexes you see all over the place these days. The ground level comprises a row of shops or 'units' as they prefer to call themselves.

There is a travel agent's, a health food shop, a video centre (when shops are not called units they are now called centres), a franchise picture framer's and a so far unoccupied 'unit under offer'.

I expect it will be a greetings card centre or a candle boutique. Ever since shops became units or centres they have stopped being what you might call proper shops. What we need on that row is a good wet fish shop and a nice deli. But with these Toytown developments fetching Bank of Fun rents no one could afford to open a wet fish unit or cheese and salami centre.

I don't know what impact the architect thought his row of shopping units would have on the street. I suppose they are an improvement on the hole in the ground that was previously there but the effect they have on me, whenever I walk past them, is one of almost clinical depression.

It is not only that they are not proper shops, it is that they do not even look like proper shops. They are uniformly lit in that shadowless white strip lighting that you get in accident clinics. Their plastic, penny-plain facias are of the utility type that you see adorning launderettes and while-U-wait heel bars. Their interiors, as viewed through floor to ceiling plate glass, are barren.

Only the health food shop boasts what you would call a real shop counter. The rest have a dead, empty look, with a jointly forlorn air as if they were pining for their spiritual home in an industrial estate on the outskirts of East Croydon.

Now it is surely not the function of a row of shop fronts to induce gloom and despondency. Shop fronts should achieve the opposite – they should lift the spirits, otherwise they are better off bricked up like hypermarkets off motorway slip-roads. They should make the passer-by feel good, make him want to go in and buy something. Shop fronts should be sirens. The ones I have been describing have the come-on appeal of traffic wardens.

I have been reminded of what shop fronts should look like and what they did look like and what, touch mahogany, some of them still look like, by a little book by Alan Powers called, appropriately enough, *Shop Fronts*, one of a series put out by Chatto & Windus on 'curiosities of the British Street' – troughs and drinking fountains, manhole covers, telephone boxes and so on (£4.99).

It is a photographic record of the way our High Streets used to be, with their white-tiled Welsh dairies and glazed terracotta provision merchants, their butcher's shops (or meat purveyors as they preferred to call themselves) richly decorated with masonic-looking motifs of dead sheep and beef cattle. Then of course there is the higgledy-piggledy ironmonger's shop with as much stock outside as in, every square inch crammed with brooms and bins and bags of nails.

Here is Boots the Cash Dispensing Chemists, Parfumiers & Stationers &c &c, with its elaborately lettered roller shutters. Here is Burton's, the Tailor of Taste, with its decorated clerestory glazing (as I now learn is the term for Burton's old distinctive frontage) and doubtless a billiard hall upstairs.

Here is Sainsbury's in its pre-supermarket era with its shop sign in gold wooden lettering. Here is W H Smith's in its Arts and Crafts phase with its arcade frontages and mullioned windows. Most towns of any age would have a few doll's-house double bow-fronted shops in whose dark mahogany interiors you half expected to encounter Jane Austen shopping for gloves or smelling salts. A few of these establishments miraculously survive, as do some robust outposts of shop frontery such as Hatchard's in Piccadilly or that exuberant umbrella emporium James Smith & Sons in New Oxford Street, a riot of ornate fairground lettering on glass panels.

But with suchlike notable exceptions the tendency has been for shop fronts to deteriorate into drabness over the years. Look at the cheap plastic facias in your High Street with their shoddy design, indifferent lettering and functional lighting and you could imagine that they had all been hurriedly, and ever so temporarily, rebuilt after a tremendous explosion. The clapboard Main Streets of the California Gold Rush looked more permanent – and more exciting.

There are all sorts of reasons for the decline. One is the hatred of tidy-minded planners for street clutter such as awnings and canopies. Another is the ingrained belief of our captains of commerce that getting up to date means erasing the past. Then there is the craze for the corporate image where cheap and nasty chainstore shop fronts, apparently designed by cost accountants, are universally inflicted on buildings from Dover to Dundee regardless of how they clash with their surroundings.

But I am afraid that what we must face up to is that the attractive shop front is becoming a lost art. I sometimes find the odd bread shop or book shop or delicatessen or greengrocer's or antique dealer's that can lure me inside with its upbeat design plus its lively window display, but my local chemists, stationers, ironmongers and so on are all now shops for firmly walking past unless there is something I specifically want. They are just not interesting enough to give reason for pause.

I wonder if that remaining 'unit under offer' might be open to a better offer than it is likely to get from the greetings card centre. Maybe I could convert it into a shop . . .

Monday, May 1, 1989

Who mislaid the mischief?

Traditionalists will be pleased to note that November 5 falls on November 5 this year. That is to say, Bonfire Night happens to fall on a Saturday. These days the burning of the guy usually does take place on a Saturday – but the Saturday doesn't usually turn out to be November 5. Like most other festivals with the exception (so far) of Christmas, Bonfire Night has been shifted from its historical date to the nearest weekend.

At least the institution survives – just, though for how long is anybody's guess. In a society which is increasingly being urged to wear a woolly vest and not go out without its wellies, a bonfire is a nasty, dangerous, unwholesome thing best left to the council leisure department to control and coordinate.

But while, for the nonce and after a fashion, November 5 will happily be celebrated on November 5, I am reliably informed that November 4 will not be happening at all.

I do not know whether you are familiar with November 4. If of southern extraction, probably not. November 4 is – I should say was – largely a northern red letter date going under the official name of Mischief Night.

Mischief Night was when the urchins of any given neighbourhood were allowed carte blanche, or at any rate took carte blanche, to roam the streets creating havoc on a reasonable scale. The mischief centred largely around letter boxes. You connected somebody's letter box to a dustbin lid with a piece of string, banged on the door and then retired to observe the clattering fun from a prudent distance. Or you tied the letter boxes of adjacent doors together, with equally satisfying results. Or you tied black cotton to a letter box and rat-a-tatted it from afar, to the bafflement of the occupant. All good clean fun.

Other aspects of Mischief Night involved raiding one another's Guy Fawkeses and supplies of bonfire wood, frightening old ladies by tapping their bedroom windows with bits of twig dangling from clothes props, and – more reprehensibly – chucking fire-crackers around, sometimes, I regret to say, through the aforementioned letter boxes. But on the whole it was a harmless little curtain raiser to Bonfire Night, which somehow has fallen by the wayside.

I have made inquiries but have been unable to find out what happened to Mischief Night. Northern friends, questioned keenly as to when they had it last, are unable to remember. They think it just sort of withered away. Or, as one of them put it grimly, 'Every night's Mischief Night these days.'

Which is true enough. For paradoxically, as long as it lasted – and the custom goes back to before Guy Fawkes Night itself, probably originating in the old Halloween celebrations – Mischief Night kept children out of mischief. With that safety valve, there was no all-year-round vandalism and very little hooliganism in general.

Mischief Night performed the same service, if you can call it that, for mischief-making as the soccer stadium has performed for those anti-social activities we like to group under the heading 'mindless' – that is to say, it contained the trouble-mongering by providing an outlet for it. I have been saying for years that the more we control soccer violence with identity cards and whatnot, the more it will spill out into the streets. Behold it happening.

There was a time, I believe, when it was compulsory to celebrate Guy Fawkes Night on pain of having an ear lopped off or something. I would not go so far as to make Mischief Night compulsory, with council mischief wardens and sponsored tying of letter boxes to dustbin lids, but if I heard of its revival I should not regard it as another victory for the forces of darkness by any means.

Mischief Night served a good social service, which is why parents and police put up with it. Besides, it was a lot of fun.

Thursday, November 3, 1988

2000 things to go wrong

As the year 2000 looms we are being subjected to more and more predictions of what life is going to be like in the 21st century. Whether they are big, bold forecasts of cities on the moon or cosier projections of how we will all be doing our shopping by computer, they have one thing in common. They have seen the future and they think it is going to work.

Nothing, it would seem, can go wrong. You will tap a couple of keys to summon up a jar of marmalade, a packet of margarine and a tube of toothpaste and lo and behold, half an hour later a van will glide up from the computerised warehouse with a jar of marmalade, a packet of margarine and a tube of toothpaste as requested. Everything will run smoothly. There will be no hiccups or human error.

I don't believe a word of it – not because I am a cynic or a pessimist but because the world doesn't work like that. There are occasions, indeed, when the world doesn't work at all, no matter how much you shake it. Cars still break down 140 years after the invention of the internal combustion engine. Planes still crash after eighty years of flight. My phone still goes on the blink 113 years after Alexander Graham Bell dialled the first wrong number. What makes them think it's all going to be different when my mantelpiece clock strikes thirteen to signal the start of the year 2000?

I will tell you exactly what life is going to be like in the 21st century. You will send out a computer request for a jar of marmalade, a packet of margarine and a tube of toothpaste and after you have waited in all day the van still won't have turned up.

You will ring the computerised warehouse but they won't answer the telephone. After hanging on for half an hour you will get a listless voice saying: 'Could you hold on a tick, I'm on the other line.' After another half an hour you will finally be transferred to an apparent halfwit who will deny all knowledge of your order, and will furthermore refuse to take it down on the telephone as everything has to go through the computer.

Next morning you will repeat the order and after three days it still won't have arrived. You will go round to the computerised warehouse in person where you will be told they're very sorry for the delay but they have four men off with bad backs. But you won't be able to purchase your groceries on the spot because they have to go through the computer.

A week later you will once again sit down at your keyboard and request a jar of marmalade, a packet of margarine and a tube of toothpaste, and lo and behold, half an hour later a van will glide up with a sack of coal. The driver will produce a printout proving incontrovertibly that that is what you ordered.

You will send the coal back and re-order a jar of marmalade, a packet of margarine and a tube of toothpaste. After a delay occasioned by your instructions having been routed to Inverness due to a computer error, a pantechnicon will draw up and unload twelve gross jars of plum and apple jam, four tonnes of lard, 3,000 tubes of moisturising foot cream and a sack of coal.

At the end of the month you will receive a bill for £1,289,613.99. You will find furthermore that this sum has already been automatically debited by your bank computer and that you are now over a million pounds overdrawn. You will query the bill with the computerised warehouse where you will be told that there is nothing they can do at the moment as their computer is down.

You will decide to transfer your custom to another computerised warehouse only to find that your own computer is down and that the rental company have no idea when they can come round to repair it because they have four men off with sprained wrists. In despair you will walk round to your corner supermarket only to find that it has been driven bankrupt by the computerised warehouses . . .

You still think it's all going to run smoothly in the 21st century? I haven't told you the worst yet. Come the year 2000, Sharon and Tracy will still not be in their thirties.

Thursday, February 9, 1989

When the Bill hits the fan

Q I am a soccer hooligan and I have had the Football Spectators Bill read out to me, but there are some fings in it what I do not understand. F'rinstance what is this Bill anyway? Does it mean the Old Bill?

A Effectively yes, but do not worry your shaven noddle about that for the moment. What we have here is a new law which converts paying customers into authorised spectators, Saturday's game into a designated match, and hooliganism into a relevant offence.

Q How will that affect me?

A As well as a better vocabulary you will need a Hooligan Card to get into the ground.

Q Coo, fanks very much. Does that mean I don't have to pay no more?

A On the contrary, it will probably mean you have to pay a good deal more, to finance the scheme. But that is the whole idea. With rising admission prices for designated matches there will be fewer authorised spectators and so relevant offences will drop.

Q Can I get credit wiv my Hooligan Card?

A No, you are mixing it up with Access.

Q Don't I get no access wiv the card, then?

A Only to a designated match.

Q What does designated mean anyway?

A In your case, Slobsville Wanderers and whatever load of rubbish they happen to be playing against.

Q What if I lose my Hooligan Card in a ruck?

A Then you will have to go in the family enclosure with your Dad.

Q But he is an even bigger hooligan nor what I am.

A That is beside the point. Families are exempt from having to carry a Hooligan Card and that's that. So, by the way, are disabled fans.

Q So if I disable a Chelsea supporter on the way to Stamford Bridge, he don't need no card?

A That is correct.

Q What difference will the Hooligan Card make on the terraces?

A Upon committing a relevant offence with half a brick, you will have to surrender it to an authorised person.

Q You mean another fan?

A No, the Old Bill.

Q What will happen then?

A You will be thrown out of the ground and brought before a Justice of the Peace.

Q But that's the same as what already happens.

A Ah, but now that you have a Hooligan Card, they can take it away from you.

Q Then why did they give it to me in the first place?

A God knows.

Q Do I need my Hooligan Card to go on the rampage outside the ground?

A No, but eventually you may need a rampage card. They're working on it.

Thursday, January 19, 1989

Arnold on the lines

'And finally, the railway that's disappearing into its own shunting shed. Following a loss of 23,000 passengers a day, British Rail hopes to halt an expected £84 million shortfall with wide-ranging cuts including the loss of up to forty-eight rush-hour commuter trains a day. Here from our Bournemouth studio to discuss the implications of that is British Rail's brother-in-law Arnold. Good evening, Arnold.'

'Good evening, Jeremy.'

'And the first thing concerned commuters will want me to ask, Arnold, is how is your wife Moira?'

'Still a martyr to indigestion, Jeremy, but my sister Elaine – you know, the one who married British Rail – has put her on to some blue pills that she has to take instead of meals, so we're hoping they'll do the trick.'

'And the boys, Arnold?'

'Kevin's waiting for his GCSE results and lucky little Rory's gone to stay with his Aunt Noreen in Barbados, would you believe? If you remember, Jeremy, she married one of the water companies so they can well afford a time-share flat.'

'Now the next thing the disgruntled public are asking, Arnold, is this. How does your brother-in-law justify charging more and more for less and less?'

'Well, Jeremy, you've got to remember he has an enormous wages bill and it's rising all the time. Three hundred and fifty per cent increase last year – and that's only his own salary.'

'No, I didn't mean your brother-in-law the water company, Arnold, I meant your other brother-in-law British Rail.'

'Oh, I see, you mean Barry, the one who's married to Elaine. He's very well, Jeremy, in fact we had a game of golf only yesterday.'

'And what did he have to say about British Rail's apparent strategy of trying to cut its losses by getting rid of its passengers?'

'Customers, Jeremy. Never say passengers, always say customers. That's what I've drummed into my brother-in-law and he's never looked back since. See, for passengers you've got to provide trains, but for customers you've only got to sell tickets. I've said the selfsame thing to my other brother-in-law Lionel, the water company. Don't call them consumers whatever you do, Lionel, I tell him, otherwise they'll all be clamouring for water to put in their hosepipes. Call them customers and all you have to worry about is sending out the bill.'

'But the question remains, Arnold – whenever British Rail is faced with a huge revenue deficiency, it tries to balance its books by putting up fares and reducing the service.'

'That's not a question, Jeremy, it's a statement. You'd better be very careful – I have another sister, Beryl, who happens to be married to the BBC.'

'Let me put it this way, then, Arnold. Can we expect British Rail standards to get worse as more and more customers drop away?'

'No way, Jeremy. For one thing, fewer customers means less crowded trains – that stands to reason, now doesn't it? And fewer trains leaving the station means fewer trains arriving late – that's another plus. Also, if the worst comes to the worst, Barry can always revise the fares structure.'

'You mean put the fares up again?'

'There you go, Jeremy, always looking on the black side. Listen, I'll tell you in the strictest confidence what my brother-in-law said over that game of golf yesterday. Arnold, he said, we'll never get it 100 per cent right until we make such a gigantic cock-up of the railways that the Government either has to sell them off or come to the rescue.'

'So the rundown services are all part of a grand long-term strategy?'

'You've got it, Jeremy. But will the powers that be listen? Of course, you know where the Government made its big mistake, don't you?'

'What was that, Arnold?'

'It should have married my eldest sister Louise when it had the chance.'

Monday, July 22, 1991

Upward with the people

W e have just had one of our periodic talkings-to from on high, this time from Sir Kenneth Durham, president of the British Association for the Advancement of Science, who warns that Britain will become a second- or even third-class nation if we do not place more importance on science.

Sir Kenneth blames every sector of British society for what he describes as 'technical Ludditism'. Sit down, Arthur Scargill – I'll answer this.

It is not for me to tangle with a man of science, but far from us being a nation of technological illiterates who are apathetic towards all things scientific, as the British Association's president contends, my impression is that technology is so high on our national agenda that we rarely talk about anything else.

Fleet Street hacks, whose conversation in their low taverns once centred on mere scoops and suchlike tittle-tattle, now swap notes on how to download their personal computers' keycode translation software from a cold start. They spend their days crouched over flickering screens calling up text input in green letters where once they scribbled in spiral notebooks.

This very column, I am here to tell you, is no stranger to the Tandy 200 which transmits these pearls of wisdom from the Royal Borough of Earl's Court to the *Daily Mail* merely by calling up the code-word HELP! Time was when this column's idea of advanced technology was liquid Tipp-Ex.

In literary circles, where the talk used to be of post-modernism and the possible winner of the Booker Prize, they now drone on about word processors. Sir Kenneth, who is the author of *Surface Activity And Detergency*, may complain that it is more prestigious to read classics at Oxbridge than to go into engineering at Salford, but does he realise that those who do read classics now file their notes on Beowulf and Chaucer in computer memory banks? I will have him know that I have met stoop-shouldered dons so hell-bent on selling the new technology that they are like Moonies handing out carnations at an airport departure lounge.

Sir Kenneth recommends communicators to be sensitive to developments in areas such as the transmission of stimuli along nerve fibres. I can tell him that many communicators talk about little else. Go into a TV studio these days and the chit-chat is not about the star's latest toy boy but about the back-room-boy toys that can bounce images across the world like frisbees.

I know of no walk of life which is not responsive to science and technology. Even Sharon and Tracy, bless their ten-denier extra-sheer seamed stockings, are computerised up to their plucked eyebrows, being programmed with a dozen variations of 'I'm ever so sorree, but the computer lost your order.' The truth is that all this talk about our being a nation of Luddites is old hat. The newspaper industry may have seen a Luddite skirmish or two (after all, as older readers will remember, Fleet Street is where Lobby Ludd was born – or was he a different chap?) but it now goes singing and dancing into the 21st century. The same kind of transition, less dramatically and less ostentatiously, has happened or is happening in every other branch of industry.

I have always maintained that the British have never been as resistant to change as we have been cracked up – or cracked down – to be. We are against change for its own sake, and why not? What has the invention of Avon, Humberside and Cumbria done for anybody? But we have embraced every beneficial new development with enthusiasm, which is why we gave a welcome to the Industrial Revolution, sliced bread, the desktop computer and the day-glo highlighter.

For Heaven's sake, we are talking about an upwardly-mobile people who have gone from the Home Service to the video recorder without a murmur.

Very quietly, even the most rigid and romantic opponents of technological advancement have begun to tiptoe forward instead of lagging back. They have seen the future and, unless the lines are down or the acoustic coupler is in the wrong socket or everything has been erased or the screen goes blank, it works.

Thursday, August 27, 1987

A flag flies in Clogthorpe

A special meeting of Clogthorpe District Council's General Purposes Committee was convened last evening to consider the borough's stand on the Gulf War.

Cllr Bulge (Chair) said that the Council faced a dilemma which might be said to be crystallised in the slogan SADDAM HUSSEIN IS A RATBAG which some mindless vandal or mindless vandals unknown had daubed on the south wall of the Civic Centre in vermilion polyurethane paint.

If the Council erased the slogan it could well stand accused, particularly by elements of the gutter press such as the *Clogthorpe Free Advertiser*, of being yellow-livered and siding with the enemy. If on the other hand the Council let the slogan be, it could cause offence to a certain ethnic minority. It was a puzzle and no mistake, the solution to which would need the wisdom of Solomon.

Cllr Nepworth opined that if the Chair was referring to Mr P J Solomon, the Borough Treasurer, it was a bit out of the latter's province, except insofar as the cost of turps or other paint remover was concerned.

Remarking that by the left, some mothers did have them, the Chair reminded Cllr Nepworth that the Solomon in question was the biblical one, as in the Song Of.

Cllr Parkin, after stating that it did not matter two shakes of a pig's bottom whether the Chair was referring to Solomon Grundy, the Solomon Islands or Solomon Isaacs the bloody pawnbroker, asked what was wrong with putting out a statement on the lines of, 'While this Council wholeheartedly endorses the sentiment that Saddam Hussein is a ratbag, it in no way approves of causing offence to the borough's ethnic minorities and points out that defacing a public building is an offence punishable on conviction by a £400 fine.'

Cllr Elland said he would like to widen the discussion by asking who the blue blazes had put out the order to council street cleaning operatives to remove the Union Jack from the back of council dustcarts.

Cllr Potter said that he himself had given the order, in his capacity of Chair of the Council Cleansing Department. Street cleaning operatives were well aware that the only political material they were allowed to display were officially-approved stickers reading Clogthorpe Is A Nuclear-free Zone and Clogthorpe Says No To The Community Charge.

On a point of information, Cllr Nepworth stated that the Union Jack was not political material.

Cllr Potter stated that it was an emblem. If street cleaning operatives were allowed carte blanche to decorate council dustcarts with emblems, the next thing anybody knew they would be painting them in the colours of Clogthorpe Wanderers.

Cllr Tweedyman asked what was wrong with Clogthorpe Wanderers.

Cllr Nepworth said nowt that a kick up the goalkeeper's backside wouldn't cure.

Reminding the Committee that they were straying far from the point, the Chair said that Union Jacks had been mentioned. He would ask for a view on the question of minicab drivers flying Union Jack pennants from their radio aerials.

Cllr Potter said the practice should be stopped off.

Cllr Tweedyman asked what was wrong with flying the flag.

Cllr Potter said nowt, so long as the flag was in its proper place, which was up a flagpole. Flags flying from minicab aerials were an anomaly. They were not authorised. If the Council allowed minicab drivers to get away with flying flags, other drivers would want to emulate them. It would set a precedent. You would get an unruly element daubing the Union Jack on bedsheets and flying them out of bedroom windows.

Cllr Tweedyman asked what was wrong with flying Union Jacks out of bedroom windows.

Cllr Potter said they were dangerous. They could blow away. They could land up on the windscreen of a moving vehicle and cause an accident. They could wrap themselves round little old age pensioners and knock them off their feet. Besides, if tenants on the Herbert Morrison estate flew Union

Jacks out of their bedroom windows they would be in breach of council regulations and could be evicted. That was just what Saddam Hussein wanted. The Council would be playing into his hands.

Appealing to the Committee to keep politics out of their deliberations, the Chair said he would like to move on to another matter. There had been complaints from the Clogthorpe Women's Peace Movement about the Boys' Brigade flute and xylophone band playing Land of Hope and Glory at their Sunday church parade. Bearing in mind that the borough was a nuclear-free zone, he would ask for assistance in formulating council policy in the matter.

Remarking that Clogthorpe would not remain a nuclear-free zone for long if a flaming Scud came flying through the council chamber windows, Cllr Tweedyman asked what was wrong with Land of Hope and Glory.

Cllr Potter said it was jingoistic.

Cllr Tweedyman said that he had said it before, on the occasion of the Falklands how-d'you-do, and he would say it again. Cllr Potter was nobbut a bloody conchie.

Cllr Potter issued an invitation to Cllr Tweedyman to step outside and repeat his statement.

Cllr Tweedyman said that if Cllr Potter liked he would broadcast it on Radio Clogthorpe. He wouldn't say Cllr Potter had a yellow streak a yard wide but if a car parked next to him and there was a traffic warden around, it would get clamped.

Asking the Chair to hold his coat, Cllr Potter stated that he would swing for Cllr Tweedyman before he was finished. There was an interruption, and the meeting was adjourned.

Monday, January 28, 1991

102

Shar & Tray go Green

Sharon and Tracy, having exhausted the humour to be got out of the possibility of their store supervisor Mrs Potts having contracted Mad Cow Disease from the canteen mince, next turned their seething brains to the topic of Miss World.

'I see where it says in the Miss UK contest this year, you won't have to wear a swimsuit no more,' said Sharon, outstaring a potential customer who appeared to be nurturing a hope that Toiletries and Perfume would sell her a lipstick if she stood there long enough. 'And they're finking of bringing in the same law for Miss World.'

'Coo!' exclaimed Tracy, applying to her rose-bud mouth the very brand that the frustrated customer was anxious to purchase. 'Does that mean Miss France and Miss Venezulu and Miss Paranoia and all them won't be wearing nuffin but their sashes?'

'No, sillee!' said Sharon. 'They've got to wear long dresses, haven't they? And instead of giving their hobbies as travel and meeting people, they have to answer questions about the thingy, the environment, and prove that they done community service.'

'What for?' inquired Tracy.

'So that the punters won't fink that just because they're beauty queens, they ain't got nuffin between their heads.'

'Shane's done community service,' said Tracy. 'Cos don't you remember, he got 200 hours for getting in that ruck with them Leeds United supporters?'

'I don't fink it's that kind of community service,' said Sharon, her brow furrowing in thought. 'I mean to say I can't see nobody being made Miss World just for kicking in free shop windows and resisting arrest. I fink you've got to do it voluntry, like picking up litter and that.'

'I don't believe it,' said Tracy, dabbing her refurbished lips with a tissue and discarding it on the floor. 'I mean to say, can you just imagine that Judith Chambers or whatever she's called saying Right, ladies and gentlemen, our next contendant is

Miss Peruvia, and her intrests are making her own dresses, doing the Lambada and picking up litter? Leave it out, Shar.'

'You don't understand, Tray. If you want to be in with a chance of being Miss World these days, you got to fink green.'

'I go green every time I see the flipping line-up,' grumbled Tracy. 'Why don't you and me have figures like that, Shar?'

'Well, I don't fink I've ever seen Miss UK sitting on a wall in the shopping centre eating pie and chips, so that might have sunnink to do with it, Tray. But now that we don't have to struggle into a swimsuit no more, and sposing we can knock the Munchie bars on the head for a few weeks, I reckon we could be in with a chance.'

'What, of being Miss World, Shar? Both of us?'

'No, not both of us, Tray. Naming no names, one of us would have to be No 1 and the other would have to be No 2. But remember, you've got to do your community service and know all about the thingy.'

'The environs,' prompted Tracy. 'I know what I could do for my community service – I could scrub all the graffiti off of the front of the public library.'

'I didn't know there was any graffiti on the front of the public library, Tray.'

'There ain't, but I could get Shane to do some, couldn't I? And as for the environs, I could go into the library and take out a book on it.'

Sharon emitted a squawk of laughter that set the chandeliers jangling in Lamps and Light Fittings two departments away.

'A book? You? You've never read a book in your life!'

'I didn't say nuffin about reading it, Shar. I'm going to carry it about on my head, like all the Miss World contendants do when they're learning how to wiggle down the catwalk.'

'But they don't wiggle no more, Tray, that's what I'm trying to tell you. Like I said, you've got to be like Ben Elton and show that as a finking beauty queen you're reely upset about the world being in such a bad way.'

'If they've done away with wiggling,' said Tracy, 'it reely is in a bad way.'

Monday, June 4, 1990

104

Here's to the
mod-con man

Why have estate agents got such a bad name? I mean apart from the fact that some of them – an unrepresentative minority, I dare say – are idle, incompetent, avaricious, devious, two-faced, dishonest and complete strangers to the truth?

In Edwardian public schools, if you wanted to say something really cutting about Jones Minor, you would taunt him with having a grocer for a father (meaning Daddy had bought a peerage out of the proceeds from cornering the market in lard). If you want to be insulting nowadays, when the father of She Who Must Be Obeyed really was a grocer, you say your enemy has the values of an estate agent.

The worst thing, the very worst below-the-belt thing that Gucci socialists can find to say about Mrs Thatcher is that she has made this a land fit for estate agents. They make Knight Frank & Rutley sound like seedy, velvet-collared characters in Minder's Winchester Club hissing 'Psst! Wanna buy a used house?'

Even estate agents themselves are so concerned about their image that they are falling basement over attic to support a new Government code of practice which will no doubt lay it down that broom cupboards may no longer be described as spare bedrooms and 'unspoilt' will have to stop standing in as a synonym for 'roof falling in'.

Of course it's high time that estate agents set their des res in order. It is, for example, highly reprehensible that any Tom, Dick or Harry can set himself up in the business for all the world as if selling houses required no more expertise than selling bars of soap – or bars of gold. I know I am on firm ground here because it happens that there was a time when I was in with a chance of becoming one of those Toms, Dicks or Harrys myself.

It is a little known fact – I hope my Boswell is taking notes – that early in life I toyed with the idea of becoming an estate agent. Or to be more exact, the idea was toyed with by my grandmother, who in the belief that the lad would get nowhere without letters after his name, enrolled me in a course of studies for the Incorporated Society of Valuers and Auctioneers.

To give me practical experience of the difference between freehold and leasehold and how to spot whether all that messuage and curtilage situate and known as No 5 Rat-droppings Lane was suffering from a terminal case of rising damp, I was signed on as an office boy to a firm of estate agents. Among my duties was framing the property ads for the evening papers – you know the kind of thing, where 'close to transport' means opposite the marshalling yards. It must have been that training which persuaded me there was a living to be got out of writing fiction.

I also had to issue prospective purchasers of outrageously priced £650 semis with orders to view, sometimes accompanying them if there was anything we wished to divert their attention away from such as the fungus on the back bedroom walls. And I took the coal orders. To this day I have no idea why so many northern estate agents sold coal on the side. Maybe it was because they didn't sell many houses.

It was dull, boring work and after a few months of it I decided that I could live without those initials after my name. But for what it was, it was honourable work. People did not wrinkle their noses in distaste or vomit into their hats when you confessed to being an estate agent's clerk. And estate agents themselves were pillars of society, members of the Chamber of Commerce and leading lights of the Ebenezer Chapel.

Why, then, has their image changed? Principally, I would say, because they make lots of easy money – still the unforgivable sin even in Thatcher's Britain. Estate agents used to be men in crumpled suits and Fair Isle pullovers who went home by bus to the kind of property described in their own classified ads as 'compact bungalow with manageable garden'. Now they dress like pop stars' road managers, drive flash Jaguars and live in riverside penthouses straight out of their own full-page ads in the glossy magazines.

It was with great glee, come the property slump, that the nation learned that not every estate agent can now make five grand simply by lifting his car telephone. We felt they had richly earned their come-uppance.

Yet – allowing that there are bad apples in every barrel, including apples that would sell the barrel itself while their own granny was still living in it – who was it gave the property market a bad name? Property owners. Who forced up prices? Property owners. There may be estate agents who connive at and even manipulate the gazumping game – but who are the gazumpers? Take a look at that chap with the pipe in his mouth, mowing the front lawn of Dunroamin.

But no one ever talks about greedy home-owners or get-rich-quick householders. You do not accuse a neighbour who has made a 500 per cent profit on the sale of his house of 'cashing in'. You do not hear Hampstead Fabians sneering that Mrs Thatcher has made Britain a spivs' paradise for the residents of Acacia Avenue.

Every era has to have its villains and Thatcherism seems to have done for estate agents what Nixonism did for used-car salesmen. Doubtless there are some of them you would not care to introduce to your mother but I can only speak as I find, and what I have found is that all the estate agents I have had dealings with down the years have been chaps I would gladly have bought a second-hand house from, and indeed usually did. Let's hear it, for a change, for the mod-con man.

Thursday, June 22, 1989

107

Bring back the money box

A report entitled Spoilt Brats, to be published this week by a leading advertising agency, sounds like good additional dialogue for the Lamentations of Jeremiah. It projects a dismal picture of the children of the Nineties. Far from being the hoped-for caring generation who are into recycling and saving whales, they will be, if the researchers have got it right, consumer gluttons who have it all and want still more.

The typical product of the Me-Me-Me Age is already demanding a TV set at ten, drinking lager at twelve and having sex as thirteen; and in what used to be thought of as pre-adolescence possesses material luxuries for which most of us had to wait until we were thirty or so.

Doubtless the next step is that tobacconists will be getting fined for illegally selling the little shavers Corona Coronas at age nine. At any rate it is going to get worse – or as they would have it, better. Young persons aged fifteen to twenty-four in 1995 will be the most affluent generation in our history – and how dare they?

You and I, who got fourpence a week pocket money and had to make our own television set from an old packing case and a sheet of Cellophane, can see that no good will come of it. But we get the blame for it. It is the parental passion for the good things of life that makes them so materialistic that half of the youngsters interviewed in this survey regard 'looking after number one' as what life is all about.

I must say that as a child I was never totally convinced that the price of a Meccano set cannot buy true happiness and I spent a good deal of my time buttering up rich kids with access to such goodies. So I am not against a certain amount of youthful affluence.

With us – the luckier ones, that is – it was bicycles and roller skates. With them it is personal TV sets and hi-fi systems. With us it was the furtive Woodbine and snogging in the back row of the Regal. With them it is keg lager and sex at thirteen. That is how the world turns – and if it is turning a damn sight too fast for some of us there is little we can do except get off.

And yet. A little cameo from before Christmas sticks in my mind. I was in W H Smith's looking at calendars when I saw a mother give her daughter of about nine or so a ten-pound note and tell her to go and choose a present for Daddy.

Nice lady. Nice child. And at least the tot had been allowed the initiative of picking Daddy's present herself. But I did wonder: whatever happened to saving up?

Moppets of nine should not be wandering around Smith's with ten-pound notes. They should be wandering around Smith's with a purseful of small change, wondering what they can buy that doesn't cost more than fifty pence. They should have been saving up for weeks, and at least once daily they should have opened up their Mickey Mouse money-box and counted the coins to see if their £1.21p had miraculously become £1.25.

Being given money to buy presents was regarded, in the circles I moved in as a boy, as a social stigma. It was like being bailed out by the IMF. You had recklessly squandered your weekly income on aniseed balls and all-day suckers and now you had to go begging for the wherewithal to purchase a bath cube and a bar of soap in the shape of a lemon.

Saving up was part of the rich pattern of childhood and never more satisfactory than when you were saving up for some longed-for treasure – a scooter, say, or a model typewriter. You augmented your pocket money with cash earned from odd jobs and donations from rich uncles and the tooth fairy – and in this case there was no shame in accepting a little parental help, which usually came in the form of matching your savings penny for penny.

But how, except by their turning to crime, can we expect today's children to raise the money for a TV set or home computer? That's a hell of a lot of car-washing and errand-running. And how, when they fail to come up with the cash, do we deny them these toys when every other kid in the street has got one? In the age they're living in, which is more than one jump ahead of the age their parents are living in, you might as well try to deny them an electric light bulb in their bedrooms.

It's a hard world, this world of ease and plenty, and it is not going to get any easier and certainly not any cheaper. It may, however, be of some grim satisfaction to reflect that by the year 2020 the Spoilt Brats of the Nineties, now grown up or anyway of parental age, will be experiencing the same problem themselves – but in spades.

Bring back the Mickey Mouse money-box, that's what I say.

Monday, January 15, 1990

Child's guide to that tax

The proposed replacement of the dog's breakfast tax by a childishly simple dog's dinner tax has caused some confusion among the class of people who get a throbbing headache every time the subject is mentioned. I have been asked to set their troubled minds at rest.

Q How will the new tax work?

A It won't.

Q All right, then, Clever Dick, how is it supposed to work?

A It will be a childishly simple property tax like the rates.

Q Then why don't they just come straight out with it and say we're going back to the rates?

A Because there are some childishly simple people around who would scoff and jeer at the sight of the Government being forced to perform not so much a U-turn as a spectacular high-speed reverse down the hard shoulder.

110

Q In what way, if any, will this childishly simple new tax differ from the childishly simple rates?

A It will be based on a childishly simple valuation of the capital value of your property.

Q Who will have to pay it?

A You will.

Q What I mean is, will it be a childishly simple roof tax, a childishly simple head tax, or what?

A If you mean will the legendary little old lady living alone in a big house have to pay the same as the equally legendary family of six living in the slum next door, as in the bad old days, the answer is certainly not. She will have to pay more.

Q So who will decide the value of my property?

A A great straggling army of licensed valuers roaming the land with tape measures around their necks and dry rot meters in their pockets, who will cast an expert eye on your Spanish patio, carport, fitted kitchen, granny flat and patch of rising damp, and after sucking their hollow tooth for a while will make an assessment of what your house would be worth on the open market if you had to sell it to pay the dog's dinner tax.

Q Sounds like an awful lot of paperwork.

A Not at all. It will be put on computer. Bit like a floppy disk Domesday Book, really.

Q Supposing I don't agree with the valuation?

A Then you have the right to appeal by voting for the Liberal Democrats in any future by-election. Alternatively you can start a riot. This should bring down the value of your property.

Q Supposing my house is valued at £100,000 but then I put it on the market and it only fetches £80,000, do I get a rebate on my dog's dinner tax?

A Sorry, that would be administratively impossible.

Q All right, then. Supposing my house is valued at £100,000 but when I put it on the market it fetches £120,000, would I have to pay a supplementary dog's dinner tax on the difference?

A The details have not been worked out yet, but the answer to your childishly simple question is very probably yes.

Q That doesn't seem very fair.

A Listen, buster, you'll be lucky if the local council doesn't gazump your would-be purchaser and force the selling price up to £150,000.

Q Supposing I don't own any property. Do I still have to pay this childishly simple tax?

A Afraid so. If you cannot afford to buy the house or flat you live in, you will be taxed as if you had just finished paying off the mortgage.

Q But if I can't afford to buy my house, how am I expected to be able to afford to pay a dog's dinner tax based on the assumption that I own the place?

A Worry not, there will be procedures for people like you. Send for our childishly simple free leaflet 'How to dodge the dog's dinner tax without being thrown into jail'.

Q Supposing, after paying my dog's dinner tax, I am reduced to living in a cardboard box. Will I still be taxed?

A Let's get this straight. You are not taxed at all. That is the beauty of the scheme. The Government, in its benevolence, is actually abolishing a tax – got it? It is your property that is taxed. So if you are living in a cardboard box, it will be taxed on the value of its contents before it was thrown away. Therefore be sure not to doss down in anything that comes from Harrods.

Q From what you are telling me, it sounds as if the dog's dinner tax is going to be as much of a fiasco as the dog's breakfast tax.

A That's the idea. You see, when the tax is implemented and armies of demonstrators are burning down their town halls, heaving bricks at policemen and overturning safe Tory seats at by-elections, people will start to demand: 'For heaven's sake, why doesn't the Government simply cut its losses, admit it's all been a terrible mistake, and go back to the old poll tax?' It's childishly simple, really.

Thursday, March 14, 1991

Yobs and non-yobs

That we are two nations was first observed by Benjamin Disraeli – since when the phenomenon has been remarked upon almost daily, the current example being the newly-published Gallup Survey of Britain. A majority of us rightly perceive this country as deeply divided, split between the haves and have-nots of the south and north respectively.

The survey shows too that half of us see ours as a violent society, that we are dissatisfied with our children's education, that nearly three-quarters of us believe our moral conduct is getting worse, and that only one in four thinks we are still a good-mannered people.

All of which brings me to a social divide unobserved by Disraeli and unsurveyed by Gallup. Our amoeba-like tendency has taken a new and unpleasant turn, our latest exercise in the two-nation splits being to realign us into one nation of yobs and another nation of non-yobs.

To be sure, yobbism has always been with us – a recurring blot on the unfolding tapestry of our island's history. What is new is that yobs are no longer drawn pretty well exclusively from the underclass of the slums and stews. There are now yobs to be found in every social class.

Take for instance that sturdy upholder of traditional values, the British bobby. That Gallup survey finds over half of us dissatisfied with the way the police conduct themselves – and not surprisingly. Everyone you meet these days has anecdotal evidence of police yobbism – of doors smashed in, of needless violence, of hassling and harassment, of wild over-reaction, of riding roughshod over the innocent. It is no longer a case of a few bad apples. There is the decent, civilised police force we have always been blessed with – the non-yobs – and there is the new and identifiable and powerful constabulary of yobs.

Confrontation politics, it has to be said, are inclined to bring out the yob in even the most even-tempered of coppers. And confrontation politics are themselves the result of the yob/

non-yob divide. The first action of Arthur Scargill's miners in their disastrous dispute was to stand up and be counted in their respective ranks of yobs and non-yobs. Mr Murdoch's sacked printers and their supporters outside the barbed wire of Wapping followed suit. The trade union movement marches into its decline under the twin banners of missile-hurling, cat-calling yobbism and respectable law-abiding non-yobbism.

So does the Labour Party, which chooses to use the term militants and moderates for its yobs and non-yobs. The Tories, while unlikelier than Labour to saddle the next Parliament with a clutch of yob MPs, have nevertheless a strong Yob Tendency of their own, though they prefer to call their yobs Young Conservatives in the hope that they will grow out of it.

Away from the mainstream, single issue politics have seen the emergence of the yob in such causes as animal rights, women's lib (female yobbism is a phenomenon within the phenomenon), race relations, the peace movement. Thanks to the calibre of caring persons attracted to the social services, there is now such a creature as the compassionate yobbo.

'Here we go, here we go, here we go!' is the national anthem of the yob – now sung at election meetings and union rallies as well as on the terraces which were, of course, the spawning ground of yobbism. But sporting yobs – still called 'an unrepresentative minority' by despairing managers – no longer confine themselves to football. Witness the oafish scenes at the Bruno–Witherspoon fight last week, when we exported our yobbism to the world.

Yobbism knows no boundaries. If there is no out-and-out Royal yob there are Royals – not all of them sprigs – who have their yobbish moments, and doubtless some future Prince Yob is in the Palace pipeline to counter-balance the once taken-for-granted non-yobbishness of the monarchy.

There are City yobs pulling in millions by putting their yobbishness to work for them on sharp property deals or in the money market; land-owning yobs, whose conifer-planted, satellite-dish-sprouting, guard-dog-infested estates march with the clover meadows of the gentle squirearchy; yobs in the cloisters of Oxbridge, born with silver spoons up their nostrils.

Commuter non-yobs from the leafy suburbs perforce stand in the aisles of their trains with empty drink cans washing around their ankles, discarded by commuter yobs sprawling their feet across two or even four seats. Holidaying non-yobs take the Channel ferry crossing their fingers against this once most agreeable means of reaching the Continent being yet again over-run by drunken, brawling, holidaying yobs. Motoring non-yobs tootling along the M1 at 60 mph are harried by the Colonel Bogey klaxons and flashing lights of motoring yobs.

You have only to walk the streets for half an hour to observe, from the litter, the graffiti, the vandalism, and not least the slouching presence of the yobs in person, that we are indeed most remarkably two nations.

Did the twain never meet – were there a kind of benevolent apartheid to prevent their paths crossing – it would hardly matter. But it is becoming increasingly difficult for a non-yob to get through the day without a yobbish encounter, direct or indirect.

How did our new two nations come about? I don't say this is the complete answer but it is noticeable that the rise of yobbism has coincided with the decline in education. Yob teachers have a lot to answer for.

Monday, July 28, 1986

It's all on the cards

I t is a week now since the first card of Christmas plopped through my letter box. As usual it was a study of some countryside in adverse weather conditions and as usual it was signed Scribble.

I do not know who Scribble is except that he or she holds no certificates for penmanship and lives in SW1. I have many friends of varying degrees of legibility in SW1 and so it could be any one of half a dozen of them who is always first with these indecipherable tidings of great joy.

Scribble is the only Old Reliable among my Christmas card correspondents, not counting a firm I last did business with fifteen years ago, which annually sends me a photographic view of some London landmark for no other reason than it cannot get my address out of its computer.

The rest of my friends are as erratic and unpredictable about sending cards as I am myself, one year sucking up to the Post Office by getting the whole thing over by December 1, the next year staggering the operation with scattered showers of robins and snowmen right up till Christmas Eve, the third year being seized with inertia and not sending any at all until equally seized with guilt as D-Day approaches.

There are, of course, those creatures of habit and regularity, prune-eaters fixed in their ways, who on the second Sunday afternoon of each and every December sit down and methodically work their way through the Christmas card list, debating long and earnestly, when they come across a name lacking a tick signifying the receipt of a reciprocal card last year, whether to give the backsliders another chance.

But even these settled souls are subject to the variations and fluctuations which attend the Christmas card rigmarole. These come in endless permutations. They also tend to come in cycles.

First there is the size factor. The pattern appears to be: Year One, despatch cards as big as bedsheets. Year Two, go to the opposite extreme and send out titchy little things the size of postage stamps. Year Three, tall thin oblongs. Year Four, novelty cards that fall over if anyone breathes on them. Year Five, standard 40cm × 25cm. Year Six, back to the bedsheets.

Then there is the subject matter. Year One, Dickensian. Year Two, Old Masters. Year Three, jokey. Year Four, outbreak of French – Joyeux Noel and all that. Year Five, chaste pen and ink sketch of single candle. Year Six, back to the old-tyme waits, skaters and stagecoaches.

Within the subject matter variation there is also the selection factor. Year One, pick cards all the same. Year Two, four or five different categories. (There is a further sub-option here: do you throw last year's surplus cards away or send the same cards out two years running to your more myopic friends, hoping the Victorian tobogganing scene won't look too familiar?) Year Three, all different. Year Four, all identical again, overprinted with sender's name and address for good measure.

Quantity: Year One, send cards to everyone in your address book, including that couple you met in Torremolinos this summer and someone called OK Taps who turns out to be a 24-hour plumbing service. Year Two, close friends and family only. Year Three, just Granny and a couple of spinster aunts who'd be miffed if they didn't get one. Year Four (after receiving only half a dozen cards last Christmas), everyone in the address book again, if not everyone in the telephone directory.

Cost: Year One, money no object. Year Two, guilt reaction – charity cards only. Year Three, bumper bargain pack bought in last January sales. Year Four, think 'what a ridiculous price to pay for a few bits of pasteboard' but stump up just the same.

Message: Do you just scribble your name (in Scribble's case, literally), or do you add a personal message to each card – 'Hope you are well and that Madge's leg will not trouble her in 1987'? The answer is that the average Christmas card sender alternates between one and the other. And does only one of you sign the cards while the other addresses the envelopes, or do you both sign each card individually? Same rule applies.

Reciprocation: Year One, meticulously send cards to everyone who's sent you one, including your insurance company and a mini-cab firm. Year Two, don't bother. Year Three, exhaustive search for addresses of all people missed out, insurance companies and mini-cab firms excluded.

And so on.

So to sum up, that annual casual-sounding question, 'What are we doing about Christmas cards this year?' is a compendium one incorporating, 'How many – if any – are we going to send, and to whom; when are we going to post them; how much shall we pay for them; what size and shape should they be; are we going in for Bruegels, Snoopies or yule logs this year; what shall we write in them; do we keep the odd dozen cards on one side in case we've missed anyone out; and when Prince Albert started this stupid tradition did he realise what he was letting us all in for?'

All of which is a lead-up to what I set off to say in my column this morning:

Happy Christmas, Scribble, whoever you are.

Monday, December 15, 1986

A name for Europe

Proceedings of the European Community Regulatory Body on Harmonised Nomenclature or a Name for Europe. Day One.

Mr Bratwurst (Germany) said that what the committee was looking for was a name that would encapsulate the hopes, dreams and aspirations of a European Federation, that would trip off the tongue, that could not be mistaken for an international parcel delivery service, and that would look good on road signs. Call Mr Bratwurst prejudiced if the committee liked, but he could think of no more suitable name than Germany.

Mr Pommefrite (France) said the problem with calling a Federated Europe Germany, delightful name though it was, was that it was not standardised. Some people would say Germany but others would be going around saying Deutschland, while a significant minority would prefer l'Allemagne. It could be very confusing – ask Terry Wogan.

Mr Bratwurst said all right then, if Mr Pommefrite could think of a better name, let the committee hear it.

118

Mr Pommefrite said he had always fancied the name La France.

Mr Fruitcake (UK) said that was the most stupid idea he had ever heard in his life. Fancy calling a loose federation of countries The France. It sounded like a bloody cruise liner or a one-star hotel. Now if the committee wanted Mr Fruitcake's suggestion as to what a united Europe should be called if there ever was a united Europe – and mind, he had said nothing – then what better name than United Europe? It had many distinguished precedents such as United Kingdom, United States and United Biscuits.

Mr Waffle (Belgium) said the problem with United Europe was that the noble conception of a community of nations with a single currency, a single market *sans frontières*, and a standard width between tram lines, might stand in danger of being mistaken for a football team. What was wrong with continuing to call the EC the EC? That, after all, was what was printed on about three billion tonnes of headed writing paper, which would have to be put in the shredder if the name were changed.

Mr Taramasalata (Greece) said he hoped the committee's vision extended beyond the contents of the stationery cupboard. Now it so happened that Greece had a terrific Name for Europe. It was a winner. It could not fail to win the hearts and minds of all true Europeans. How about, wait for it, Boom-bam-a-bam?

Mr Poteen (Ireland) said he would award the Greek contribution no points – *nul points*.

Mr Mortadella (Italy) said he was just running this one up the flagpole to see if anyone saluted, but how about all the nations of the Community just sticking the prefix Euro- in front of their names, so that you would have EuroFrance, EuroGermany, EuroItaly, EuroTheNetherlands and so on?

Mr Smorgasbord (Denmark) said he liked it, he liked it.

Mr Fruitcake said he was not too sure. He could see difficulties. Supposing, for example, one former Prime Minister of a particular member of the Community wanted to call another former Prime Minister a pig-ignorant old bat for knowing point nought nought one per cent of damn all about European culture, he would have to rant on about the EuroGermans being European, the EuroItalians being European, the

EuroFrench being European and so on. It was a bit of a tongue-twister. He would finish up frothing at the mouth.

Mr Gateau (Luxembourg) said the committee was beating about the bush. If there was to be a federation of European states then it would have to call itself the Federated European States. What more suitable name did objectors have in mind? Mavis?

Mr Sardine (Portugal) said all right, supposing for the sake of argument the committee decided on Federated European States, what would individual nations put on their signposts?

Mr Bratwurst said there would no longer be any individual nations.

Mr Sardine said that was the very point he was making. You would have a big sign at one end of the Channel Tunnel saying 'To the Federated European States' and another big sign at the other end saying the self-same thing but pointing in the opposite direction. He had heard of all roads leading to Rome but this was ridiculous.

Mr Smorgasbord said that speaking of road signs, what size lettering would they be in? He knew it was early days yet, but the committee would not want different transport ministers authorising road signs in different sizes from one region to another. They would all have to be the same.

Mr Bratwurst said that went without saying, and a sub-committee was working on it.

Mr Pommefrite said and they would all have to be in the same language, preferably French. That was another problem the committee would have to face up to sooner or later. How could you have a Federated Europe when individuals were gabbling away ten to the dozen in Portuguese, English, Spanish, Walloon et cetera?

Mr Bratwurst said another sub-committee was drafting a standardised European language, a streamlined version of Esperanto with all the words the same length. Talking of standardisation, he knew of a restaurant where they had twelve identical lobsters, so how about a spot of lunch?

The meeting adjourned.

Thursday, June 20, 1991

Chinese chatter

According to reports in the Chinese Press, too many state employees are spending their time idling and sipping tea, with up to eighty per cent of China's white-collar workers not doing a full day's work.

I call that rather reassuring, as my friend Ned Sherrin used to say. It is always a relief when the inscrutable Chinese show scrutable signs of being a bit like us. Next, we shall be hearing that they are always taking days off with bad backs and that they throw their Crispy Rice wrappers down in the street.

But perhaps you want evidence that Chinese office workers are only human? Over, then, to the Ministry of Certain Things, where two clerks, Ke Vin and Bri An are supposed to be filing ball-bearing production returns. But are they? Let us listen in.

'Did you see that smashing programme last night, "Self Reliance and Arduous Struggle as a Means of Increasing Agricultural Norms"? It was really good.'

'No, but I taped it. I was watching the last episode of "On the Correct Handling of Contradictions Among the People".'

'Load of rubbish. I only saw the first one – I can't stand that bloke who's in it. What's his name, the one who did the voice over in "A Visit to the Prosperity Through Better Understanding Tractor Factory".'

'It got better as it went along. Last night they were on about the achievement of unity through self-criticism and correcting mistaken ideas. It was terrific. I hope they do another series.'

Meanwhile, across the office, Sha Ron, Tra Si and Ca Thi should be typing up next month's quotas for the Diligence & Frugality Scrap-iron and Old Bones Collective. But Ca Thi is on the telephone, Sha Ron is painting her nails and Tra Si is running off a recipe for dumplings with yellow-bean sauce on the office photocopier . . .

'. . . So she says, she says, "I thought you were going out

with Ba Ri," she says, "So why are you making eyes at Roh Ni?" she says. Oo, she's a spiteful little cow. So I turned round and said, "Look, Deh Bra," I said, "if it's any of your business," I said, "just because Ba Ri took me to a public discussion on the Orientation of the Youth Movement it doesn't mean to say we're going steady," I said. "It just so happens that he offered me a lift on his bike, if you want to know. And as for making eyes at Roh Ni," I said, "since when has there been a law against talking to someone just because someone else once invited him to a reading of Problems Of Strategy In China's Revolutionary War, only he stood her up . . . ?"'

Bored of listening in to Ca Thi's conversation, Sha Ron and Tra Si resume their own.

'Are you going to that lecture on Integrating the Intellectuals With the Broad Masses of Workers and Peasants at the Palace of Youth Culture tonight, Sha Ron?'

'No, I'm staying in to wash my hair. Besides, I don't want to risk bumping into that creep who's always hanging about near the statue of Industrious & Conscientious Young Revolutionaries in the entrance hall, combing his hair. He doesn't half fancy himself. He's a right bighead.'

'Who – Teh Ri? The one who looks a bit like that feller who played the combine-harvester driver in "The Youth Shock Brigades Are Our Future"? I think he's quite dishy.'

'He's a drip. He asked me to go with him to do voluntary rice-picking in the No 14 Agricultural Producers' paddy fields next Sunday. I told him to get lost.'

Back in the filing section, the tea mugs have been pushed aside and some paperwork appears to be getting done at last. But are Ke Vin and Bri An really attending to their duties?

'Have you got Peking Wanderers and Canton Rovers down for a draw, Ke Vin?'

'No, I reckon Peking will walk it now; they've got that new striker. Canton are in all kinds of trouble.'

'I can't agree with you. Didn't you see him miss that goal in that replay with Shanghai Wednesday the other night? He lost his feet totally. I tell you, when Canton get in that park on Saturday, it will be like taking sweets from a baby.'

'So who are your First Division draws, then?'

'Hengyang United and Tailyuan Argyll, for one. On present form I shall be really choked it if isn't a goalless draw . . .'

At this point Pah Tsi from the typing pool comes into the room with a collection tin and a jokey greetings card for Ke Vin, Bri An, Sha Ron, Tra Si and Ca Thi to sign. It appears that Cri Si in Accounts is taking half a day off to have a baby and they are having a whip-round.

Pah Tsi accepts Sha Ron's invitation to stay for a cup of tea since the kettle is just boiling again. There is just time for a little office gossip.

'You know that Bar Bra? Yes you do – our deputy supervisor. The one that doesn't wear glasses. Oo, she has turned nasty. Ever since she went on the course on How Leadership Must Serve The People And Set Examples, she's become a right bossy little madam. Anyway, don't let on I told you this but . . .'

But now it is time to leave the staff of the Ministry of Certain Things to their tea and chit-chat. Quite the home from home, isn't it?

Monday, March 23, 1987

Chucking the pilot

A meeting of Clogthorpe District Council's informal but influential Ginger Group was held behind closed doors last night to discuss the council's growing leadership crisis.

Opening the proceedings, Cllr Parkin said that not since the late Alderman Cuthbertson fell off the perch had the District Council seen a better chairperson that Cllr Enoch Bulge. He had given the best eleven years of his life to the town, turning it from something the cat had dragged in to the forward-looking conurbation it was today. He had put Clogthorpe on the map.

But the fact had to be faced, he was clapped out. He was doolally. Cllr Parkin was not being disloyal in any way but it was time Cllr Bulge was shown the red card and sent packing.

Responding, Cllr Nepworth said it could not be denied that Cllr Bulge was over the hill. His mind was going. The other day he had chaired a meeting of the Parks, Recreation Grounds and Leisure Committee in the belief that it was the Housing Committee, and had proposed converting the Clogthorpe Wanderers terraces into old people's flats. But how to get rid of the beggar? Cllr Bulge was on record as saying he would stand down when carried out in his wooden overcoat, and not before. Who was going to tell him?

Cllr Tweedyman said there was such a thing as procedure. Under standing orders, any councillor could challenge Cllr Bulge for the leadership, and if that challenger got a majority vote the old sod was out on his neck with the council's warmest thanks for services rendered. There were no two ways about it.

On a point of information, Cllr Potter asked who, considering how few councillors were fit to lick Cllr Bulge's boots, let alone step into them, reckoned himself to be up to the job.

Cllr Parkin said he hoped Cllr Potter was not looking at him (Cllr Parkin). He had brought up the matter of Cllr Bulge being two Green Shield stamps short of an electric toaster only because he considered it his public duty to do so. He himself had no leadership ambitions in any shape or form. He would not accept the chairpersonship if it was offered to him on a dinner plate with rabbit gravy. He was not interested.

Cllr Elland asked what was wrong with Cllr Sludgeworth. While Cllr Sludgeworth could not be at the present meeting owing to having to go over to his mother's with a red cabbage from his allotment, he had indicated, in private talks at the Limping Cockroach Doubles Bar last evening, his willingness to stand. Admittedly, he had had a few at the time but his colleagues could go further and fare worse.

124

Stating that he would go to the foot of his (Cllr Nepworth's) stairs, Cllr Nepworth said he had a budgie at home that would make a better chairperson than Cllr Sludgeworth. If that was the calibre of leadership material that was putting itself forward, he had a bloody good mind to stand himself.

Reminding the Ginger Group of Cllr Nepworth's tenure as chairperson of the Finance Committee, when owing to inexperience and over-indulgence at the Limping Cockroach he had signed over the town hall to a rag-and-bone man in exchange for a windmill on a stick, Cllr Parkin announced that if only to save weak-minded councillors from the consequences of their own folly, he was now after all prepared to allow his name to go forward in the leadership contest. Not that he had ever wanted this high office, it had never crossed his mind, but it was his duty to save the party he loved.

Wondering how Cllr Parkin could look himself in the face when he shaved of a morning, Cllr Potter said that there was only one place he (Cllr Parkin) was capable of leading his fellow-councillors to, and that was oblivion. Cllr Potter urged his colleague to stick to the devil they knew and reaffirm their loyalty to Cllr Bulge.

Cllr Nepworth said that while he yielded to none in his admiration of Cllr Bulge, the silly old fool was past it. He wanted chucking in the canal.

Cllr Potter said in that case there was only one course open, and that was for himself (Cllr Potter) to stand for the leadership. He had not sought this demanding role, but now that it looked like being forced upon him he would do his level best to serve his fellow-councillors and the people of Clogthorpe.

Stating that he had known Cllr Potter pull some strokes in his time, Cllr Parkin added that this one took the cream cracker. He wanted it put on record that he was inviting Cllr Potter to step outside.

The doors being opened at this juncture, Cllr Bulge (Chairperson, Clogthorpe District Council) fell into the room. Cllr Bulge, on a point of information, informed the Ginger Group that chancing to be passing on his way to the stationery cupboard for a ballpoint pen, he had paused to tie his shoelace and had thus heard every word.

Cllr Bulge had never come across such an ungrateful,

spineless, cowardly, conniving, double-crossing bunch in all his born days. Were he a younger man there would be members of the Ginger Group now lacking teeth. It would serve his colleagues right if he resigned there and then and let them stew in their own juice. But he was not going to do that, oh no. If there was any resigning to be done it was for the likes of Cllrs Parkin and Potter to lead the way. For himself, Cllr Bulge proposed to remain in office until he was carried out of the council chamber feet first, so his colleagues could put that in their pipes and smoke it.

The meeting was adjourned.

Thursday, November 15, 1990

Egging the pudding

I had better make it clear from the start that this is just a Christmas story, to be read over a mince pie and a glass of mulled wine. It is not true. It is a legend. Any suggestion that it could be even remotely based on fact, as you will see, must be dismissed as absurd.

Are you sitting comfortably? Then I'll begin. Once upon a time, in a far-off kingdom, there was a terrible hullabaloo about Christmas puddings. You see, many of the King's subjects had become ill and some had even died from eating bad Christmas puddings.

But that was not the reason for the hullabaloo. Oh dear me, no. I forgot to say that this far-off kingdom was a rather peculiar far-off kingdom, and little matters such as a few peasants

126

being struck down with Christmas pudding poisoning were of small concern to the King, provided the victims did not pester him for free hospital beds, which owing to the great hospital bed shortage were not to be found, except in hospitals suffering from the great blanket shortage.

No. The way of the hullabaloo was this. The King in his wisdom had appointed a Minister of Silliness, whose function was to draw attention away from the great hospital bed shortage and the great blanket shortage by coming out on to the palace balcony from time to time to make very silly proclamations.

For instance, the Minister would tell the populace that if only they wouldn't eat so much, they would be a healthier populace and wouldn't need to go to hospital; but that if they did need to go to hospital and were willing to pay for a bed (for even with the bed shortage this was entirely possible, as it was to hire blankets), they could raise the money by selling their hovels.

The more commotion these proclamations caused, the sillier they became. The King's subjects simply roared with laughter when the Minister of Silliness told them that if they were cold in winter they should burn their furniture; or when he warned travellers that if they consorted with the women of neighbouring kingdoms their noses would drop off.

When the Minister of Silliness decided to tell the people about the dangers attendant upon eating bad Christmas puddings, they didn't know what to make of it. Some thought the Minister was being even sillier than usual and went on stuffing themselves with Christmas pudding. But others, including many who were sillier even than the Minister himself, grew alarmed and swore that not a crumb of Christmas pudding would pass their lips again.

How many of the King's subjects really gave up eating Christmas puddings we shall never know. What we do know is that the Christmas pudding makers wrung their hands and beat their breasts and declared that they were ruined. Saying which, they climbed into their golden coaches and drove pell-mell to the palace where they demanded to see the King.

In vain did the King try to quell their wrath by making a public announcement that he had had a Christmas pudding for his tea that very day, and that parts of it had been excellent. In vain did the Minister of Silliness's fellow-minister, the Minister of Seriousness, try to reassure the populace that it was perfectly safe to eat Christmas puddings except for that trifling number containing bits of dead rat. The Christmas pudding makers demanded satisfaction.

There was nothing for it. The Minister of Silliness was led out into the palace courtyard and beheaded, and then the whole matter was put into the hands of the Minister of Christmas Puddings.

Now why on earth, you may wonder, should this peculiar kingdom have boasted a Minister of Christmas Puddings, of all things? Why not, then, a Minister of Pencil Boxes or Bed Socks or Top Hats? The answer, I fancy, is that many of the King's favourite courtiers were themselves part-time Christmas pudding makers.

Without wasting a moment, the Minister of Christmas Puddings bustled off to the King's counting house where he procured many bulging sacks of golden florins and put them into the clamouring hands of the Christmas pudding makers.

Then he caused a Great Decree to be inscribed on vellum and read out to the populace in every corner of the kingdom. This declared that all must surely see that the number of the King's subjects falling prey to Christmas pudding poisoning was very small if only they would think of the large quantity of Christmas puddings eaten; that for those not prone to Christmas pudding poisoning, no harm whatsoever could come from eating Christmas puddings provided they did not contain bits of dead rat; and that the Christmas pudding makers were now working on the dead rat problem and had even issued a Code of Practice advising, 'Please wash your hands before chopping up dead rats.'

Some of the King's subjects made so bold as to ask why, as they had been eating Christmas puddings since time immemorial, it was only now that the Christmas pudding makers had decided to see what could be done about bad Christmas puddings. To which the answer was: If you want to ask a silly question, you must first appoint a Minister of Silliness.

The Christmas pudding makers, clutching their bags of

128

money, drove off in their golden coaches, and soon the great Christmas pudding hullabaloo was forgotten, and there was peace again in this far-off kingdom.

And everyone lived happily ever after – except, of course, for the very few who continued to die of Christmas pudding poisoning.

Thursday, December 22, 1988

Waiting for Wayne

I am about to tell you of a conversation that did not take place with an antique shop assistant after I had bought from him a charming if overpriced nineteenth-century chest of drawers for £360.

'Thank you, sir, and we'll deliver it some time next Tuesday.'

'Oh, will you? But isn't it up to me to decide when it's convenient?'

'No, I'm afraid that's not possible. We have an awful lot of antique furniture to deliver and all our customers are in the same boat.'

'Then at least give me a time when you'll be bringing the chest of drawers round.'

'No, I'm awfully sorry, I can't do that.'

'Morning? Afternoon?'

'I really couldn't say. You'll just have to be in all day.'

'But this is ridiculous. Why on earth should I put myself out to take delivery of £360-worth of furniture? Get the manager.'

Enter the manager, who most graciously concedes that if I will be so good as to call his delivery department they should be able to tell me whether a.m. or p.m. Finally a time is fixed – between nine in the morning and eleven.

That conversation, as I say, did not take place. Nor, on the appointed day, did the antique chest of drawers fail to arrive within the allotted hours. Nor was it impossible to get in touch with the delivery man to find out what the hell he was playing at because he had either switched off his radio phone or did not have one – the shop seemed unsure which. Nor, when I rang the antique dealer with the same question, did he fail to ring me back.

The following didn't happen either.

11.30. Call the antique shop to say that I have now been waiting in for two-and-a-half hours and have to go out very soon so what is going on? Told that the delivery men have been given a specified time but 'it is entirely up to them whether they make the delivery or not.'

12.20. Antique dealer finally rings back with the big news. The men are in the area and will be along in about ten minutes. Point out that I have an urgent appointment down the street and am going to be out for half an hour. Antique dealer says I had better stay in. Point out that I have stayed in all bloody morning and since he has kept me waiting for nearly three and a half hours it is not entirely unreasonable for me to keep his delivery men waiting a lousy half hour, particularly as it must be their lunchtime by now. Antique dealer gets on high horse. I get on even higher horse and tell him that he either delivers the chest of drawers when it's convenient to me or we can forget the whole thing.

2.00 p.m. To cut a long saga short, the chest of drawers finally arrives, three to five hours after the promised delivery time, and without a word of explanation or apology.

I repeat: none of the above happened. Nor, in a million years, could it ever have happened – for any antique dealer behaving in so stupid and surly and lackadaisical a fashion would have gone out of business quicker than he could say: 'Screw the customer.'

But now behold. Substitute the words 'London Electricity Board' for 'antique dealer' and 'cooker' for 'chest of drawers' throughout, and you will readily see that of course it did happen, and in spades.

And I will tell you another thing. As the two youthful and barely civil delivery blokes – Wayne and Shane, would it be? – trundled the old cooker into their van, my mind went back twenty years to when I bought it. And when I went through exactly the same scenario of waiting in all morning, passing the time in enraged telephone conversation with well-meaning but utterly useless Sharons and Tracys.

Twenty years. If, in the entire region covered by the smug LEB, only half a dozen irate persons a day have been ringing up to ask where their flaming cooker is and doesn't LEB realise that they have children to pick up from school or a dentist's appointment to keep or a job to go to, then that is 30,000 disgruntled customers for electricity. And nothing done about it.

Twenty years – in which time we have seen the development of so much high-tech wizardry in the field of communications that there is nobody on the face of the earth, given the proper equipment, who cannot be contacted at a second's notice, whether on the move, in somebody's kitchen running up a £19.95 connection charge for all of five minutes' work, enjoying a bacon butty break in Fred's café, or propping up the wall of the depot. And still the London Electricity Board cannot get its act together.

An undertaker who told a bereaved family that he would be along at the cemetery some time between nine and twelve and who then kept them waiting until two before he trolled round with the hearse would end up face down in the family burial plot.

So what is so special about delivering an electric cooker and isn't it about time the LEB treated itself to an electric clock?

Thursday, March 15, 1990

131

Green grows the AAAA

Apostrophe House has been besieged with calls from members demanding to know what has happened to this year's Annual Apostrophe Show in Hyde Park. The answer, I am afraid, is that under pressure from environmentalists the show has been called off.

It has been discovered that aberrant apostrophes are ozone-unfriendly, constituting a major pollutant which is responsible for the so-called greengrocer effect.

The greengrocer effect is caused by a build-up of billions of unnecessary apostrophes which go floating off into the sky where they are trapped in the atmosphere. They then come fluttering down like flakes of soot to contaminate greengrocery stalls, causing widespread outbreaks of banana's, tomato's, potato's, Brussel's sprout's and even watercres's.

The infected fruit, when ingested by signwriters, printers, secretaries and so on, can cause aberrant apostrophes to spread far and wide. For instance, a single barrel of apple's sold at New Covent Garden is believed to be responsible for an offer of holiday bargain's from the British Telecom Shop in Warrington, a sale of sofa's in Oxford, a Simon Elvin Valentine Card with the greeting 'Just how much you're love could grow', a sale of tree's, shrub's, conifer's and heather's from a garden centre in Liverpool, and an alarming new mutation, an advertisement for load'sa furniture by a second-hand store in West London.

Speaking at a seminar on the safe disposal of toxic apostrophes at St Anne's on Sea yesterday, the Life President of the AAAA (Association for the Annihilation of the Aberrant Apostrophe) said: 'We have always known that aberrant apostrophes are a blot on the landscape and a source of illiteracy and high blood pressure, but it is only recently that we have come to realise that they are a menace to Planet Earth itself.

'Apostrophes escaping from a damaged sealed drum in an abandoned Cornish tin mine have been traced as far afield

132

as Wigston in Leicestershire, where they had lodged in an advertisement for a local swimming pool: Birthday Partie's – All Facilitie's Available – Include's a Swim.

'It is now well established that the sharp end of a single aberrant apostrophe can puncture the ozone layer. Unless something is done now to stem this tide of dereliction at a cost of, oh, call it a billion pounds to be going on with, then future generations will not know their ear's from their elbow's.'

Meanwhile a consignment of AAAs (appallingly aberrant apostrophes) from Canada has been blocked at Liverpool docks by the newly-formed Green Apostrophe Movement. The Greens claim that the untreated contaminated apostrophes, if released into the atmosphere by militants of the Apostrophe Liberation Army prising open their lead-lined containers with crowbars, could poison the entire English language.

The danger ship has been re-routed to an unnamed Middle East port where it is hoped that the offending apostrophes will be mistaken for Arabic letters by illiterate dockers. The move has infuriated liberal thinkers, one of whom raged yesterday: 'This is absolutely typical of the Green Apostrophe Movement. So long as our own language is kept pollution-free, they don't give a hoot about the Third World where your average peasant wouldn't know the difference between an apostrophe and a semi-colon. Once Moslem fundamentalists see what a sprinkling of these deviant apostrophes could do to their political slogans, for instance changing "Hang President Bush" to "Good Old Bushy", it will make the Salman Rushdie affair look like a mosque tea party.'

But a spokesperson for the Green Apostrophe Movement, hitting back at the attack, said that if an Apostrophe Armageddon is to be avoided, there must be a new approach to the whole wasteful practice of incinerating aberrant apostrophes. Except for the really virulent strain found in it's, your's, and their's, there was no reason why extraneous apostrophes, properly treated, should not be recycled.

A pilot scheme by Green Apostrophe Movement technicians has already successfully transplanted the aberrant apostrophes on a flower seller's placard in Rutland – 'We supply Flower's, Bouquet's, Spray's, Wreath's according to customer's' requirement's' – to a childrens bookshop in West London, the slogan 'Heres Harrys' outside a Fulham café, and several signboards at Kings Cross station, where apostrophes were missing. If aberrant apostrophes could be reclaimed on a national scale, it would save enough money in paint and printer's ink to train 5,000 English teachers.

Is, as some grammar-watchers believe, the growing Green Apostrophe Movement poised to take over the role of the AAAA? In a statement issued last night the Life President of the AAAA said: 'Such a radical, forward-thinking, wide-sweeping reform of our great cause would be carried out only over my dead body. While we welcome any constructive suggestions by the Green Apostrophe Movement, such as "apostrophe-free" labels for greengrocers' products and apostrophe-resistant paint for signwriters, we must not forget for an instant that we are dealing with a bunch of cranks and loonies.

'Our policy here at Apostrophe House will be the same as that of both the Government and the Opposition parties towards the political wing of the Green Apostrophe Movement – nick all their best ideas then show them the door.'

Thursday, August 17, 1989

Joy for the joiners

Since nature abhors a vacuum it will be interesting to see with what ism or ology she fills the awesome void created by communism disappearing up its own annual congress.

The process has of course already started. From Moscow to Moldavia and from Kiev to Kazakhstan, the political leopards are scrubbing off their spots to replace them with the stripes of the paper tiger. Former lifelong communists are now lifelong Democrat Socialists or Social Democrats or any other combination of those two useful words that may occur to them.

Here at home, where the dear old *Morning Star* reproaches the media for 'doing its best to present these painful events in a way intended to undermine confidence in Socialism', the Communist Party of Great Britain months ago determined to change its name by deed poll to the Democratic Left and its ideological goals to controlling the manufacture and distribution of the ozone layer.

But to what great lost cause will the kind of person who used to join the Communist Party now turn? After all, even in the Soviet Empire – even in China – it was never compulsory to be a Party card-carrier, although it was always a good career move; so it is not enough to say that the obvious alternative to joining the Communist Party will be not joining it.

There are people set down on this earth to be natural joiners, and in Russia and its satellites the ideologists among them will continue to labour for one state of affairs to be changed to another – whether for better or for worse is irrelevant – while the opportunists will continue to support whatever political affiliation offers them the best chance of a new video recorder.

Here in our capitalist backwater the starry-eyed will still be able to join the tiny but exquisitely-formed New Communist Party, known to former comrades as 'the tankies' because of its unswerving belief that while Uncle Joe Stalin may have made a few mistakes, you cannot make an omelette without breaking a few million eggs. But it is something of a backwater in which to clutch communism's remaining straw.

What does the political future hold for the idealist who joined the Communist Party in youth, switched to some obscure splinter group because it wasn't far Left enough, and after a certain amount of mature (ie, immature) student agit-prop settled down to become a Left Wing moderate – possibly even a Labour MP? What does the natural joiner join now?

As so often when contemplating what the larger lunacy has in store for us, we must look across to the United States where the cult of the Politically Correct – a Stalinist concept if ever there was one – is slithering its tentacles from the universities into the schools to produce a generation of right-thinking, non-drinking, non-smoking, non-sexist zombies.

The kind of American academics who are rewriting the history books with the same assiduity and obedience to the party line (which is that black wimmin invented the telescope and discovered China) as their Russian opposites used to rewrite the Great Soviet Encyclopedia, are the same breed who only a few years ago were telling their classes that Castro's Cuba was a great social experiment on America's doorstep. PC, condemning 'inappropriately directed laughter' on the campuses, is Marxism without the economics. To each according to his needs – if what he needs is absolute conformity.

It will happen here, of course, and indeed it is happening here. A tiny illustration: some time ago I did some radio interviews to promote a little book of mine on our language called *English Our English*. A (white) headmaster on one of these programmes, who had never even held the book in his hand, much less read it, told me it was a 'sinister' title because it could be interpreted as racist. There, I thought, is someone who is politically at a loose end.

Militant feminism, black activism, health fascism and a morbid interest in the ecology are among the isms and ologies that are replacing the vacuum of communism. It is no coincidence that these preoccupations are planks in the new platform of the born-again British Communist Party, the Democratic Left.

We are, in short, entering an era of nuisance politics, where the kind of political obsessives and hyper-activists who in the old Cold War days had no more chance of influencing events than a cabbage white has of changing back into a caterpillar, now see to their great joy a golden opportunity for bossing people about and stopping them from doing things. Put that cigarette out – the times they are a-changing.

Thursday, August 29, 1991

136

Service with a Wossname

Every garage should have a customer relations trouble-shooter to deal with motorists' complaints, says Prof Krish Bhaskar, head of East Anglia University's Motor Industry Research Unit, in a report on public dissatisfaction with the motor trade.

Immediately, my friend Percy applied for the job. Percy has been servicing my cars since I was knee-high to a Morris Minor and what he doesn't know about customer dissatisfaction would fit into the hollow tooth he sucks while scrutinising my engine. Yesterday I interviewed him on the subject.

Percy, what is the greatest single cause for complaint, in your vast experience?

The wossname, Keefy, definitely.

What might that be?

The bill style of fing, Keefy. Nine times out of wossname, the punter starts out by taking one look at it and saying Gorblimey O'Riley, stone the crows style of fing, I'll have to take out a second bleeding mortgage to pay this.

Why does the bill appear to be too high?

The VAT, Keefy. It is diabolical, I kid you not. Without the VAT style of fing, the wossname would definitely be wossname per cent lower.

But even discounting VAT, aren't the bills astronomical?

To the layman, yes. But when you explain, the average wossname comes to realise he's laughing and giggling style of fing.

When you explain what, exactly?

That he is definitely out of order and if he don't pay the Jack and Jill, he don't get his jamjar back style of fing. Also, you point out how in actual fact, if he did but know it, he has got his wossname done dead cheap. See, what the punter forgets is that as well as the wossnames what have got to be paid for, we have to charge for the wossname.

The wossnames being what?

137

Parts. Your accessories, Keefy. They don't grow on wossnames.

And the wossname that you have to charge for?

Labour, Keefy. It don't come cheap. Even when you fink the mechanic's done sod all you're paying for his expertise style of fing. See, it's like the old story about the wossname who charges fifty knicker for knocking out the wossnames in a wossname style of fing. The punter says: 'Stone me, that's a bit steep for five minutes wossname ennit?' So the plumber says: 'Right, I'll give you a detailed breakdown. For knocking the wossname out of the wossname, one knicker. For knowing where to find the bleeder, forty-nine wossname.'

I appreciate that, Percy, but are these charges always justified? For example, when I brought my car in to have a cracked wing mirror replaced, I noticed you charged me for changing the oil and fitting a new clutch.

Yeh, you was dead lucky there, Keefy. By rights, we should have charged you for a 50,000-mile wossname, which was wot we had you booked down for by mistake style of fing. But seeing as it was our wossname, we stood for it, so you got a full service thrown in for sweet Fanny wossname.

So in your capacity as trouble shooter, what would you say to the customer who complains his bill was too high?

I'd tell him to wossname off. But I definitely wouldn't sort him out, Keefy, not unless he wanted to have a go. You have got to fink of your public wossname style of fing.

And what other ways are you working on to improve your public wossname?

Starting tomorrer, Keefy, we shall be speeding up wossnames by taking on two new receptionists style of fing. Right little darlings they are, Keefy – I fink you know 'em. Sharon and Wossname.

Monday, June 22, 1987

Shar & Tray in Essex

To take their minds off the horde of customers milling around Toiletries and Perfumes and showing dangerous signs of wanting to do their Christmas shopping, Sharon and Tracy were having one of their meaningful discussions.

'How many Essex girls does it take to change a light bulb?' asked Sharon.

'I dunno,' confessed Tracy after giving the matter due consideration. 'How many?'

'I dunno,' said Sharon. 'I did know, but I've forgot. How does an Essex girl put the light on after making love?'

'Open the car door, I spose,' said Tracy carelessly.

'That's fantastic, Tray! How did you know that?'

'Isn't that what everybody does? Anyway, woss this moody about Essex girls all of a sudden, Shar?'

'It's just that they're bringing out the *Official Essex Girl Joke Book* – it's being publicised this week,' said Sharon knowledgeably. 'Like what does an Essex girl say after sex? Do you all play for the same team? Boom boom.'

'Which team is that?' asked Tracy.

'It don't make no difference which team, Tray. It could be any team.'

'It couldn't be no one in the Scottish League for a kick-off,' pouted Tracy. 'Not unless they was playing away to Billericay Town.'

There was a pause while an irate customer informed Sharon that if she was not given some service that instant she would buy her husband's aftershave at Selfridge's. Having given the lady directions to Oxford Street, Sharon continued: 'What happens if you shine a torch froo an Essex girl's ear?'

'I dunno.'

'Her eyes light up.'

'I fink that's reely stupid, Shar,' said Tracy. 'I mean to say it's just not possible. Because shall I tell you why? Her brain would get in the way.'

'It's sposed to be a joke, Tray,' pointed out Sharon. 'It's funnee.'

'Well, I don't fink it's funnee, Shar. It's just people having a go at people just cos they come from Essex. Why don't they have Sussex girl jokes or Somersetshire girl jokes? It's just stereographic.'

'Pardon, Tray?'

'Where people fink you're a particular kind of person just cos you happen to be black or a woman or fat or a dwarf.'

'But Essex girls ain't black, Tray. Well I spose some of them are, but I know what you're getting at. It's stereotyping.'

'No, that's where you have these headphones clamped over your ears and you have to type out what comes froo the tape. Cos don't you remember, that was what they tried to make us do when we was office temps that time?'

'I fink that's called audio-typing, Tray,' said Sharon gently. 'Stereotyping is laughing at women just cos they've got big boobs.'

'Are Essex girls sposed to have big boobs?' asked Tracy.

'Not only that but they're sposed to be dim.'

'Well I don't fink it's fair,' said Tracy firmly. 'Not that it's any skin off our noses, Shar, seeing as how we have the good fortune to come from Dagenham.'

'What's the difference between an Essex girl and Mr Gorbachev?' asked Sharon.

'Who's Mr Gorbachev?'

'It don't matter who he is, Tray. He's a Russian leader, that's all you need to know. What's the difference between him and an Essex girl?'

'I give up.'

'At least Mr Gorbachev knew the names of the eight who screwed him on holiday.'

'I don't get it,' said Tracy, her pretty brow corrugating in puzzlement. 'What's the joke, Shar?'

'I was hoping you'd tell me, Tray.'

Monday, November 4, 1991

140

Order of service

Then, speaking unto the persons that shall have been watching the programme since dawn, shall that Commentator which shall be without Clarence House say: And now at last the moment this great crowd has been waiting for as the fairytale glass coach comes into view on the long-awaited start of its historic journey to the Abbey.

And the crowd shall say: Ooh, isn't she lovely.

And an Japanese tourist shall say: Excuse please, which is Serene Highness Princess Fergie?

And a woman up from Brighton shall answer: The one that's waving, ducks.

And the woman up from Brighton's companion shall say: She's lost a bit more weight, unless it's the dress that makes her look slimmer.

And a woman up from Brighton shall answer: White suits her.

Then shall the Commentator say unto his congregation: And viewers at home ahead of the 1,800 guests waiting in the Abbey now have the very first glimpse of Sarah's wedding dress which of course has been under wraps until today and here's fashion editor Sophie Hicks to describe it.

And an viewer at home shall say unto her hubby: Turn the sound up, Walter.

And the viewer at home's hubby shall say: Good God, woman, they can already hear it three streets away.

And the viewer shall say: Stop moaning, Walter, it's been moan, moan, moan ever since I got you up at six this morning. For heaven's sake, we only have a royal wedding once in a blue moon.

And the viewer's hubby shall answer: You what? We have one every bloody month if you ask me.

Then shall that Commentator which shall be without Westminster Abbey say: And any moment now the fairytale glass coach will be arriving with the bride accompanied by her father Major Ronald Ferguson.

And an American tourist shall say: Excuse me, is this the Changing of the Guard?

And an Cockney Sparrer shall say: That's right, mate, and this is the Tower of London where they takes the salute.

And the Cockney Sparrer's trouble and strife shall say: Here she comes, bless her.

Then shall the crowd cry: Hurrah, hurrah, good luck Fergie, all the very best love, sock it to him Fergie, I see you're not dressed up as a policewoman today, then.

And that Commentator which shall be within the Abbey shall then say: And now to the strains of a fanfare sounded by Her Majesty's Royal Marine School of Music, the bride on the arm of her father Major Ronald Ferguson enters Westminster Abbey.

And an viewer at home shall say: She looks really radiant.

And that viewer's hubby shall say: That's the tenth time this morning you've said that. Put another record on.

And the time appointed for the solemnisation of Matrimony having come, then shall the Archbishop say: 'Dearly beloved, we are gathered together . . .'

And the hubby of an viewer at home shall say: Any chance of you cutting some sandwiches?

And the viewer at home shall answer: If you want sandwiches you can get yourself down to the pub. Now shut your mithering before we miss the marriage service.

And the hubby shall say: Look, it's not a criminal offence to ask for a cheese and chutney sandwich. Anyway, it's just the same as any other marriage service, you know. Once you've seen one royal wedding you've seen them all.

And the viewer at home shall say: I wouldn't know, would I? Because all through Charles and Di's wedding service you were going on about how you didn't half fancy a pork pie.

And then shall the man which is being married take the ring and place it upon the finger of the woman which is being married. And that hubby at home shall say: I could murder a pork pie now, since you mention it.

And the viewer which is his wife shall sob: There you go, spoiling all my pleasure as usual.

142

And the hubby shall say: So now you know how I felt when I was trying to watch the World Cup and you were going on about taking the dog for a walk.

And the viewer shall say: All I can say is I hope you're getting all this on video.

And the hubby shall say: Oh, crikey, no, I forgot.

And the viewer shall rise and go forth unto her mother's.

And the Archbishop shall say: I now pronounce thee man and wife. Those whom God hath joined together let no man put asunder.

Monday, July 21, 1986

The ash-tip of affluence

It is not very edifying, the sight of long queues of claimants outside the DHSS offices, waiting to be told how much poorer they are in these prosperous times. Even some Tory backbenchers are shocked – in moderation, of course. But for all that, we do not yet seem to be suffering a crisis of conscience.

There have been noises from the pulpit, but these days the bleatings of bishops count for little, except among politicians outraged at the Tory Party at prayer, as the C of E used to be, turning itself into the Labour Party at Sunday School.

The latest denunciation of the Thatcher ethic was from the Roman Catholic Archbishop of Liverpool, who this weekend challenged the assumption that wealth accrued by making the very rich richer somehow trickles down to the deserving poor.

Such protests as Labour has been making – and they are curiously muted, these days – have been entirely put in the shade by the headline-grabbing antics of its new pygmy breed of obscure backbenchers.

That, failing any intervention from Prince Charles, leaves us to do the caring – and we have had remarkably little to say on the fact that the new social security arrangements consolidate and isolate a solid underclass of no-hopers, doomed to a mad nightmare world where thrift is punished and work penalised, a world of forms and small print and strangely precise petty sums like £12.54, and interview cubicles where the DHSS clerk sits behind reinforced glass and the chair is bolted to the floor for fear it may be used as an offensive weapon.

That was how the world turned in the Thirties, and such was our sense of moral outrage that when we put those bad old days behind us it was in the belief that ordered penury, the state-registered breadline, was now securely locked in the past. There is little moral outrage at its escape into the Eighties.

Yes, there are letters in the papers – but they are practically all from the victims themselves, drawing pitifully detailed attention to the £5 a week social security supplement now reduced to 12p a week, or this and that vital allowance lost for the sake of a pathetic £1.25 a week increase. Incidentally, let no one tell us these new measures are reforms. A reformed social security system would sweep away all the nitpicking, dignity-sapping anomalies and absurdities attendant on drawing benefits, not create new ones.

'There have to be winners and losers,' declares the sanguine Mr John Moore. The new losers are estimated at a million. More human clinker for the ash-tip of affluence. Who cares?

Don't we take in all those stories of pennypinching and grinding poverty? Have we convinced ourselves – or allowed ourselves to be convinced – that the underclass consists entirely of feckless single-parent scroungers smoking forty a day and picking up their dole in taxis? Do we think young drifters sleep in cardboard boxes for fun?

Or is it, as I believe, that we prefer to distance ourselves from such problems, that we look to officials to sort these things out? The welfare state, even though it is now relegated to the gutter like the rest of the down-and-outs, remains the conscience of the nation. What do we want with individual consciences?

True, we are a charitable lot. Indeed, the DHSS depends on us being a charitable lot, for with its lorry-loads of new forms and explanatory leaflets, it has been sending out guides to the various charities to which claimants may be referred by its harassed clerks. But charity begins in the bank book, and hard-pressed organisations such as Age Concern and the Salvation Army look to us to keep them in the black.

We are in fact donating more to charity in the Thatcher years than ever before in our lives. But while this is highly commendable, and St Paul would give us a glowing reference, it does rather make my point that we look to others to minister to – the very phrase now has an old-fashioned ring to it – 'those less fortunate than ourselves'.

When I was a child the lady who lived in the Big House next to the park used to distribute her cast-off clothes among the needy. The girl next door minced around in a pair of purple dancing shoes she had been given. Nowadays our local Lady Bountiful would give her old clothes to Oxfam.

Give to the Sally Army but not to the huddle of rags in the shop doorway – he'll only spend it on drink. Give to the Save the Children Fund but don't save a child yourself. Here we really do distance ourselves, with the neighbours of parents ill-treating their kids dumping the problem on social workers who have demonstrably proved themselves to be ill-trained and incompetent.

Do I blame Thatcherism for our lack of direct concern, for leaving it to the community authorities and agencies to do the caring? How can I, when Thatcherism preaches precisely the opposite – that it's up to people to help themselves?

Precisely because of that oft-reiterated message: it's up to us to help ourselves. If she's ever said it's up to us to help others, I can't have been listening.

Monday, April 18, 1988

The good companion

I t is agreeable when old friends who have somehow drifted apart stumble across one another again after many years. I had such a chance encounter the other day – though I have to say that this particular friend did not so much drift apart as fall apart at the seams.

My former bosom pal was known to acquaintances simply as *Everybody's Pocket Companion.*

Close buddies, however, knew it more familiarly as A Handy Reference Book of Astronomical, Biblical, Chemical, Geographical, Geometrical, Historical, Mathematical, Physical, Remedial and Scientific Facts, Dates Worth Knowing, World Sports and Speeds Records, Mythological, Physiological, Monetary, Postal and General Information – a name we took pride in being able to recite in full.

I recognised its distinctive blue jacket from across the street. Lying there on the junk stall my Pocket Companion (Interesting & Useful To Young & Old) was just as I remembered it – a bantamweight of a book, only six inches by five, but bulging with facts, from the family tree of the House of Windsor on the inside front cover to Domestic Hints (Blood stains: use cold water containing salt and soda) on the back.

Packed into the eighty pages of closely-printed tables and tabulations in between there still reposed all the information in the world as drunk in by the fact-sated Waterhouse light years ago. Thus:

A bucketful of water weighs approx 30 lbs. The skin contains more than 2,500,000 pores. The average height of a man is 5ft 8ins. Receipts should be kept for six years from the date of payment, after which no action can be brought concerning the goods received. Printed by Thomas Hope & Sankey Hudson Ltd, Owners of the Copyright, at Crusader Works, Manchester 1.

As I recall, *Everybody's Pocket Companion* cost a bundle of old comics or what have you at street prices, or if you wanted a first-hand copy, three old pence from Woolworth's.

The reason it was so expensive was that owning it was the next best thing to being given a leasehold on the Seven Wonders of the World (p. 46) or a charabanc tour of the principal rivers, lakes and mountains (p. 17).

From Abbreviations, common, to Zone, standard time, the *Companion* was a cornucopia of the kind of imagination-firing knowledge that, back in the cigarette card era, urchins would thirst for.

We would drink as deeply and as gratefully from its list of the World's Biggest Things (the longest railway platform in the world is at Sonepur, India – 805 yards) as from the chained iron cup of the park drinking fountain.

Apothecaries' weights and measures, the dominions and colonies of Oceania, freezing, fusing and boiling points, the velocity of light and sound, English kings and queens, Gunter's chain square measure, the specific gravity of solids – what schoolteachers went prematurely bald trying to drill into us, we guzzled down from the *Companion* as if the Table of Scriptural Measures (one Sabbath Day's Journey equals about 279 paces) were made of nougat.

Everybody's Pocket Companion was well named in that, in my neck of the woods at least, it was as ubiquitous a handbook as that other popular source of knowledge, *The Red Light.*

It was the accepted authority in any dispute concerning the longest ship canal in the world (Baltic and White Sea – 500 miles), the nomenclature of a twelfth wedding anniversary (silk) and the capital of Alaska.

If you said Anchorage, move to the back of the class. It is Juneau, as any member of our street Mastermind team could have told you.

Along with French cricket, hopscotch and relieve-oh, the general knowledge quiz based on facts gleaned from the *Companion* ('All right, cleverclogs, what's the height of Mount Everest?') was an established childhood pursuit, rivalled only in popularity by who could spit the farthest.

As I say, my copy of the *Companion* literally fell apart, disintegrating from wear and tear and the ravages of an inquiring mind.

The table of Roman numerals went adrift, and the page on orders of chivalry and rates of service pay for senior officers, then the centrefold on coefficients of heat expansion and all that; until at last there was nothing left but the area and population of the world and the capitals of Europe, Asia and part of Africa.

And those tattered blue covers with the name of the author, A Mercer MRST, regarded by his fans as The Man Who Knew Everything.

Well, at not much more in real terms than its original price, *Everybody's Pocket Companion* and I have now renewed our companionship.

It is evidently a later edition than the one I treasured, since it gives the recipe for the atom bomb and the information that the first aluminium alloy lifting bridge was opened in Sunderland on November 26, 1948; but it still carries me back to a world where there were 240 pence to the pound and 16 drams equalled one ounce, when there was a Belgian Congo and a French Equatorial Africa and I knew the capitals of both, and all the facts in the universe were at my fingertips.

Thomas Hope and Sankey Hudson Ltd, I gather, are still with us under a somewhat more streamlined name, but their *Everybody's Pocket Companion*, alas, continues not.

Since I gather there is still a keen demand for it, it must be that in these high-tech times there is now too much knowledge about to cram into eighty pocket-sized pages.

Monday, August 11, 1986

Umbrellas and rainbows

Big fat volumes have been written about it. Reports have been issued on it. Committees have pondered it. Parliament has debated it. Professors and pundits have pontificated upon it. But there is no single, universally accepted theory as to why Britain's downward spin into economic oblivion continues despite all efforts to reverse the process.

It is a very large question to which we are accustomed to getting very large answers, usually embracing the Industrial Revolution, World War II, the loss of Empire, the education system, Japan, the trades unions, myopic manufacturers, snobbery, managerial incompetence, spiritual sloth, sexual permissiveness, the BBC, and the British disease.

Yet big questions sometimes have small and simple answers and it may be that had we been in the gallery of Bow Street Magistrates' Court on Monday of this week, we should have settled for what we heard there as the solution to our national conundrum.

For on that morning, in that court, a man was fined £30, plus a fiver costs, for selling umbrellas in the rain.

The charge was obstruction, the Piccadilly Circus street trader's wares having attracted such a crush of eager buyers in the torrential downpour that passers-by – presumably those who had umbrellas already – were forced to put themselves to the slight inconvenience of stepping off the pavement.

Not only was the entrepreneur fined for following the elementary commercial principle of meeting demand with supply, but he spent the night in clink – there to ruminate, possibly, that he would have been better off spending that wet Sunday in bed.

And there is the small answer to our big question. Britain went into decline and remains in decline and will continue in decline because it is, always has been as far back as anyone can remember, and ever shall be for the foreseeable future, a country where men are locked in the cells, hauled into court and fined for selling umbrellas in the rain.

We may try to stimulate the economy with the application and diligence of a market gardener forcing rhubarb. We may launch business incentive schemes until hell freezes over.

We may introduce one youth opportunity programme after another. We may hand out job-creation grants and allow tax and rates concessions to encourage new factories. We may create freeports and planning-free zones. We may announce dynamic new plans for revitalising the inner cities.

We may take the burden of red tape off the small business-man. We may encourage investment with business expansion schemes. We may encourage growth with enterprise allow-ances and share schemes and loan guarantee schemes.

And after all that we may trumpet over and over again and ever more loudly that Britain has turned the corner at last – but we might just as well confine our efforts and exertions and ingenuity to the pursuit of the crock of gold at the end of the rainbow, so long as in the summer showers that bring forth that rainbow and its elusive prize, we penalise a man for selling umbrellas.

Thursday, August 7, 1986

Shar & Tray on holiday

Sharon and Tracy's charter flight to the Costa del Rat had been delayed for the third time and the delectable duo were growing restless. Five hours was not a long time for them to spend looking at a television screen, but when it showed only departure times its entertainment value began to flag.

They had had their fill of fizzy drinks, queued four times over for the loos, read the pictures off their mags and bought souvenir Tower of London ashtrays for Wayne and Shane in the belief that they were duty-free, and now they were bored.

'Know what, Shar?' sighed Tracy, as she returned from staring at a wall. It had not been a pleasant experience – it had reminded her of being at work.

'No, what, Tray?' sighed Sharon.

'I don't fink we're gonna get away before midnight,' said Tracy. 'Cos see that lady over there eating the banana? She was here before us and she reckons their flight's been held up until one in the morning.'

'Yeh, but she's going to Florida,' Sharon pointed out.

'So what? Her flight's still before ours in the queue.'

'No, it don't work out like that,' said Sharon knowledgeably. 'See, Florida's an American island, so they don't have to fly over Europe, whereas we do. So whereas their delay must be down to engine trouble or sunnink, ours is down to the French air controllers.'

'The French air controllers?' queried Tracy.

'According to Wayne,' said Sharon. 'They're on strike or sunnink.'

'But we're not going to France,' said Tracy.

'Aren't we?' asked Sharon uncertainly.

It was Tracy's turn to be knowledgeable. 'Course not, sillee. Look what it says on your currency.'

Sharon stared uncomprehendingly at her wad of pesetas. 'I can't understand it, it's in Spanish,' she said at last.

'There you are then,' said Tracy. 'So where do the French air controllers come into it?'

'I dunno,' admitted Sharon. 'I fink they're in charge of all the air. That'll be why they're called air controllers.'

'How can they be in charge of the air?' demanded Tracy. 'The air belongs to everybody. It's what you breathe.'

'No, it's not that kind of air,' asserted Sharon. 'When you get up to the sky, you run out of breathing air. According to Wayne.'

'So how do we manage to keep on breathing when we're up in the flipping aeroplane?' asked Tracy sceptically.

'Cos the aeroplane's already full of breathing air when it leaves the ground,' said Sharon confidently. 'But outside, it's just sky. And that's what these French air controllers have been put in charge of.'

'Why the French? I mean to say why not the Norwegians or the Belgians?'

'Because it's Europe,' said Sharon. 'All the European sky comes under the French, same as all the American sky comes under the Americans.'

Tracy was beginning to get one of her headaches, but she persevered. 'All right,' she said. 'So why can't we fly round the edge of Europe instead of over it?'

'I fink it's too far,' said Sharon. 'We'd run out of petrol.'

'Don't be sillee,' said Tracy, drawing on her own knowledge of the stratosphere. 'Once you're up in the air it's all the same distance, ennit?'

'How do you make that out?' asked Sharon.

'Cos up there there's no such thing as corners,' said Tracy. 'Whichever way you go, it's a straight line.'

'Is it?'

'According to Shane.'

'In that case,' challenged Sharon, 'how come it's further to the Costa del Rat nor what it is to Peckham?'

'Cos you don't fly to flipping Peckham, sillee!' said Tracy in exasperated tones. 'Anyway, I didn't say nowhere was further nor anywhere else, I just said that everywhere's in a straight line, that's all.'

With another sigh, Sharon unwrapped her fifth Munchy bar of the day and offered a bite to her pulchritudinous pal. 'So long as we take off soon, Tray, I don't care whether we go in a straight line or round in flipping circles.'

'Me neither,' said Tracy indistinctly as she chomped her piece of Munchy bar. 'Know what worries me, Shar? It's the thought of arriving there in the dark.'

'I spect they'll have street lamps,' said Sharon, comfortingly. not that, Shar, it's when we get to the hotel.'

'They'll have lights too,' promised Sharon. 'It said so in the brochure.'

'That last hotel we stayed at didn't,' recalled Tracy.

'Only cos they still had the builders in, Tray. This place is definitely finished. Look at the brochure, you can see the roof.'

Tracy, still apprehensive, studied the brochure. 'It don't show you what I'm looking for, though, Shar. What's bothering me is when we get up to our room how will we know where to find the light switch?'

'I see what you mean,' said Sharon slowly.

As her forehead corrugated in thought, an announcement crackled over the Tannoy. Bucketshop Charter Airways regretted that their flight to the Costa del Rat was now delayed until noon the following day.

Sharon's furrowed brow cleared. 'One problem solved, Tray. Come on, let's go have another burger. After all, we are on holiday.'

Thursday, August 3, 1989

English, our English

The class had been asked to write something about their families. The quiet boy at the back produced something like this: 'My father loves us but he is dead. He went to work and brings home wages for my mother. He is always here but now he is gone.'

The teacher who marked this touching, lyrical effort commented succinctly, and with the sensitivity of a poker dipped in soot, 'Mixed-up tenses'.

I can't think of anyone, in or out of the education world, who would call that good English teaching. On the other hand, when I was visiting schools and teacher training colleges as a member of the Kingman Inquiry into the Teaching of English Language, a puzzled student teacher asked me, 'What's this syntax you're all banging on about?' That young lady is now a qualified teacher. I don't call that a very satisfactory situation either.

She didn't know anything about syntax because her own teachers had told her next to nothing about grammatical rules – either because they didn't think it was necessary or because they were unsure of the rules themselves. More than one in four teachers of secondary school English have no qualifications in the subject beyond O-level. Even peasant cultures know their own grammar. We stand in danger of losing ours, of the language eroding into a semi-literate scrubland like badly-husbanded soil.

I don't know whether it was as the Life President of the AAAA (the Association for the Annihilation of the Aberrant Apostrophe) or what that I was press-ganged by Education Secretary Kenneth Baker into the Kingman team of educationists, academics and literary folk. It was an offer you couldn't refuse if you've spent much of your life banging on, as that student teacher would put it, about declining standards of English.

It was a gruelling fourteen months of listening and learning and argufying and trying to blend into the woodwork in classrooms and ploughing through the six-foot mini-mountain of evidence and papers which accumulated just to the left of my typewriter. Learning before you chip in with your two-penn'orth is the essence of this kind of exercise, and the prejudices I brought to the task were not always confirmed.

I acquired a new respect for teachers. None of the slogging pedagogues I met was anywhere near the disastrous image projected by their NUT activists on the TV news. The abiding picture in my mind is of a plumpish educational Mother Earth in an infants' school in a run-down part of the North, comforting a child with bellyache in her arms while giving equal attention to two other mites plucking at her skirts with stories hot off their exercise books, and at the same time explaining to me the complexities of an exciting new system, mugged up in her own free time, of developing children's writing from scribble.

But respect for dedicated teachers didn't always extend to their teaching methods or to the rationale of those who teach the teachers. I was angered to read in papers presented in perfect English that perfect English isn't important, dismayed to hear it argued by people so grammatically articulate that they did not so much as misplace a preposition, that grammar needn't be taught.

Why, like the grammar-school-educated Labour politicians who destroyed the grammar schools, do they want to saw the rungs off the ladder they themselves climbed up? Above all, why do they want to withhold from children, as if it were a dangerous drug to be put on a high shelf, knowledge they already have themselves? That seems to me an educational sin – the refusal to pass on information for doctrinaire or faddish reasons.

The most faddish of teaching fads, the belief that children's writing should be 'creative' regardless of grammar or even comprehensibility, has thankfully been long on the wane, although you do still see on classroom walls 'poems' written on sugar paper which consist entirely of nouns and participles ('Breezes blowing, leaves swirling' etc). But there are still a lot of teachers about who believe in talking to their pupils 'where they are' – which could well be something worse.

Talking to children 'where they are' means acknowledging that since their only reading outside school is comics, the workbooks used in schools should be the *Dandy* and the *Beano*. Nothing that was said or shown to me could persuade me that this theory isn't the utmost tosh. Teachers have a duty to expand children's horizons, not to work within their existing limitations. But protest that children must be exposed to good literature and many of them will argue, 'Ah, but who's to say what's good literature?' If that means they don't know, as I suspect it does, then they must be shown.

And so what about grammar? I began with a bias towards assimilating formal grammar by rote as a subject in isolation, as it was learned by so many of my generation who by now would be hard put to distinguish between a gerund and a gerbil. I came round to the realisation that grammar has to be a live, integral part of learning about the English language. But learned it must be. Using English without knowing the parts of speech is like painting without knowing the colours in the spectrum.

The Kingman Report is only one piece of the education reform jigsaw. For fourteen months' hard work it is a slim document, but I could make it even slimmer by summarising it in two sentences. It is the job of teachers to pass on what they know. If they don't know, they themselves must be taught.

Monday, May 2, 1988

Clogthorpe in combat

An emergency meeting of Clogthorpe District Council's Finance Committee was held at the Clogthorpe Heritage Park Hotel and Leisure Complex yesterday to consider the implications of the poll tax.

Opening the meeting, Cllr Bulge (Chair) said that there was now nobbut ten days to go before the balloon went up. There was no use beating about the bush, the Finance Committee could expect trouble. There was an element going round the town saying couldn't pay, wouldn't pay, and there had been talk in the Snivelling Coalman public house of burning down the Civic Centre.

Cllr Parkin asked the Chair to tell the Finance Committee summat it didn't know. Already council tenants on the

Clement Attlee Estate had climbed up on their roofs and were chucking slates. It was like World War II.

Cllr Hopcraft said he wished to place on record that he did not agree with the poll tax.

Cllr Bulge said that by the left, nobody agreed with the bloody poll tax. That was not the point. The point was how the council was going to go about collecting it.

Cllr Tweedyman asked what was wrong with the rentman.

Cllr Ackerman said that what was wrong with the rentman was that he was hobbling about in a zimmer frame, and that was just the result of trying to get rent arrears out of that unrepresentative minority of trouble-makers in Nelson Mandela Approach. God knew what they would do to him if he went round asking for £327 a head poll tax. They would string him up.

Cllr Bulge said the Finance Committee ought to take cognisance of what some other local authorities were doing. Rhymney Valley Council in Wales had bought an armoured van as a mobile collection point, capable of resisting chainsaw attacks and with an emergency ventilation system in case of gas attacks.

Cllr Hopcraft said he didn't believe it.

Cllr Bulge said that Cllr Hopcraft had not yet heard the half of it. Cambridge Poll Tax Office had got reinforced counter screens and an alarm linked to the police station. Lichfield, Staffs, had bullet-proof glass. Poll tax staff in Lothian, Scotland, had been offered martial arts classes. Other councils were issuing high-pitched personal alarms and fitting panic buttons in their community charge offices. And all Cllr Tweedyman could suggest was leave it to the bloody rentman. He (Cllr Tweedyman) wanted putting away.

Cllr Tweedyman said all right then, how about putting sandbags round the old Rates Office and Administrative Annexe where the poll tax staff were now housed.

Cllr Ackerman asked if Cllr Tweedyman had ever been hit in the mush with a flying sandbag. If the Finance Committee asked him (Cllr Ackerman) anything, he reckoned that they should cut the cackle and explore the legal position of equipping all poll tax clerks with Armalite rifles.

Cllr Parkin said that hand grenades would be better suited

to the purpose, adding that it would be all right by him if they wanted to lob a few into the Clement Attlee Estate by way of target practice.

Cllr Hopcraft said that speaking as a pacifist he could not go along with any of this.

Cllr Bulge said that while the Chair respected Cllr Hopcraft's sincerely-held beliefs, this was no time to be a bloody conchy. There was going to be blue bloody murder in Clogthorpe come poll tax day and it was up to the council to be prepared.

Cllr Nepworth said that if gossip in the Snivelling Coalman was anything to go by, there was a detachment of SAS at that army barracks over on Pothole Moor. Cllr Nepworth was only thinking aloud now, but could not the council parachute the SAS into the Clement Attlee Estate as poll tax collectors?

Cllr Bulge ruled that while the powers vested in Clogthorpe District Council under the Local Government (Finance) Act 1988 were great, he begged leave to doubt whether they gave it jurisdiction over the bloody army. He would remind the Finance Committee that lunch awaited them in the White Rose Rib Room and would beg them to get their thinking caps on.

Cllr Ackerman asked how it would be if each and every poll tax official in Clogthorpe were to be issued with a Rottweiler apiece.

Cllr Bulge said that was the best bloody idea he had heard all morning. How much were they?

Cllr Parkin said that he had a cousin down south who bred pit bull terriers. He could probably do the council a couple of dozen wholesale.

Cllr Tweedyman asked who would train them.

Cllr Ackerman said they didn't need training, they just had to be kept without food for three days and then turned loose on the Clement Attlee Estate. The unrepresentative minority of troublemakers in Nelson Mandela Approach would then be begging on their bended knees to pay their poll tax, mark Cllr Ackerman's words.

Cllr Hopcraft said that he had a better idea. The Chair had pointed out that there were still ten days to go before poll tax day. The borough of Clogthorpe was twinned with the soot manufacturing town of Zkrjcrw in Albania. The Finance Com-

158

mittee had a standing invitation to visit their opposite numbers in Zkrjcrw to study how they budgeted for the drains. Such a visit could take days or it could take weeks.

Cllr Bulge said months, even. He would ask someone to propose that the Finance Committee did adjourn to the White Rose Rib Room for lunch and then run like the clappers to Thomas Cook's in Scargill Shopping Mall and book the air tickets.

The motion was adopted.

Thursday, April 19, 1990

Our life and time

The Museum of Mankind – which I hope has not spent too much of its budget on headed notepaper, since by and by it is bound to change its name to the Museum of Humankind under pressure from mankind's other half – is compiling a catalogue of time capsules.

These are those buried cylinders containing such social bric-a-brac as credit cards, zip-fasteners, digital watches, wartime ration books and so on, by which we hope to throw some light for posterity on how we live now.

It seems there are time capsules buried all over the place, with examples of the squirrelling urge going back to 3000 BC. Come to think of it I know personally of one example going back to 1939 AD.

This was when, inspired by the news that a time capsule had lately been sunk into the foundations of the New York

World's Fair, I decided to communicate personally with posterity by constructing a time capsule of my own and burying it in our back garden.

It consisted of a screw-top bottled beetroot jar purloined from the larder and it contained, as I recall, a bit of chalk, a marble, a cigarette card, a piece of Meccano, a lead cow with three legs and several other artefacts including a wrapped toffee.

But for that toffee my time capsule would by now have been under the ground for exactly fifty years and I should be sending the Museum of Mankind a map of our back garden with X marking the historic spot. As things turned out, I found myself so maddened with a craving for toffee half an hour after burying my treasure that I dug it up again. Alas: before, dribbling and slurping contentedly, I had chance to rebury it, my mother came out to peg up the washing and the beetroot jar was reclaimed.

The recollection has set me wondering idly what I would put in a time capsule today if I knew where to lay my hands on a large steel cylinder, this apparently being the kind of receptacle now favoured by the capsule fancy over your conventional beetroot jar.

Into it, without hesitation, would go a squashed lager can, a crisp packet, a half-eaten doner kebab, a ghetto blaster, a tattooing needle, a nose-ring, a video nasty, an aerosol paint spray, a pair of bovver boots, a soccer identity card and a song sheet with the complete lyrics and music of ''Ere we go, 'ere we go, 'ere we go.'

Then we should have to have a wedge of contaminated cheese, a suspect egg, the 'best thrown in the bin by' label off a dodgy vacuum-packed portion of Belgian pâté, and a jar of babyfood containing a bit of glass. And Edwina Currie.

What else? A poll tax form. An official Government announcement claiming that you can get Aids from pretty girls (they would have caused less offence, and been no less misleading, had they said you can get it from lavatory seats). A British Steel share certificate.

And talking of privatisation, a message from the ten water and sewage businesses of England and Wales boasting that they are working for us. Plus another message from some of

160

the same authorities informing us that the water has been cut off and warning us not to drink it when it comes on again.

A British Rail announcement regretting late departure of trains owing to late arrival. A London Underground announcement regretting that passengers may experience intervals. Ron Todd.

The Greens have to be represented if future generations are to get some idea of how we ran our little corner of civilisation and so I should include a bottle of polluted river water, that picture of Mrs Thatcher picking up litter in St James's Park, some dawn-plucked pesticide from Rosycheeks Farm, a phial of leaded petrol, some items picked up on the average beach other than pebbles, and Ben Elton's novel *Stark*. Oh yes, and Ben Elton.

Plus a dead partridge in a blighted pear tree. And my simple message to posterity would be, 'So you think you've got problems?'

Monday, July 31, 1989

Leave it to Arnold

L oitering on Victoria Station with intent to catch a train, I couldn't help overhearing a telephone conversation between British Rail and British Rail's brother-in-law Arnold, which some incompetent had unaccountably plugged into the Tannoy system. Since my train was the 8.54 and it was only just gone nine, I had plenty of time for eavesdropping.

'Arnold? Barry this end. How's tricks?'

'Barry! Long time no hear! How's Elaine?'

'A lot better than she was under her new doctor, but of course we're all suffering from the side-effects of these tablets she has to take six times a day. How's Moira and the kids?'

'Moira's fine, Barry, and the kids are shooting up. Listen – I was just off for a round of golf with British Telecom. What can I do for you, sunshine?'

'We have a problem, Arnold.'

'Your problems are my problems, Barry. What's the trouble?'

'Wet leaves.'

'You call that a problem? How many do you need?'

'We don't need any, Arnold – we're trying to get rid of them.'

'Oh, I see. Well to tell you the truth, Barry, there isn't much of a market for wet leaves. I'll ask around, but quite frankly I think you've got a tricky one there. How much did you pay for them?'

'You don't understand, Arnold. These are not our leaves – they're leaves that are falling off the trees at the side of the tracks.'

'Yes, they would do, Barry. It's what we call the autumn effect. It happens to us all – don't worry about it.'

'But they're screwing up the timetables, Arnold. As we keep explaining to the customers, due to an overnight build-up of wet leaves on the railway lines which have become compacted and turned into a sticky residue causing trains to lose adhesion, all services are subject to delay. But will they listen? No.'

'Maybe they think you're pulling their plonkers, Barry. I mean to say wet leaves – it does seem a bit far-fetched, doesn't it?'

'It's a big headache, Arnold.'

'I can't see why it should be. They don't have a wet leaves problem on the Continental railways.'

'Arnold, I did not ring you up to talk about the Continental railways. I have had it up to here with the clever-dick Continental bloody railways. This is British Rail we're talking about and these are British leaves.'

'What kind of leaves, Barry? Oak? Sycamore? Weeping willow?'

'What the hell does it matter what kind of leaves? All I want to know is how to keep them off our railway lines!'

'Calm down, Barry – you know what the doctor said about

your blood pressure. All right, now as I understand it, you'd be a happier man if these wet leaves didn't keep falling on your track, right?'

'Right. Any bright ideas?'

'The solution's staring you in the face Barry. You glue the leaves to the trees.'

'Have you been drinking, Arnold?'

'When did you ever know me take a drink, Barry, except for that one glass of champagne when I sold you on the Channel Tunnel? Listen to what I'm telling you – this is lateral thinking. Problem: the leaves are falling off the trees, right? Question: how do we stop this process? Answer: glue.'

'But what about the cost, Arnold?'

'Not your pigeon, sunshine. Who owns all these trees – not you, I sincerely hope and trust?'

'No, they're owned by all sorts of people. Farmers, mainly.'

'So these farmers are allowing the leaves off their trees to trespass on your track. Have they got tickets?'

'Pardon?'

'I'm asking if these leaves have any kind of authority to be on British Rail property. If not, you have got their owners by the short-and-curlies.'

'Do you know, Arnold, I think you've got it. So we get the British Rail solicitor to send out letters requiring the farmers to glue the leaves to the trees?'

'You've got it, Barry.'

'Just one snag, Arnold. What if the glue melts?'

'No problem, Barry. You put up a notice saying that owing to wet leaves losing adhesion, all services are subject to delay.'

'Brilliant, Arnold. Love to Moira.'

'Any time, Barry. Remember me to Elaine.'

Monday, November 11, 1991

163

Health takes a holiday

T hat busy body, the Government-funded Health Education Authority, has produced half-a-million leaflets
advising holidaymakers to drink less alcohol if they
want to avoid hangovers and stomach upsets.

I don't know where these leaflets are to be distributed –
perhaps the Authority plans to trawl the Continental resorts
looking for half-a-million drunks wearing Union Jack T-shirts.

It is typical and timely advice this caring quango is offering,
however. Up until now the connection between the consump-
tion of twelve Margaritas and the room spinning round
has escaped your average visitor to the Costa Del Hell, who
has put his raging headache down to eating too many ice
creams.

The 'drink wisely on holiday' leaflet contains Awful Warnings in its illustrated examples of Uncle Clarence, who became
blotto at the station and had his passport, money and baggage
stolen; Ginger Robinson, who was arrested on a cross-Channel
ferry after taking too much whisky, gin and rum on board;
and Charlie, who returned from holiday 'strapped for cash'
because he had spent all his money on cheap drink.

I must say that, given the choice, I would sooner be on
holiday with the likes of Clarence, Ginger and Charlie than
with the Health Education Authority. In fact the Health Education Authority on holiday, doing everything in moderation
and cleaning its teeth in mineral water, fills me with a great
depression.

I should think, though, that the chances of bumping into
Clarence, Ginger and Charlie and the Health Education Authority in the same lowdown bar in Majorca are slim. I cannot
imagine the Health Education Authority, with its horror of
rich greasy food, ever taking its holidays in germ-ridden
foreign parts.

No, I can see the HEA, on its fortnight off from haranguing
the public about the perils of cigarettes, strong drink and sex,
staying either at a quiet English spa or – having checked that

the beach and the bathing are pollution free – a no-smoking hotel down in Devon.

As to what the HEA actually does on holiday, I'm none too clear. Cream teas are out for a start, obviously. There will be no holiday romance (Aids, you know), and pony trekking can be dangerous if you fall off on the edge of a cliff. Washing the picnic lettuce (use carefully boiled water with a few drops of TCP) can only account for a small part of the day, so after it has performed its morning exercises what does the Health Education Authority do with itself while all the other guests are down at the village pub?

I don't know; but if I could make the HEA a present of the Perfect Day Off, it would go something like this. After breakfast (muesli, prunes, one slice dry wholemeal toast, rose-hip tea and one teaspn honey), the Health Education Authority cleans its teeth and jogs down to the beach. Not to swim – that can be fatal so soon after a meal – but to relax and thus eliminate stress.

The HEA settles itself on a Li-lo and dips into the rucksack for some sensible reading. This consists of an enticing wad of pamphlets with titles like *Avoiding Heart Attacks*, *Safe Sex*, and *What To Do About Nosebleed*.

It is a hot day, even in the shade away from the harmful rays of the sun. Presently the Authority, like everyone else who has tried to dip into its magnum opus, *Smoking at Work: How To Persecute Offenders*, nods off to sleep.

Unwisely, and very uncharacteristically, the HEA has failed to check the tide tables. Soon the sea begins to lap against its air-bed. Then, very gently, and still snoring fitfully, the Health Education Authority floats slowly out to sea.

No one observes the occurrence. All the holidaymakers are down at the Cross-eyed Ferret drinking scrumpy with Clarence, Ginger and Charlie. The lifeguard is indoors eating a chip butty.

A lone camper, cooking eggs, sausage, bacon and a fried slice on a spirit stove high on the cliff top, thinks he sees a figure bobbing up and down far out to sea. And then he hears – is it the wind, or is it a thin reedy voice crying: 'Help! Swimming out of one's depth can be dangerous to health, as well as a hazard to fishermen!'?

The camper shakes his head. Obviously a figment of his imagination, probably brought on by indigestion caused by last night's pork pie. He applies himself to his breakfast. On the far horizon, a hand clutching a leaflet entitled *Mouth To Mouth Resuscitation* waves feebly, there is a glugging sound, and the Health Education Authority vanishes for ever.

Thursday, July 5, 1990

Off the pedestal

I n the extremely unlikely event of the French having given the Statue of Liberty to us instead of to the Americans – they may have hated our guts but it would have saved humping the thing across the Atlantic – it is not difficult to imagine how she would have been received on these shores. You need go no further than Customs and Immigration . . .

'Anything to declare?'

'Oui, a 152-foot statue of a woman.'

'Oh, yes? Saucy, is it? Is she completely stark bare naked, or is she wearing some of these frilly ooh-la-lahs you have over in Gay Paree?'

'Au contraire. She is clothed from head to foot and holding a torch.'

'A torch, eh? What's her game, then – one of these foreign anarchists, is she?'

'Non, non, non, she represents ze spirit of Liberty.'

'Come again?'

'Liberty, M'sieur.'

'What – free love, nude sunbathing, open-toed sandals, that style of thing?'

'Just Liberty, M'sieur. She will stand on ze Isle of Dogs, a beacon for huddled masses yearning to breathe free.'

'She will, will she? Do the council know about this?'

Or perhaps I'm being unfair. We are talking, after all, about a century ago, when although we had little time for the French we took a much more benevolent view of public statuary than we do now.

It was then impossible to stand in a town square and throw a tomato without it hitting the granite top hat of some alderman or benefactor on a plinth. As for statues of Queen Victoria, if you had abstracted half a sovereign from the privy purse for every one sighted up and down the land, she would have died a poor woman.

While, say, the hundredth anniversary of the unveiling of the Black Prince's equestrian statue in Leeds City Square (no one is quite sure what he is doing there since he is not known to have been a Leeds lad) did not attract quite the razzamatazz centring on the Statue of Liberty this July 4, we used to have quite an extraordinary affection for our public statues.

Every town had its own popular mythology concerning its bronze or granite or marble monuments – usually touching on their ability to come to life on the stroke of midnight.

The circle of scantily-draped nymphs surrounding the Black Prince were said to be in the mischievous habit of changing plinths.

In the Yorkshire model mill town of Saltaire (where Sir Titus Salt's statue caused considerable offence by having its back turned on the town he built), their four stone lions, Peace, War, Determination and Vigilance, were supposed to go down and drink from the River Aire each night.

Probably Londoners had some romantic fable about Eros shooting his arrows at the flower girls when Big Ben struck twelve, but if so it is forgotten now (and anyway the flower girls have been moved on for obstruction). When Eros was recently restored to his rightful place in Piccadilly Circus the event raised hardly a ripple.

Why has this engagingly ponderous art form, descending in

a hitherto unbroken line from the Parthenon to the corporation ornamental drinking fountain, fallen into disfavour?

Partly, I suggest, because we no longer put our eminent personages on pedestals – it would be a brave commemorative committee indeed these days which tried to fund the effigy in bronze of some local or national worthy by popular subscription.

Another hazard is the element of spite that has entered into public life. I can think of no monument from Cleopatra's Needle to the Albert Memorial that would not nowadays be violently opposed on political grounds – with many of the objectors equipped with hammers, paint sprays and balaclava helmets.

But mainly I put down our growing lack of interest in street sculpture to the philistine gullibility of cash-bloated local authorities who were conned into commissioning twisted girders and lumps of concrete to set in front of their new civic centres and leisure complexes, in the belief that anything the ratepayers couldn't understand must be art, and anything they actively hated must be very good art indeed.

I don't suppose the soot-caked, pigeon-baptised likeness of Alderman Rumbletummy was so aesthetically OK that it ever made the heart beat faster but it was comfortingly there, a link, a part of your own past and – so you thought until the Town Hall Square became Peace Square and the Alderman was carried off to the knacker's yard to make way for a giant wire coathanger representing the Unknown Freedom Fighter – a part of your own future.

Ho, hum. I'd even accept a statue of Ken Livingstone if they'd give what used to be the people's art back to the people. Meanwhile, back at the Statue of Liberty . . .

'These huddled masses, then. What are they – Afro-Asians, Pakistanis, boat people?'

'Just huddled masses, M'sieur, yearning to breathe free.'

'So you keep saying. Is this statue hollow?'

'Oui, M'sieur.'

'Open it up, then. And if it's stuffed full of ethnic child brides from Bangladesh you're in deep trouble.'

Thursday, July 3, 1986

168

The thousand year yob

Let us hear it for Chelsea fan Mr Terence (Not The Fatman) Matthews, now serving a four-year stretch for causing an affray which led to a pub manager requiring 130 stitches for damage inflicted to his face by a broken beer glass.

Counsel for the defence spoke up for Mr Matthews thus: 'For 1,000 years or so we have needed tough young fellows like this who are prepared to shed blood at the drop of a hat . . . We still have not made any provision for this violent streak that the British have always had. That is why we have always done so well in wars.'

A thousand glorious years of mindless violence, eh? Let us roll back the tapestry of history to the year 989 AD. Edgar is king of all England, Eric the Red has established the first Viking colonies. Aelfric the Grammarian is working on his Latin opus. Egbert the Clod is up in court again.

Clerk: Are you Egbert the Clod, a registered serf, and do you reside on the refuse tip next to the pig sty, on the estate of Cedric the Squint-eyed?

Egbert: Pardon?

Defence counsel: May it please your Majesty, the clerk will have to speak up. My client was very properly deprived of his ears by your Majesty in consequence of his throwing a quartern of ale over Wulnoth the Bow-legged's swordsmith after the jousting semi-finals at Martinmas.

Spectators (singing): We are the champions, what a load of rubbish, go home ye bums go home, etc.

King: Silence! The court will ignore that reference to one of Egbert the Clod's many previous convictions until I find him guilty. Proceed, clerk.

Clerk: Egbert the Clod, you are charged with that on St Audrey's Day last, with divers others, you did go on the rampage in the hundreds of Wulnoth the Bow-legged, causing wilful damage to valuable peasants with a spiked ball on a chain, and uttering the words 'Wosser marrer with you, you bald-pated git?' to Bishop Athelstan the Perfect. How do you plead?

Egbert: Pardon?

Prosecution counsel: Your Majesty, this is a case where a gang of serfs, known collectively as Cedric the Squint-eyed's firm, set out to wreak their revenge on a rival gang, Wulnoth the Bow-legged's team, after Squint-eyed United had lost three-nil to Bow-legged Wanderers in the Jousting Association Buttermilk Cup Final.

Spectators: (singing) We won the cup, we won the cup, here ye go, here ye go, here ye go, etc.

King: If there is any more of this from you lot I shall have your ears removed.

Spectators: Pardon?

King: Oh, sorry, I didn't know you were my regulars. Now what has the prisoner to say for himself?

Clerk: Egbert the Clod, raise your right hand and take the oath.

Egbert: Pardon?

Defence counsel: With respect, your Majesty, the prisoner is unable to raise his right hand as a result of your Majesty quite rightly having ordered it to be chopped off for setting fire to a haywain, the property of Wulnoth the Bow-legged, at the beginning of the stag-hunting season. Your Majesty will recall that the haywain contained one of Wulnoth's foresters and a dairymaid, which as you wisely said made the offence doubly serious.

King: Has your client got a tongue in his head?

Defence counsel: For the present, your Majesty. (To Egbert, in sign language) Tell the court in your own words how you came to be allegedly mixed up in this unfortunate alleged incident.

Egbert: Werl, like we come out the wossname arter y'know the game like, then like summer vese Bow-legged geezers, they starts avin a go, don they, know worrer mean? Like callinus a loader wossnames an that. So like we wozzen stanin fer that, was we, so we done no more, we put like y'know the boot in, an next fing we knows there's this ruck goin on an this geezer crawlin abart in a pooler blood like lookin forris nose.

King: Is this man talking Danish?

Defence counsel: It is my client's idea of your Majesty's English, your Majesty.

King: He should be roasted on a slow gridiron for that alone. I find him guilty. What have you to say in mitigation?

Defence counsel: Your Majesty, for a thousand years, ever since we heaved our first rock at the Romans, we have needed tough young fellows like this who are prepared to shed blood at the drop of a helmet. When the Vikings come in earnest, we shall be glad of the likes of Egbert the Clod.

King: Absolute poppycock. Off with his ears.

Defence counsel: Begging your Majesty's pardon, but he has already forfeited his ears.

King: Not his – yours. As for the prisoner, he will be hanged in chains from the gibbet by his ankles, flayed alive, and fined one sheep; and I only wish I had the power to confiscate his jousting tournament pass for the rest of the season. Next case.

Clerk: Call Alfred the Thick.

Alfred: Pardon?

Thursday, October 16, 1986

Rhymes and reasons

It's just as well that the BBC are taking off 'Top Of The Form'. In a recent edition one school's team had no idea who wrote 'I wander'd lonely as a cloud'. Had they been asked about Masefield's dirty British coaster it would probably have finished up as the ship that died of shame.

All right, now: for ten points, what is the second line of 'Not a drum was heard, not a funeral note'; who wrote 'loveliest of trees, the cherry now'; who brought the good news from Ghent to Aix; and who immortalised the Old Vicarage, Grantchester?

If you're under thirty you probably passed on all four. The answers are 'As his corse to the rampart we hurried'; A. E. Housman; Joris, Dirck and the unnamed narrator; and Rupert Brooke (if you put Jeffrey Archer, go to the back of the class).

Those of you who got them all right may like to join with me in chanting 'Kubla Khan' by Samuel Taylor Coleridge. Altogether now: 'In Xanadu did Kubla Khan, a stately pleasure-dome decree, where Alph, the sacred river ran . . .'

Floundering already? Then how about, 'I will arise and go now, and go to Innisfree, and a small cabin build there, of clay' and how the bloody hell does it go after that?

Of clay and wattle made, actually. But I have to confess to using a crib. For as I jot down these half-remembered lines I am leafing through what is destined to become a well-thumbed book on my shelves – *The Collins Book Of Best-Loved Verse* (£9.95) chosen by Charles Osborne.

As its title suggests, it is an anthology of those poems that are part of us – the ones so familiar to us, at least in fragments and snatches (Half a league . . . Is there anybody there, said the Traveller . . . Quoth the Raven, Never more) that we seem to have been born with them in our heads – though dimly we can remember learning them by rote, on hot afternoons in classrooms smelling of melting varnish, with chalk-dust dancing in the sunbeams.

They are not all school poems, I should say – or at any rate, not all from the repertoire of the schools I went to. 'Come, friendly bombs, and fall on Slough' is there, for instance, and 'Do not go gentle into that good night', and 'Bagpipe Music' (I should think that isn't a school poem indeed, with lines like 'Their knickers are made of crepe-de-chine' and 'Sit on your arse for fifty years'). But if we did not learn them at school, we were taught at school the capacity to learn and enjoy them in later life.

And it is all gone now, or going – this golden treasury of ours crumbling and decaying like a vandalised family tomb.

A generation hence there will be hardly a soul in the land who can recite 'Abou Ben Adhem' (may his tribe increase). I doubt, even now, whether there is a single child who knows 'The boy stood on the burning deck', even in one of its unauthorised versions.

The reason for the decline and fall of our heritage of poetry, the great enfeeblement of our corporate memory of Blake and Browning, of Keats and Longfellow and Tennyson, and the crying shame of it, was encapsulated by Education Secretary Kenneth Baker in a lecture this weekend:

'It has become unfashionable to teach children the benefits of learning things by heart. Learning by heart is not only good memory training, it also gives a sense of achievement. But it need not be a chore . . .'

Well, I wouldn't say that, exactly. Learning poetry, learning multiplication tables, is a hard grind (though a rewarding one). It is because there are teachers who live in terror of boring their charges or setting them tasks too difficult that so many schools these days are places where you go to be taught, not where you go to learn, to do some of the donkey work yourself. But it is not, alas, possible to learn 'Sea Fever' by catching it contagiously from someone else.

'I suspect I shall be told by many educators that I'm old-fashioned,' continues Kenneth Baker. If that's all they tell him he is, he will have got off lightly. In some centres of learning, standard English verse is regarded as elitist, reactionary, clapped-out, jingoistic doggerel with no relevance to 'present-day needs' (but what about those who have a need for poetry?). The one-eyed yellow idol to the north of Kathmandu is probably racist, 'The Owl And The Pussy Cat' sexist, and 'The Charge Of The Light Brigade' glorifies war.

And in any case, 'the kids' (do you notice how teachers who can't teach always use this patronising term for their classes?) are all TV-orientated these days. So they are, as my generation was comic-orientated and picture-house-orientated. But they are not watching EastEnders in school hours any more than we read the *Beano* in school hours (well, only in old Softy Bates's class). However TV-orientated they may be at home, there is no reason why they cannot be 'Drake's Drum' orientated in the classroom.

Knowing poetry by heart, and having one's own little repertoire of recitations (would you like to hear me do 'Albert And The Lion'?) doesn't have to be one of the lost arts like knife-throwing or filling the stage with flags. It didn't die with the music hall. It wasn't killed by television. It was the victim of educational whim – a whim that is robbing our children of pleasures unknown to them.

As the poet said: 'When I was but thirteen or so, I went into a golden land . . .'

Monday, November 10, 1986

Twelve angry partridges

Now you have admitted that on the first day of Christmas you sent Miss X a partridge in a pear tree, and you have asked for eleven other partridges in pear trees to be taken into consideration. Will you tell the court what, over and above these items, you sent her on the second day of Christmas?

And were these the only two turtle doves you caused to be pressed upon the lady, or were there others?

Thank you. The eleven pairs of turtle doves to which the accused refers, M'lud, are those flying about the courtroom, and they are labelled exhibits A, B, C, D, E, F, G, H, I, J and K.

No, M'lud. The bird perched on your lordship's wig is a French hen. If the court usher could put it back in the crate with its colleagues, perhaps I may continue my cross-examination.

Now you have described yourself as Miss X's true love, and in that capacity you began to send her French hens, calling birds and other live poultry, is that correct?

Calling birds, M'lud, or colly birds as they have been termed in some versions of this evidence, are, I am informed, black-birds, of the variety your lordship may be able to perceive perched on the rail of the public gallery.

As your lordship pleases.

I will rephrase the question. Commencing on the fourth day of Christmas and continuing daily until your arrest you began to send the lady quantities of blackbirds, did you not? Will you please tell the court why you took this particular course of action?

Because the shop had run out of parrots, I see. And doubt-less you thought that when Miss X had got enough blackbirds she could bake them into a pie.

Let us move on now to the fifth day of Christmas, when you received by recorded delivery a letter from Miss X's solicitors requiring you to cease and desist from pestering their client with unwanted and useless gifts. But you ignored that warning, didn't you?

I see. So you're asking the jury to believe, are you, that because you'd signed for these daily deliveries of pear trees, partridges, turtle doves, hens and blackbirds in advance, you were powerless to cancel the order?

And in any case, didn't you compound the offence by adding yet another present to the list, though mercifully not of an ornithological nature?

And what exactly was she supposed to make of these five gold rings?

You wanted her to marry you. Isn't it more usual, when taking a lady's hand in marriage, for the ring to be handed over by the best man rather than delivered in quintuplicate by Brinks-Mat armoured car? And in any case, you appear to have sent five rings daily for eight days in succession. It sounds, does it not, more like an invitation to wholesale bigamy than a straightforward proposal of marriage?

Very well. We've already established that on the sixth and seventh days of Christmas you reverted to the poultry motif and began sending out geese, some of them with new-laid eggs, and swans. I would like to bring you now to the eighth day of Christmas and ask you to tell his lordship and the jury what you sent round on that particular occasion, despite a further solicitor's letter delivered to you by hand.

Perhaps these maids a-milking will refresh your memory.

And on the ninth day?

Thank you. And the tenth?

I am obliged. And the drummers and pipers in the case are assembled outside the court, M'lud, in case they should be called. Perhaps your lordship and members of the jury will accept the strains of 'Amazing Grace', which I believe we can all hear quite clearly, as evidence of their presence.

On the eleventh day of Christmas Miss X was distressed to be served with a nuisance order by the borough council as a result of the rabble of milkmaids, drummers and pipers milling about her garden, not to mention the partridges, geese, swans and so on that by now had made her home resemble a bird sanctuary.

She was therefore left with no option but to take out an injunction against you and this she obtained from a judge in chambers that same morning, when you were solemnly warned to cease your unwelcome attentions on pain of imprisonment.

But you didn't cease them, did you? No, you promptly despatched, did you not – I do not want to lead you – a troupe of dancers, eleven in number?

And so we come to the twelfth day of Christmas, when you were taken into custody and these offences came to light. The tipstaff has told the court that when he came to arrest you for contempt he was just in time to see twelve men in coronets and ermine robes leaving your premises, having been apparently instructed to take themselves round to your true love's place and leap about. Do you deny that?

Thank you. The contempt proceedings are a matter for his lordship but it is on charges of obtaining goods and services by false pretences – to wit, acquiring birds, trees and gold rings and hiring musicians, dancers, milkmaids and peers of the realm by means of a forged credit card – that you are arraigned here today. Have you anything to say about these matters?

I am obliged to you, but I fear the jury may not regard it as a sufficient excuse that none of this would have happened if only you'd been able to get through to the gorillagram service.

Monday, December 22, 1986

Shar & Tray on Sunday

S haron and Tracy, transferred for the month from Perfumes and Toiletries to China and Glassware, were
taking advantage of a comparative lull in the January
Sales to discuss revived moves to allow Sunday trading.

Frowning absently at a potential customer who was standing
by a twenty-four-piece dinner service and waving a credit card,
Sharon said: 'Wayne read it in the paper whereby they're going
to pass a law for big shops to open on Sunday afternoons and
little shops to open on Sunday mornings as well. Or it could
be,' she conceded, 'the other way round.'

'Is it compulsive?' asked Tracy, avoiding eye contact with a
woman who was desirous of buying a set of wine glasses.
It was Tracy's experience that if you were seen serving one
customer, another would at once expect the same privilege.

'I don't fink so,' said Sharon. 'I fink if you don't want to
work on Sunday you don't have to.'

'You mean same as now, where if you don't feel like coming
in on Monday your Mum rings and says you've got flu?'

'Yeah, except that under this new law you won't even need
no sick note. It's to safeguard religious maniacs, according to
Wayne.'

'What's the idea of the big shops not opening till the afternoon, then?' asked Tracy.

'Dunno,' said Sharon. 'I expect it's so we can all go on having a lie-in.'

There was a pause while Sharon directed an unusually persistent would-be purchaser of a Wedgwood tea set to another cash desk, where with any luck her colleagues Debra and Bev would shortly be back from lunch.

Applying lip gloss with the assiduity of a craftsman varnishing a piece of furniture, Tracy said: 'I'm not sure I agree with Sunday opening, I mean apart from being able to buy things you reely need to get you through the day like ciggies and mags and crisps and fizzy drinks and Munchie bars and that.'

'Same as I said to Wayne,' agreed Sharon. 'I mean stands to reason, it's got to affect the traditional British Sunday, hasn't it? I mean if everybody's out shopping what's going to happen to all those fings we've been doing every Sunday all through history, like watching EastEnders and playing compact discs and going down the video arcade and ringing up the Chatline?'

'S'pose we could catch up on our hobbies on our days off,' suggested Tracy.

'Yeah, but it's not the same as doing them on Sunday, is it, Tray? I mean to say Sunday's special. Ever since I can remember, we've gone down the shopping precinct every Sunday afternoon to lean against the window of the British Home Stores. And what's going to happen now? We'll have to go in and buy sunnink.'

'Yeah, it's reely going to affect family life, Shar,' said Tracy gloomily, adding by way of a professional aside, 'Debra and Bev are back late – that woman I sent over's getting reely impatient.'

'I wonder if this dump'll open on Sundays?' mused Sharon.

''Spect so,' said Tracy. 'Anything for a fast buck, Shar. Just so long as they don't look to us to come in.'

'We couldn't even if they offer us double time,' Sharon pointed out. 'Not if we have to go Sunday shopping.'

Monday, January 30, 1989

178

Clogthorpe considers

C logthorpe District Council's Policy Steering Committee met behind closed doors this weekend to consider the implications of the independent Audit Commission's pessimistic report on the management of London's local authorities.

Opening the discussion, Councillor Sludgeworth said that while he had not read the report, it had all the hallmarks of one more Thatcher-inspired attack on the so-called Mentally Disadvantaged Left. He recommended chucking it on the fire-back.

Requesting Councillor Sludgeworth to hold his horses, Councillor Arkwright said that the report had the gravest implications. While Clogthorpe did not get a mention, he had no doubt that it would be Clogthorpe's turn next.

The report had said, and here Councillor Arkwright quoted, 'There is a spectre hanging over parts of London. They could become all too easily like parts of New York or Chicago.'

Mark his (Councillor Arkwright's) words, the next thing the committee knew, the Audit Commission would be comparing Clogthorpe with parts of Miami and San Francisco.

Councillor Tweedyman asked what was up with Miami? He had been there on a fact-finding trip with the Parks and Amenities Committee and his only complaint was that you could not get black pudding.

Councillor Hopcraft asked what was up with San Francisco, come to that? Speak as you found, but he had been there on a fact-finding trip with the Baths and Waterworks Committee, and he had been most favourably impressed, especially by the trams.

Asking if the committee could stick to the flaming point, Councillor Bulge (Chair) said the report was far more than a routine swipe at what he believed the Tory gutter press called the Not Quite All There Left. It made serious allegations of incompetence, waste and inefficiency by local government.

Councillor Neggs said he would go to the foot of their (Councillor and Mrs Neggs') stairs.

Councillor Sibkin inquired whether this did not beat the flipping band.

Councillor Elland moved that the Audit Commission's report be banned from all Clogthorpe public libraries forsooth.

The Chair said he would direct the Secretary to minute that last word as forthwith.

Cllr Elland said he had said forsooth and he meant forsooth. It was a bloody nerve. How dare the Audit Commission, which could not run a whelk stall, let alone deploy limited resources to maintain run-down housing stock such as the Clement Attlee Overspill Conurbation, have the nerve to criticise council house management performance? All right, so there were some sub-standard dwellings on the Nelson Mandela Estate which had lacked quantities of guttering and floorboards for some years, but had the Commission never heard of having four workmen off with bad backs?

Cllr Parkin said that Cllr Elland had had his say as Housing Chairman and now he (Cllr Parkin) was going to have his two-penn'orth as Chairman of the Finance Committee. The Audit Commission had mentioned waste. He defied the Commission to come up to Clogthorpe and show where one penny had been wasted, whether on the twin-town exploratory trip to Nicaragua where the entire Council and their lady wives had travelled not first-class, but club-class for most of the way; or on the new Directorate of Publicity offices where the marble statues surrounding the ornamental fountain had been painted with ordinary gold Dulux instead of the more expensive gold leaf. Cllr Parkin pointed out that resources would only stretch so far. It was the Rates Office he was running, not the Loaves and Fishes Office.

Cllr Nepworth said he was flabbergasted by the report's charge of bad management practices. Cllr Nepworth did not know whether the Chair of the Audit Commission had ever managed a bicycle shop, but he (Cllr Nepworth) had, that time when his brother-in-law was off with his nerves. He had also had considerable experience at running a milk-round, before taking his present position as Recreational Facilities Co-ordinator in the neighbouring borough. So the Commission was talking out of the back of its neck.

Cllr Tonks said it was a case of them that could, doing, and them that couldn't, teaching. The Audit Commission, which administratively speaking could not knock the skin off a rice pudding, ought to come to Clogthorpe to see what local government was all about. All right, so what if Clogthorpe did spend more on its facilities for the maritally deprived parent than any five other boroughs put together, while on the face of it providing the poorest service? What the moaning minnies forgot was that the staff ratio was also the highest in the country, thus providing much-needed job opportunities. Let the Audit Commission put that in its pipe and smoke it.

Winding up, Cllr Bulge said it had been a full and frank debate. It was now up to the ratepayers to judge whether the Audit Commission's outrageous and biased remarks were worth the paper they were printed on. He proposed punching a hole in the top right-hand corner of the report and hanging it up in the new superbog in Nuclear Free Square (formerly Town Hall Square) where it could be scrutinised at leisure.

Monday, February 2, 1987

Going do with UK plc

Long ago there used to be a big flashing neon sign on Piccadilly Circus reading EXPORT WE MUST OR BRITAIN GOES DO. What it was supposed to say, I guess, was EXPORT WE MUST OR BRITAIN

GOES DOWN but I never knew for certain since it flashed merrily away for months without the dud letters ever being repaired.

I used to wonder what contribution the neon sign business was making to the export drive and whether some lucky fluorescent magnate would receive a knighthood for services to expo as a result of this patriotic drive.

I can't remember exactly who financed the BRITAIN GOES DO campaign but I do recall that it was very much the fashion at the time for captains of industry to go around talking about Great Britain Ltd, so probably they had a whip-round between them.

Great Britain Ltd always struck me as a pretty repulsive conception, conjuring up as it did a New Jerusalem Trading Estate of biscuit-box greenfield factories, motorway slip roads and windowless hotel conference suites awash with change-jangling businessmen sporting plastic name tags and clutching black executive briefcases.

In the event Britain did not go do but I nourished the hope that Great Britain Ltd would. Alas, the old firm has just recently resurfaced with a new logo and a new company name – UK plc. The motto, too, has been somewhat updated: PREPARE FOR 1992 WE MUST OR BRITAIN GOES DO.

If anything, UK plc is even more dispiriting than Great Britain Ltd. At least it used to be possible for old-fashioned patriots to go around snorting, 'Let's put the Great back into Britain.' Whoever heard of putting the U back in K? (And by the way, why don't the feminists among us mark the twentieth anniversary of the Women's Lib movement with a demand for a United Queendom? Just a thought, girls.)

UK plc is a place of wealth-producing juggernauts thundering round and round the M25, of shirtsleeved executives caught in traffic jams barking into cellular telephones, of primary performance targets and corporate strategies and visioning implementation seminars and, oh yes, getting out there and selling. All this and the Eurotunnel too. And undoubtedly, without all this energy and without all those charts and diagrams with the company aims set out like Wellington's plan for the Battle of Waterloo, Britain would go do.

You are doing a grand job, chaps, but does the head of the Institute of Directors really have to go banging on about UK plc like the managing director of a company with cashflow problems haranguing the reps at their annual sales conference in the Churchill Suite of a system-built hotel on the outskirts of Slough?

Mr Peter Morgan (for it is he) evidently thinks he does, and few realistic thinkers would take issue with his roasting of the Establishment at the Institute's convention last week, for all that he was saying nothing that wasn't being said when UK plc was merely Great Britain Ltd. Nor can one argue with his subsequent lambasting of the public sector and the prevailing notion that trains should be run for the benefit of railway workers – although I did rather puzzle over his demand for the ambulancemen to produce more. What are they supposed to do? Run down an old lady and then put her on a stretcher?

It is when I read headlines like 'The scourge of the Establishment predicts company managers will be the heroes of the 1990s' that I beg to differ from Mr Morgan's philosophy. Company managers will not be the heroes of the 1990s. Company managing is simply not in the heroic mould. In the past we have hung up the bunting for explorers, inventors, entertainers, Empire builders and men of war, but I do not recall that we have ever put out more flags for the likes of the marketing director of Cadbury Schweppes.

Such company managers as have caught the popular imagination have done it not by company managing but by flying about in hot-air balloons or bonking bimbos or indulging in highly-publicised boardroom battles. As an activity in itself, their company managing fails to grip.

It is a deep-felt though curious belief of top businessmen that because they themselves are fascinated by industry and commerce, the rest of us should be equally riveted by balance sheets and profit margins and the valiant efforts of our great army of executives to ensure that Britain does not go do.

They simply cannot grasp that what they do for a crust, though eminently worthwhile, can never compare with the weather or the Test score or the latest episode of Neighbours when it comes to holding the attention span of the average shareholder of UK plc.

There was a letter in one of yesterday's Sunday papers complaining of the coverage in the review section: 'Arts nine pages, books five, science one, engineering none. If these are our priorities is it any wonder manufacturing is in decline?' Dear God, can there really be people who want to read about engineering over their Sunday breakfast? 'Today, only in the *Sunday Blather*: concrete stress in motorway bridge trusses.' Thank you, I'll take the sports pages.

UK plc is essentially a boring and depressing venture and facing the challenge of the Single Market will never replace watching International Bowls as a way of passing the long winter evenings. So let those who see this country merely as one great factory site surrounded by service areas and lorry parks and conference centres get on with what they are doing and leave the rest of us to our own devices.

But they'd better fix the neon sign before UK plc goes do.

Monday, March 5, 1990

Fare to muddling

I keep reading letters in the papers from people who claim to be baffled by British Rail's fare structure. I cannot understand what it is they cannot understand.

The other day, while waiting at Brighton ticket office behind a queue of irate customers all demanding to know why they can no longer travel on a return ticket to Victoria before 9.30 a.m. (the answer is that everyone going to London by train would keep coming back), I boned up on an armful of

British Rail Supersaver leaflets and it all seems crystal clear to me.

For the benefit of my fellow-passengers, I summarise some of British Rail's bargain offers.

The Staybreak. To ease the congestion caused by customers going on Awaybreaks, British Rail is to introduce a Staybreak ticket for people who prefer to remain at home. A Staybreak ticket entitles you not to travel anywhere in the country (except from North Wembley and Liverpool Lime Street) on selected days. Queue at inquiry office for details of when free leaflet will be available.

The Saverwaiver. For less than twice the cost of a Saver ticket you can buy a Saverwaiver which relieves you of all the annoying restrictions which apply to your Saver (except on Bank Holidays and at Exeter St David's). Ring Information to hear bored clerk asking you to hold the line.

The Supersaverwaiver. This is your offpeak leisure ticket which you may produce on any train except the 20.02 to Portsmouth Harbour whenever the ticket inspector looks sneeringly at your regular Supersaver ticket and says, 'Sorry, my friend, you'll have to pay the full fare, this isn't valid on a Saturday with an r in the month, and particularly when you're travelling to Gloucester Parkway.'

The Guesswork Card. If you are in possession of a Guesswork Card (available for this month only; allow twenty-eight days for delivery), and can guess what number between 1–1,000 the ticket clerk is thinking of, you are entitled to travel offpeak to over nine stations in the vast Network SouthEast at little more than full fare. Ask your accountant for details.

The Brainstrain. So long as you have brought your accountant with you to explain the difference between a Saver return and a Supersaver return, and you intend to be away for not less than ten days but no more than nine, the pair of you can travel anywhere except Bath Spa and Effingham Junction for the price of a five-day Awaybreak. Not valid Mondays to Fridays or on certain evening peak InterCity trains from Truro.

The Grannysaver. Using your Network card, you may buy a return ticket to any station in Britain (except Birmingham New Street and Bristol Temple Meads) at only twenty-five per cent more than the price of a single, provided you are going to see your grandmother and undertake to bring her back with you on a Senior Citizens Railcard (except to Exeter via Honiton).

The Earlybird. Using your grandmother's Senior Citizens Railcard plus three Unigate red striped bottle tops (green ones not valid), you may ship the old dear to Exeter via Honiton on any milk train.

The Farecop. Using your Farecop Card plus an out-of-date season ticket from East Croydon to London Bridge, you may travel anywhere within Network SouthEast (except King's Lynn, Banbury and Dover Western Docks on a Tuesday), until you are caught by an inspector when you may face a fine of £400 or one year's imprisonment or both. Ask at your local magistrates' court for details.

The Trainfare. This unique ticket allows you to travel to the station of your choice at any time and on any day and to return when you please within three months of issue, with no messing about at the ticket office whatsoever, so long as you are a bicycle. See very small print for conditions.

Thursday, June 7, 1990

Three cheers for the AAAA

The annual conference of the AAAA (the Association for the Annihilation of the Aberrant Apostrophe) took place under conditions of the strictest security at an undisclosed seaside resort earlier this week.

Road blocks were erected around the town and car boots searched for extraneous apostrophes. Delegates were frisked with electronic devices which can detect a misplaced apostrophe even in a personal letter concealed within several layers of clothing.

Demolition squads with sniffer dogs searched the drains for exploding apostrophes which could have been planted by an organisation of disaffected teachers with the fanatical belief that there are more important things to teach children, or 'the kids' as they are known to the group, than grammar and punctuation.

A police helicopter patrolled the sky to prevent the Life President's motorcade from being bombarded with illiterate handbills from the air. A minesweeper stood guard against the possibility of greengrocers and barrow-boys smuggling in aberrant apostrophes in crates of banana's and orange's. On the eve of the conference, hotel guests were dragged from their beds in the middle of the night and made to explain what they meant by the expression 'Your's' on their postcards home.

In his keynote address, the Life President of the AAAA said that while misuse of the apostrophe was as widespread as it ever was, so long as he had breath in his body he would never give way to the forces of ignorance, apathy and sheer bloodymindedness which could place fourteen aberrant apostrophes in a single quarter-page advertisement for a £49 camera.

He would resist, however, moves by some delegates to change the name of the AAAA to the AAAAAAA – Association for the Annihilation of the Aberrant Apostrophe and Allied Anomalies. While he sympathised with delegates who complained of the misuse of 'hopefully', the use of 'you and I' for 'you and me', the belief that it was all right to write 'alright', and sundry other offences against the English tongue, the AAAA simply did not have the resources to set itself up as a guardian of the language in general.

In fact the AAAA's overstretched staff had all its work cut out simply sorting and classifying the hundreds of aberrant apostrophes which reached Apostrophe House each year, then mounting and framing them for the annual Apostrophe Show in Hyde Park.

Delegate after delegate had drawn attention to the apostrophic vandalism being inflicted in our society today. There was the official sign in St James's warning of roadworks in St James's. There was the headmaster's newsletter informing parents that their children had learn't quite a lot from a particular project. There was the carphone describing itself as hand's free. There was the company advertising for a Directors's secretary. While the Life President could not go along with delegates who demanded long prison sentences as a deterrent against apostrophic offenders, he would use all the energy at his command to stamp out aberrant apostrophes.

In its education debate, Conference called upon teachers to stop letting children leave school in the belief that any word containing the letter s has to have a little hanging comma shoved into it like a currant in a bun. In the debate on the economy, Conference demanded a swingeing tax on aberrant apostrophes displayed on signboards. In the foreign affairs debate, Conference called for a customs embargo on apostrophe-tainted material imported from Taiwan and such places.

As usual, Conference ended with three hearty cheers for the Life President. Unfortunately, security having slackened on the final day so that dissidents were allowed to get into the hall, delegates were embarrassed to find themselves giving three hearty cheer's.

Thursday, October 27, 1988

The Channel Tram

The talk is of trams. Pray do not be alarmed. Those of a nervous disposition may leave at the earliest opportunity. Please form an orderly queue at the foot of this column, where the gates will be unlocked in due course. Women, children, and those allergic to nostalgia first.

The fair city of Manchester has heard something to its advantage this week, namely that it has got the thumbs-up for a Government grant covering the £110 million cost of bringing back the trams.

The system, to be known as the Metrolink – if I had my way the grant would be withheld until it had been sensibly renamed Manchester Corporation Tramways – will connect the city's main railway stations. The street tram-lines will be the first to be laid since – well, since they foolishly dug them up about thirty years ago.

It is well known that what Manchester thinks today the rest of the country thinks tomorrow and already Leeds, Birmingham, Bristol and other cities are thinking tram. Trams are the most efficient form of mass urban transport ever devised – which is why they were so popular in the first place. They were only got rid of because they seemed old-fashioned in that era of Poulsonisation when the cities became obsessed with shaking off their sooty past.

You used to be able to travel from Leeds to Liverpool by a series of tram networks, with only a short walk over the top of the Pennines from the last stop in Yorkshire to the first stop in Lancashire. Perhaps, with this spearhead operation in Manchester, those heady days will return.

But there is more. While the homely tramcar seems by contrast with your InterCity 125s a parochial kind of vehicle, we must think European these days. Let us turn to Grenoble in France where the city fathers, in their wisdom, have reintroduced the tram after a lapse of thirty-three lost years. Vive la Grenoble Corporation Tramways.

Is this a trend I see before me? I think it is. And it is only the beginning. You have to be a visionary when it comes to tramways and I have a vision.

Ladies and gentlemen, I give you the Channel Tram.

You know it makes sense. The Chunnel operation is in deep financial trouble. The controversial high-speed rail link is in a serious state of waffle. The Channel Tram – can you not see it lumbering up out of the chalky bowels of the earth at Dover harbour, rocking and swaying and blazing with light, its roller-blind indicator proudly proclaiming DEPOT ONLY? – is the solution to all their problems.

The conversion would be child's play – all they have to do is double the height of the present Tunnel (I am assuming – nay, I am insisting – that the Channel Tram will be a double-decker) and clad it in white lavatorial tiles. Then they have to change the name of the European Community to the Corporation of Europe, and European Corporation Tramways will be in business.

Disruption will be minimal. There may be minor inconvenience to the residents of south-east Kent while tram-lines are being laid along their High Streets and Acacia Avenues, but not a single home will have to be destroyed. And can you imagine angry deputations storming the House of Commons simply because a request stop has been put up outside their homes? On the contrary, they will be signing petitions clamouring for tram shelters.

There will be no need for elaborate ticket halls at King's Cross and elsewhere. Tickets will be issued by the conductor. The service will be from Dover Terminus to Calais Terminus, with connections on this side of the Channel to Liverpool (passengers please note: a short walk over the Pennines may be necessary) and on the French side to Paris and thence to Grenoble and all other European cities.

Channel trams will run every ten minutes or so unless a convoy of half-a-dozen or more is stuck in the Chunnel when passengers may experience a short delay. Smoking on the upper deck only. No more than fifteen standing. Kindly move down the car.

A mad fancy? Compare European Corporation Tramways with British Rail's megalomaniac dream of tearing up half of Kent and tell me whose vision is the sanest.

Thursday, October 26, 1989

190

The bad books hour

I can still recall the glow of pleasure with which I antici-
pated the last hour of school on Friday afternoons. Four
and five-sixths days did we labour, but between three
o'clock on Friday and the bell that would release us charging
out into the streets for the weekend, we were not required to
do any work.

A new teacher, either unaware of the convention or unwill-
ing to abide by it, tried to introduce an arithmetic test into
that last hallowed hour. He was practically lynched. The headmaster, who came in to see what all the commotion was about,
must have subsequently marked his card, for this unwelcome
break with tradition was never repeated.

What happened on Friday afternoons was that the teachers
had to occupy themselves with administrative chores such as
marking up their attendance registers and filling in their free
milk and dinner returns. For this, they needed a period of
peace and quiet. Entirely by way of buying this peace and
quiet – certainly not with any educational intent in mind – that
last hour of the week's lessons was designated a free reading
period.

The idea was that you brought your own book to school and
got on with it. If you didn't have a book, and many didn't, you
could choose one from the school's meagre stock of tattered
children's classics. Or you could bring a library book. The
only rule was that comics were barred – though comic annuals
were not. You could follow the adventures of Lord Snooty and
his Pals between hard covers, but not in the jam-smeared
twopenny version.

Since there are a goodly number of Fridays in the school
year and our somewhat cramped homes had not room for a
library on the scale of that at Bunkerton Castle (Lord Snooty's
family seat, doncherknow), there was a good deal of swopping
of such volumes as we owned between us. Thus, in exchange
for my much-treasured book of true horror stories – only on

loan, of course, since it included a priceless authentic account of a giant orchid which eats people – I was introduced to such literary gems as the *Sexton Blake Annual*, the adventures of Billy Bunter and the *Chums Annual*. Or rather, two-thirds of a *Chums Annual*, since the last 100 pages, including, to my annoyance, the final instalment of a lurid serial, had gone adrift from their moorings.

As I say, there was no higher motive to these afternoon sessions than that of keeping us out of the teacher's hair. But they did, allowing for a certain amount of pellet-flicking, get us into the habit of quietly reading to ourselves. Of course, there were those who would sooner have been kicking a ball about in the playground, and I dare say that a good number of my fellow urchins have never picked up a book since. But others became what our mothers always called 'big readers', in danger of ruining our eyesight by over-indulgence in library books.

I thought back to those Friday afternoons when I read of the biggest survey yet into the lifestyle of today's youngsters, by Exeter University's health education unit, which shows that while four in ten boys and nearly as many girls watch more than three hours of TV a night, 68 per cent of boys and 56 per cent of girls in their fifth year at school had not picked up a book for pleasure the evening before.

I don't think the picture is entirely as gloomy as those figures suggest, since we are still spending nearly £200m a year on children's books, but there is certainly a substantial and growing class of young people who do not read at all. I believe I may have mentioned before the headmistress who remarked sadly to me on the decline of that stock school character, the girl who always has her nose in a book.

Incidentally, I see that poor Enid Blyton has got a clogging again, being deliberately omitted from a list of 227 children's writers recommended by the latest government inquiry into the teaching of English. I believe Enid Blyton's *Sunny Stories* periodical, being not quite a comic, just scraped under the wire at those Friday afternoon reading sessions of ours. Certainly she would not have been banned on grounds of blandness. We were allowed to read whatever rubbish we liked, provided that no sound came out when our lips moved. It was the Bad Books Hour.

I have, down the years, remained firmly in favour of a set period being reserved each week for children to read by themselves, without particular reference to what it is they are reading. Some schools do it, some don't. From my own limited observation, I would say that schools which allow time for silent reading produce more 'big readers' than those which don't bother.

Should the last 100 pages of the *Chums Annual* for 1937 turn up in any quiet reading period, I should be glad to hear of it.

Monday, November 14, 1988

Trust in Dunroamin

A perfectly-preserved, fully-furnished Edwardian grocer's villa, unchanged since the early Thirties and with every detail intact from the pipes and baccy on the mantelpiece to the starched collars on the dressing table, has been acquired by the National Trust.

You only have to look at the pictures of No 7 Blyth Grove, Worksop, Notts, with its 1932 calendar still hanging in the front room, to be wafted in a cloud of Cut Cavendish back to the rock-solid world of Arnold Bennett and J B Priestley and G K Chesterton and muffins still for tea.

Rightly chuffed at this most untypical addition to its collection of stately piles and stretches of coastline, the National Trust's regional director Mr James Turner confessed himself surprised that until now the Trust had not preserved a single example of what he called 'the nation's most common form of housing, a middle-class town dwelling from around the turn of the century'.

Well now, it must not stop there. For, begging Mr Turner's pardon, there is an even more common form of housing, and that is the suburban semi or bungalow that was beginning to replace the Edwardian villa even as No 7 Blyth Grove sealed itself into its time capsule.

Somewhere in these islands there must be an ossified Dunroamin with a sunburst gate, a porthole window in the front porch, a Ford Popular in the garage and a flight of plaster ducks on the wall. The National Trust must grab it.

The period in which Dunroamin is preserved in Brown and Polson's aspic could be anywhere between 1935 and 1950, provided the essentials are there. The essentials include an uncut moquette three-piece suite, a barometer incorporating twin clothes brushes on hooks, a Bakelite wireless set with a fretwork front, and if possible the odd leaded window faintly reminiscent, with its picture of a galleon in full sail, of the fish and chip saloon down on the shopping parade.

There should be a crinoline-lady cover for the telephone and the works of Dornford Yates in the glass-fronted Minty bookshelves. Further reading matter should include the *Daily Sketch*, the *Radio Times* in glorious black and white, *Picture Post* or *Illustrated*, the *Happy Mag* and a rotogravure weekly devoted to the home and electric cookery.

There would be a lozenge-shaped mirror hanging on a chrome chain above the fawn tiled fireplace, which has to be fronted by a half-moon rug. The scent of cut flowers from the garden should mingle with the heady odour of Mansion Polish. A spot of Benaresware would not go amiss and a table lamp in the shape of an electro-plated naked lady holding what appears to be the full moon is a must.

I could go on, but you get the picture. You may even live in it. For this is the Ideal Home, bright, cheerful, labour-saving, modern without going overboard, and uniquely English. Never mind whether the church clock stands at ten to three, it is whether the privet hedge needs trimming that the English muse upon when they are abroad; and they know they are back home again when they see the first avenue of Dunroamins on the way back from the airport.

No matter how much it may be dragged up to date with satellite dishes and patios and fitted kitchens, Dunroamin's heart remains in the Thirties, when a three-bedroomed share of this Blessed Plot cost as little as £350. If the National Trust does not claim Dunroamin for the nation, I may just have to do it myself.

Thursday, June 13, 1991

Plague and peasant

A leaflette warning of ye perils of ye Blacke Death is to be carried by Messenger to every hovel in ye kingdom. With passages underlyned in redde by teams of monks, ye costlie document reflects ye Government's determination that ye plague can no longer be sweppte under ye rush-matte.

Ye leaflette warns hovel-holders bluntlie: 'Ye Blacke Death can kill.' Admytting that fourteenth-century alchemy has yette come up with no cure, it puts ye task of stamping out ye pestilence firmlie on ye shoulders of ye common people.

In starke question-and-answer terms, ye leaflette spelles out what everyonne wants to know about ye Blacke Death but is afrayd to aske:

Q How would I know if I had contracted ye Blacke Death?

A You would turn blacke and then you would dye. Other symptommes are a sore throatte and people fleeing when they see you coming.

195

Q What should I do if I thynke I have gotte it?

A Do not panick. First, chalke a crosse on your doore. Second, make your peace with your Maker. Third, dygge a lyme pitte and climb into it. Observing these simple pre-cautions will prottecte your neighbores whyle your Physician determynnes whether you are dying of ye Blacke Death or merelie of a Common Coldde.

Q How is ye Blacke Death spread?

A Alchemists believe that it is carried in ye air. Therefor, lette as little air as possible into your hovel, and do notte leave ye privie door open for ye goate to gette out.

Q Can I contact ye Blacke Death from kyssing?

A Onlie if you are giving ye Kisse of Lyfe to a vyctimme of ye Blacke Death.

Q Am I at riskke by washing my cloathes in ye sewer? I do not lyke to use ye well as there has been a dead pygge in it. Also, is it safe to eat ye pygge?

A It is safe to wash your cloathes in ye sewer onlie if you are wearing glovves. Ye pygge should be rinsed carefullie in ye streame before roasting.

Q We are very fond of rattes, which run freelie aboutte our hovel. Can they passe on ye plague?

A It depends whether you keepe ye rattes for food or as pettes. A well-cooked ratte boyled in ye stockpotte should do you no harme. Physicians do not yette know whether a byte from a ratte kept as a pette could pass on ye Blacke Death, but it could certainlie give you a nastie flesh-wounde. Why not give up your rattes and keep some other domestick vermynne, to be on ye sayfe side?

Q Can I catch ye Blacke Death from an infected leech?

A Possiblie. A used leech should never be employed for lettying bloode. Allways use leeches freshlie gathered from ye drayns.

Q What can I telle ye chyldrene about ye Blacke Death without fryghtening them?

A There is no neede to alarme ye kyddies. Simplie tell them that if they go near a door with ye chalked crosse on it, a giant will come and putte them in a sacke and eatte them. Also when ye charnel-house men come round callyng 'Bryng out your dedde', they should not be allowed to play around ye cartte.

196

Q Instead of puttyng ye winde up ye entire populace, would it notte be better for ye King's Mynisters to do somethyng pracktical aboutte ye Blacke Death, like fundyng a massyve research programme?

A That question is sedytious, and we will pretendde you have notte asked it.

Monday, November 24, 1986

A taste of EuroTat

M rs Thatcher has been celebrating the thirtieth anniversary of the EEC by haranguing the EuroSummit about EuroDebt and suchlike Euro horrors. It is a pity she did not, while she was about it, give them a piece of her mind on the subject of EuroTat.

If you seek to know what EuroTat is, look around you. It is that corporate third-rateness, as exemplified by – for example – the new telephone boxes, the characterless, uniform lettering that signposts every hospital in the land, the tacky refurbishment of London's Tube stations, that permeates all our lives.

EuroTat is the conference centre, the shopping mall, the leisure complex, the hypermarket, the airport, as designed by cost-conscious drawing-board hacks with the architectural sensitivity of a cowboy builder of breezeblock privvies in a lorry park.

EuroTat is the hotel where you wake up not knowing whether you are in Manchester or Munich. It is the office that has been put into the clutches of a design consultant whose avowed aim is to obliterate all traces of individuality by the wholesale application of oatmeal wallpaper and egg-box ceiling fixtures.

It is the stunted mini-skyscraper that is equally at home, yet equally out of place, in Brussels or Birmingham. It is the pathetic British Rail spokesman speaking of 'jazzing up our image'. It is the new streamlined logo. It is the replacement of a Victorian cast-iron pillar box with a tin can on a pole which looks as if it gives preference to letters franked with triangular stamps.

Now to be sure, tat has never been a stranger to this country. But it was good English tat. From the knitted egg-cosy and the crinoline-lady telephone cover to the flying geese and the garden gnome, from the Albert Memorial to Dunroamin, our tat was home-grown, and we had a soft spot for it. We laughed at it or we waxed sentimental over it.

Nobody laughs at EuroTat. The sleek EuroTat push-button telephone with the 'feature' that can automatically re-dial and still get the wrong number isn't funny, just nasty. And I mentioned the new EuroTat phone boxes. Can you imagine anyone mourning these shoddy plastic cabins when they fall to pieces, as they are ultimately bound to do? Can you see them being exported to America as a touch of old England?

English tat is the horsebrass-festooned Pig & Whistle. Euro-Tat is the cocktail-infested Pop Inn Doubles Bar. English tat is a synthetic cream horn on a doily in a fly-blown tea-shop. EuroTat is portion-controlled Black Forest gateau from the trolley in a North Circular Road steakhouse. English tat is the old covered market. EuroTat is the new shopping centre.

EuroTat is our lasting legacy from Europe, bequeathed to us by worried-looking men in dark suits with name badges on their lapels and executive briefcases stuffed with print-outs, who shuttle backwards and forwards from one look-alike airport hotel conference suite to another, costing things, portion-controlling, eliminating 'frills' (their word for anything that smacks of service) to increase profit margins.

EuroTat man cannot see a marble pillar without wishing to enclose it in Formica ('extensive refurbishment'), cannot enter a large room without experiencing an uncontrollable desire to lower the ceiling ('eliminating heat loss'), cannot encounter a wall without wanting to knock it down and replace it with room-dividers ('most cost-effective use of unit space').

Good design matters not a hoot to him. Standard design does. Everything must look the same. Not only does it do wonders for the corporate image but it eliminates profit loss by making the most cost-effective use of a central stockpile of EuroTat furnishings and fittings that look as if they had been bought at a fire sale. EuroTat is the unacceptable face of modernisation and the unacceptable backside of harmonisation.

The aim of EuroTat, secondary to that of making a fast buck, is to cause as little trouble as possible (that's not to be confused with causing as little offence as possible, which would be a fruitless ambition). EuroTat offers no challenges, takes no risks, aspires to no new horizons. Thus we have the paradoxical situation that while EuroTat jars every nerve and has the effect on the bystander of fingernails scraping down a blackboard, it is at the same time as bland as strained baby-food.

EuroTat is that aimless music in the lift, it is the subdued lighting, it is the carpeted foyer and the row of glass doors with the notice 'Use other door'. It is the ultimate portion-controlled cocoon of the motorway slip road hotel where, if EuroTat Man had his way, we would all permanently live in square, featureless rooms with make-your-own-bloody-coffee facilities 'for your convenience'; and name-badges on our lapels, and black executive briefcases containing the Expo InfoPak (there is EuroTatspeak, too) for the perpetual conference downstairs in the Churchill Suite to which we would be doomed to yo-yo up and down for the rest of our lives like so many EuroTat Flying Dutchmen.

Hang on to those flying geese.

Thursday, July 2, 1987

199

Messing about with bikes

I n a week in which the CBI announces the fullest order books for ten years it is sad, though not surprising, to learn from an exhibitor at the Olympia cycle show that the British bike is all but extinct.

Raleigh – what a splendiferous name for a bicycle – is now American-owned. The BMX boom has bubbled out. Where twenty years ago we imported only 5,000 bikes but exported a million, last year we imported 600,000 and exported just 150,000, and even they sported tyres, tubes, saddles, brakes, gears and chains manufactured in some other country.

In the circumstances, it seems tactless for Norman Tebbit to have advised the unemployed to get on their bikes – since the bikes they got on would very likely have been made in Taiwan.

It is the old story of a complacent industry just letting the competition ride all over it, but what makes it especially depressing is that there is something essentially English about the bicycle.

A bike, no matter how souped-up and new-fangled, conjures up images of leafy lanes and bowling home for tea by the light of a 'Voltalite' dynamo lamp ('No batteries! British made! Refuse substitutes! Send for testimonials!').

Pooter fans will recall how prominently the *Bicycle News* figures in *The Diary Of A Nobody*. Jerome K Jerome's three men, when they were not in a boat, were on their bikes, touring Germany (where pedals now come from). Sherlock Holmes rode a bike, though not so often as he took a cab. Jeeves rode a bike, but only in the country.

Nearer our own day, and more to the point, I myself rode a bike. Indeed, I came from a home which had bikes the way some houses have mice. My elder brother owned two (he still does) – a racer and a sit-up-and-beg. On wet days the racer, anointed in Vaseline, was brought into the living-room and propped against the sideboard. It could not be left in the scullery because that's where the sit-up-and-beg was, propped against the mangle.

Other bikes belonging to other brothers festooned the house and garden. I did not personally own a bike, but by virtue of being senior paper-boy I had first call on the newsagent's delivery bike, as sturdy a boneshaker as ever hurtled down a one-in-five hill with the rider's feet on the handlebars. The huge wicker pannier – over the front wheel – was felt to preclude me from membership of the Cyclists' Touring Club, but there were no other snags. Biking was bliss.

Few and forlorn were the dispossessed in our street who did not have access to a bicycle. But apart from the odd junior bike – fairy cycles, as they were known – magicked into the neighbourhood by Father Christmas, you never heard of anyone actually buying a bike, certainly not first-hand.

You swopped Brownie cameras and Meccano sets for bikes, you borrowed bikes, you – shall we say – acquired bikes. But you never went down to Curry's cycle shop for any item more substantial than an Ever-Ready lamp or a celluloid-sheathed pump (Made and Guaranteed by the Apex Inflator Co, Birmingham). In the dumps the British bike industry may be now, but it would have been in them four decades sooner had it looked to us for its profits.

The great thing about those biking days was that unlike skating or tree-climbing or sledging, where you were expected to maintain a certain standard if you wanted to keep your street credibility, you could pick your own level of involvement. Perhaps there was an idea among fixed wheel fans that freewheeling was for cissies, but that apart you took your cycling as seriously or as frivolously as you liked.

You could pack your saddle-bag with sandwiches and Tizer and head for Scarborough, perhaps getting as far as the local park boating lake – or you could never go further than the top of the street. You could regard your bike as a kamikaze instrument and career round the rim of a disused quarry on one wheel (the 'bucking broncho' position) or you could lean on your crossbar outside the public library and chat up girls. You could live in fear of getting your front wheel trapped in a tram-line or go out and do it on purpose.

Mending punctures, with a bowl of water to trace the

rupture with tell-tale bubbles, was great fun, as was giving your machine a coat of 'Club' enamel paint. You could, in fact, put in so much time tinkering with your oilcan or replacing accessories such as brake-blocks and shock-absorbers that your bike was rarely seen upright. But as Ratty didn't quite say in *The Wind In The Willows*, 'There is nothing – absolutely nothing – half so much worth doing as simply messing about with bikes.'

And now we're importing them from Taiwan. Oh dear. I do hope we're still making our own John Bull puncture outfits.

Thursday, March 26, 1987

Shar & Tray's Christmas

'Do you know what reely gets up my nose this Chrissy, Tray?', pouted Sharon, putting the finishing touches to the tinselled collecting tin with its Day-Glo inscription: STAFF BOX – A HAPPY XMA'S TO ALL OUR CUSTOMER'S. 'It's having to come back to work next Monday, just because they want to open for the sales. I call it reely mean.'

'So do I,' sulked Tracy, popping a Pina Colada chocolate liqueur into her rosebud mouth. 'Because don't you remember, when we had them office jobs, we used to get nearly a fortnight off for Chrissy?'

'*And* they always had this reely trif office party with green Chartreuse and blackcurrant and that, *and* sent you home in a taxi if you happened to feel a bit groggy style of thing,' sighed

Sharon, blowing a pink bubble gum bubble the size of a party balloon. 'Be lucky if we get so much as a packet of wine gums with this lot, stingy cows that they are.'

'Still, we do get staff discount, so mustn't grumble,' Tracy pointed out. 'I mean to say, it's the one time of year I wouldn't reely mind being stuck behind the perfume and toiletries counter if it wasn't for the flipping customers. What are you giving your Mum for Chrissy, Shar?'

'Perfume,' said Sharon. 'What are you giving yours?'

'Same here,' said Tracy. 'And I'm giving my Dad aftershave and Gran an avocado soap on a rope, and I might give Wayne some Oh-de-toilet if I'm still going out with him.'

'Oo, are you thinking of packing him in, Trace?' asked Sharon, her Barbie doll face for once betraying signs of animation.

'I am if he doesn't stop acting like a complete Wally,' said Tracy. 'He can be a reel pain sometimes, honestlee.'

'Why, what's he done, Tray?'

'Only let his Mum talk him into stopping at home over Chrissy and watch telly and pull crackers and that, instead of having a few frozen daiquiris down the Purple Pussycat then crashing into the disco, like everybody else. He's reely weird.'

'Still, without taking Wayne's side, I can see his Mum's point of view,' said Sharon. 'Because my Mum's like that about Chrissy. It's like a religion with her – she's reely traditional. I mean to say she sits through that Bing Crosby film year after year, even when she could be watching Bruce Springsteen on the other channel. She's ever so funnee.'

'What's she giving you for Chrissy?' enquired Tracy.

'Money,' said Sharon. 'She wanted to go up West and choose something for me, but I said to her, I says, Do leave it out, Mum, I says, because you'll only come back with the wrong thing, I says, and you don't want to go traipsing back on your bad feet to get a refund, I says, and besides, I says, you know what the shops are like at this time of the year, I says, it's just impossible to get served, I says.'

As Sharon concluded her narrative, Tracy gave her a little nudge and asked in a low voice that carried no further than the gloves and scarves department at the other end of the store, 'Shar, why is that bloke staring at us?'

'Which bloke?'

'The one standing at the counter waving his American Express card about.'

'Dunno,' said Sharon, having appraised the man in question. 'Mebbe he fancies you.'

Tracy giggled. Sharon giggled. Tracy gave Sharon a push. Sharon gave Tracy a shove. Presently the man went away. The delectable duo resumed their conversation.

'What are you giving Shane for Chrissy, Shar?' asked Tracy.

'Ciggies.'

'What's he giving you?'

'Ciggies.'

There was a long pause, in which Tracy assumed the air of frowning, fevered concentration appropriate to one nearing the solution of the formula for splitting the atom. At last she said: 'But if you're giving Shane ciggies and Shane's giving you ciggies, it just cancels itself out style of thing. I mean to say you might as well not give one another nothing – specially as you both smoke the same brand.'

'I know, but Shane said it's the thought that counts.'

'Coo, I never thought of that,' said Tracy.

'Neither did I,' admitted Sharon. 'He comes out with some reely brainy things sometimes, does Shane. F'r instance, only the other day he was saying, if we had peace on earth and goodwill to all men and that, he says, there wouldn't be no more wars, he says, so all these summit conferences style of thing, they could be done away with.'

'I dunno,' said Tracy uncertainly. 'I never did geometry at school.'

'Yes, you did, you silly cat,' said Sharon. 'Because don't you remember, Trace, when Miss Bates asked you where Bethlehem was, and you turned round and said Egypt?'

'I never, Shar! I said it was in Cairo!'

'Ah – you know that now, but you didn't know it then. Anyway, roll on six o'clock and getting home for a nice bubblebath. Happy Chrissy, Tray.'

'Happy Chrissy, Shar.'

Monday, December 21, 1987

Prophet motive

G reater Manchester police chief and AIDS scourge James Anderton made it known this week that he believes himself to have been chosen by God to be a prophet. You may have been wondering how this selection process came about.

God was in His heaven but all was not right with the world. The planet Earth was playing silly beggars again. Really, You could not turn Your back for five centuries. If it was not war it was famine, and if it was not famine it was pestilence.

God had come across a few plagues in His time but this AIDS epidemic was something else. It was getting to be like Sodom and Gomorrah all over again down there.

Something would have to be done. God raised a golden horn to His lips and summoned the Recording Angel.

'Park yourself at My right hand,' said God. 'The world is getting up My nostrils again and I want someone to go round putting the fear of Me into these people. How are we off for prophets?'

'There is no shortage, O Lord,' said the Recording Angel, producing a parchment scroll the size of a cable drum. 'Let's see – we have Abraham, Moses, Isaiah, Ezekiel, Daniel, Zephaniah, Obadiah, Habakkuk . . .'

'You are getting into the minor league now,' said God. 'Who was that fellow we used to have who was very hot on lamentations?'

'Jeremiah, O Lord,' said the Recording Angel. 'You know best in Your infinite wisdom, of course, but isn't he a bit gloomy for modern tastes?'

'Prophets are meant to be gloomy,' said God. 'They are not supposed to be a bundle of laughs. But I catch your drift. We need someone with a more up-to-date approach. Someone who can really get My message across in the media, rather than bellowing it from a rock and hoping his voice will carry.'

'There is always Bob Geldof,' said the Recording Angel.

'Yes, I know there is,' sighed God. 'But he would expect to be in my New Year's Honours List and I do not want to create any life saints. Who else have you got?'

'Richard Branson?'

'I want a prophet, not a pickle manufacturer.'

The Recording Angel held his peace. With billions of names on the books, God sometimes confused one soul with another. But you could not argue the toss. If He thought Richard Branson was a pickle manufacturer, then a pickle manufacturer he was. God was infallible.

'Keep them coming,' said God.

'The Archbishop of Canterbury?'

'No churchmen. No one ever takes a blind bit of notice of them, as I know to My cost.'

'Terry Wogan? Derek Jameson? Sir Robin Day? David Frost? Clive James? David Dimbleby? John Pilger? Michael Parkinson?'

God shook His head. 'They are all very good names which would look good on the credit titles of a prophesy, but I will tell you what the trouble is. They none of them have beards. Call Me old-fashioned, but I like My prophets to have beards.'

'How about Esther Rantzen?' asked the Recording Angel.

'Remind Me – does she have a beard?'

'No, O Lord, but she would glue one on for a giggle.'

There was a clap of thunder as a frown crossed God's brow. 'This is a full-scale plague we are talking about, not a mass outbreak of inefficiency by the Gas Board. Be serious.'

'If it is beards You are looking for,' suggested the Recording Angel, 'You could go farther and fare worse than Terry Waite.'

'You are on the right lines, but being omnipotent I happen to know that he is up to his eyebrows in missions of mercy. Name Me everyone else on the list with beards.'

The Recording Angel drew a deep breath and began at the A's. 'Anderton, Cyril James.'

God raised a finger. 'Anderton, Anderton, Anderton.' He mused. 'Don't tell Me, don't tell Me, it is on the tip of My tongue. I've got it – he is the chap who sold Britain on back-garden air raid shelters when they had that big War down there, am I right or wrong?'

God was infallible. There was no machinery for His being wrong. 'You are right, O Lord' said the Recording Angel. 'Mr Anderton popularised the Anderson shelter.'

'And you're sure he has a beard?'

'Absolutely, O Lord.'

'Then he's our man. Anyone who can get the British to dig six-foot trenches in their flower beds must have them eating out of his hand. They would follow him anywhere.'

The Recording Angel tried to sound a cautious note. 'The Big War was nearly fifty years ago, O Lord. You are going back a bit.'

God waved an airy hand. 'We talk in millennia up here, Sunshine. Fifty years is but the bat of an eyelid. I want this Anderton signed up as My personal prophet. Tell him to put out a Press release. And see that he keeps his beard.'

'Yes, O Lord.'

Thursday, January 22, 1987

The knell of St Clement's

Visiting an infants' class in a poor quarter of Greater Manchester a while ago, I was saddened to hear that most children starting school did not bring with them so much as a scrap of the old nursery rhymes or skipping rhymes. They knew the theme song from Neighbours, though.

Yesterday I was just as saddened to read that children in Stoke-on-Trent are having to be taught playground games. Their headmaster is commendably enterprising but it is on a par with them needing a crash course on Father Christmas.

It is a bleak moment we have arrived at when six-year-olds have to learn their hopscotch from a council Community Recreation adviser.

The games children play used to be part of their corporate intelligence. You assimilated the rules of hopscotch while you were still in your push-chair. Indeed, you mastered the rules of three versions of hopscotch, each more complex than the last, and you knew the words of In And Out The Windows better than that little moppet in Lionel Bart's commercial knows the words of There's An Abbey Ending.

Children's games had their golden age when there were streets to play in and no TV to watch. There must be pockets of small-fry civilisation where they survive but they are getting fewer. A mother got in the headlines the other week because her small daughter came home reciting One Potato Two Potato in Hindi. At least she had learned it, and the little Hindu girl who had taught it to the class had had it handed on to her. A cheering little story rather than otherwise, I thought.

It has always been a mystery about street games and their accompanying songs and rhymes how children from one end of the land to the other knew the rules and the words and the music without them ever being written down, or certainly not written down where children had access to them. I remember a few years ago teaching London Bridge Is Falling Down to a Russian kindergarten. I cannot have played London Bridge since I was three, yet there it still was, lodged in my mental golden treasury and just waiting to be passed on.

Another mystery of street play was how anyone knew when the season for a particular game started and finished. One evening you would go to bed sated with a month-long marbles tournament and the next day you would go out with your pockets full of marbles to find the street alive with whip and top.

You would dig your old whip and top out of the boot cupboard and refurbish the top with coloured chalks, but then lo and behold when you got out into the street with it, whip and top was already passé and the game of the moment was hopscotch, or French cricket, or tig, or rounders, or relieve-oh, or piggy in the middle. And this was not only in your street but over the whole city and indeed throughout the country, even throughout the entire world for all I know.

Did children have the instincts of migrating birds and if so, where is that instinct now?

Those indefatigable chroniclers of the lore and language of children, Iona and Peter Opie, scoured the land tracing singing games and clapping songs reaching back into antiquity. Oranges And Lemons, for instance, dates at least from the early eighteenth century, and its intricate rules were explained to the Opies by a nine-year-old urchin from Stepney:

'You 'ave to pick Oranges or Lemons, see. Two people 'ave to pick what they are, Oranges or Lemons, and the person who's 'ad their 'ead chopped off 'as to say Oranges or Lemons, and they go on their side and then in the end there's a tug-of-war and see who wins.'

The obscure rules of the Eton Wall Game can be no more elaborate, yet they were passed on by generation after generation of street arabs. Hands up everyone under twelve who knows Oranges And Lemons by heart today.

There is a haunting little scene in George Orwell's *1984* where an old man (who turns out, incidentally, to belong to the Thought Police) shows Winston Smith a fading print of St Clement Dane's church and says: 'Oranges and lemons, say the bells of St Clement's . . . That was a rhyme we had when I was a little boy. How it goes on I don't remember.' Who said Orwell's prophecies didn't come true?

Monday, May 14, 1990

Clogthorpe's day of rest

Clogthorpe District Council's General Purposes Committee met in emergency session yesterday, Sunday, to discuss the implications of the Sunday trading laws.

Cllr Bulge (Chair) said the Appeal Court had set the cat among the pigeons. If the Borough Solicitor had got his facts right, any council taking out a temporary injunction to stop a shopkeeper from opening on a Sunday could be liable for heavy damages if that injunction was later quashed.

Cllr Nepworth said he was sorry, the Chair had lost him.

The Chair said if Cllr Nepworth would put down his *Whippet Fancier's Telegraph & Greyhound Argus* he would explain. To take an example, the Savewise Supermart down the road reckoned on taking £10,000 a day.

Cllr Tweedyman said he was not bloody surprised, the price they charged for back bacon.

The Chair said back bacon was not at issue. What was at issue was that if the Council stopped the Savewise Supermart from trading on Sunday, and the Savewise Supermart fought the case, the Council might have to cough up what the store had lost in profits by not opening. It was a rum do.

Cllr Parkin said if the Savewise Supermart was making £10,000 a day it was a wonder they wanted to go to the bother of opening on a Sunday in the first place.

The Chair said he was not saying they did want to open on a Sunday. He was saying *if* they wanted to open on a Sunday. He was quoting a hypercritical case. Maybe he should have taken the example of the Clogthorpe Garden Gnome Centre, which he knew for a certain fact would give its right arm to trade on Sundays.

Cllr Potter asked why people couldn't buy their garden gnomes on a Saturday.

Cllr Tweedyman said it did not matter whether they bought

garden gnomes on Saturday, Sunday or Pancake Tuesday. The point was, if he had understood the Chair rightly, that if the Council served an injunction on the Clogthorpe Garden Gnome Centre to stop it opening on Sundays, and that squint-eyed sod of a manager took the Council to court over it, the General Purposes Fund would stand liable to fork out for about five hundred quidsworth of garden gnomes, birdbaths, sundials, urns, plastic cherubs and terracotta little lasses.

The Chair said and the rest.

Cllr Elland said he had an interest to declare. He was the owner of a stall in Clogthorpe covered market trading in Elland's Original Fudge and Marzipan Teacakes Since 1948. Was the Chair now saying that after working all the hours God sent through the week, he now had to open on Sunday?

The Chair, asking Cllr Elland not to be more doolally than he could help, said not had to, could do. That was if Cllr Elland was prepared to put his hand in his pocket and sue the Council if, in its wisdom, it made him shut down again.

Cllr Potter said he could not see the covered market opening on a Sunday just for the sale of a quarter of a pound of fudge and a few packets of wine gums.

Cllr Parkin reminded Cllr Potter that there were other traders in the covered market. Cllr Parkin's sister Beryl, for example, had a stall selling bargain crockery, which without blowing anybody's trumpet he could recommend most highly as being cheaper even than Woollie's. Not that she would be taking advantage of any relaxation in the Sunday trading laws, as she always went to her mother's for a custard and rhubarb tea on Sundays.

Cllr Nepworth said that was just as he had always said it should be. He had been telling the Council for years that if Sunday trading came in, some shops would open and the others wouldn't. It would remain a free country. Cllr Elland would open on a Sunday and Cllr Parkin's sister would remain closed.

Cllr Elland said he had no wish to open on a Sunday.

Cllr Nepworth said he could stay in bloody bed, then. He could please himself. What was wrong with shops opening or closing as the fit took them?

The Chair said the Council had always pursued a policy of Keep the Clogthorpe Sunday Special.

Cllr Potter said it was a pity that policy did not seem to extend to a certain person, no names no pack drill, who was in the habit of selling blue cabbages and King Edward potatoes from his allotment out of the back of a van on Sunday mornings.

Cllr Tweedyman asked if this was a reference to himself.

Cllr Potter said if the cap fitted Cllr Tweedyman, he should wear it.

Calling the meeting to order, the Chair said that if Cllr Tweedyman was trading in blue cabbages and King Edward potatoes on a Sunday morning, then he should have declared an interest. How much were they?

Cllr Tweedyman said he could do the Chair and other councillors, with the exception of Cllr Potter, a special price. The van was parked outside the Snivelling Coalman public house and would be open for business in about fifteen minutes. If members of the General Purposes Committee were at all interested in dawn-plucked cauliflowers, there were none better in Clogthorpe.

Stating that the Committee was never going to have a better opportunity of studying the pros and cons of Sunday trading at first hand, the Chair ruled that the meeting be adjourned to the Snivelling Coalman.

Monday, May 6, 1991

212

Shelf-room for reading

In my bumper catalogue of things that are no longer what they used to be, there is a special place for the public library. What was once a cloistered haven of serendipity where you could discover enchantment as well as the occasional kipper pressed into service as a bookmark, now frequently has the desolate air of being run by the social services department.

The joint is festooned with leaflets advising readers of their rights in various obscure areas where most of us didn't know we had any. The assistants wear boiler suits and look as if they disapprove of elitist books like *Alice In Wonderland*. The library is milling with people of all ages engaged in various activities such as working the photocopier or playing with the toys, but no one seems to be doing any actual reading.

The name of the game, as any librarian will tell you, is 'accessibility'. This is very much a buzz word in educational circles these days. Because children supposedly 'relate' (another buzz word) more to living composers than dead ones, Andrew Lloyd Webber is thought to be more accessible than Mozart. Strip cartoons are more accessible than Shakespeare. And a public library where the punters are not necessarily drawn in by love of books is more accessible than the stuffy old building smelling of Mansion polish where love of books was the sole reason for using the place.

A Government Minister (though a thousand miles away from the Arts, thank God) once boasted to me that he could transform the library services by introducing modern marketing techniques. His plans included live music, craft and poster shops, previews of the latest video releases and whatnot. Reading, as I recall, did not get much shelf-room in this grand design. The frightening thing is that if this chap had Arts Minister Richard Luce's job he would have half the libraries in the country with him.

Mr Luce himself has just published proposals for the future

of public libraries which would widen their scope but do not, I am relieved to note, envisage the installation of fruit machines and video games. Nor is the cornerstone of the library service, free borrowing, as yet threatened, though the idea of a special charge for newly-published novels and biographies may be the thin end of the chisel. It certainly seems a rum way of assuaging Mr Luce's anxieties over the fact that half the population never read books.

However, the Arts Minister's Green Paper has not gone down too well with the public library lobby, which complains that Mr Luce makes 'an increasingly artificial distinction between books and information on computers'. As Alan Beevers, national secretary of the Libraries Campaign, puts it: 'It is essential, if libraries are to continue to be guarantors of access to information and ideas, that technology should be available.'

We are back to 'accessibility'. And accessibility to libraries is no longer about books exclusively, or indeed books at all in some cases, but to access to information. Hm.

Anyone who uses the public libraries knows that they are obsessed with computerisation. Where once you had a neat card index in a polished mahogany nest of filing cabinets, you now have an electronic slum of sprawled print-outs and scattered microfiches. Doubtless the computer is enormously useful to librarians wishing to check that the book they have not got is equally unavailable in other branches, but I don't see why it has to be inflicted on the customer.

The fact is that most electronic gadgetry is the enemy of literature, while libraries are supposed to be the bastions of literature. The ubiquitous photocopier (battening on to a scandalous shortage of school books which is near-criminal in a nation drifting remorselessly towards mass sub-literacy) has created a system where children study one page of a book instead of the book itself. The equally ubiquitous video recorder has led many librarians to the extraordinary conclusion that since there are people who watch videos instead of reading books, they had better be catered for by the public libraries. This puts the libraries on a par with the fish and chip shop which starts selling pizzas and doner kebabs because the demand is there.

Fish and chip shops are about cod and rock salmon and libraries are about books, or should be. They are not, or shouldn't be, about any means of passing the time which does not involve taking a volume off a shelf and opening it at page one. 'Access to information', I will grant, calls for computer screens in the reference library. But the public lending library has no business to be all that very much different, except for the titles and better lighting, from its Victorian foundation.

If the day comes when the libraries stand empty because no one can be bothered reading any more, then so be it. They will have to find a fresh use for their premises, as the churches had to do. But there is no need to hurry the process along.

Thursday, February 25, 1988

Gory of the garden

Gardening hint. So many people do themselves a nasty injury by poking themselves in the eye with garden canes when bending over to sniff the flowers that the Consumers' Association recommends putting yogurt pots over the tops of the offending canes to prevent such painful occurrences.

All together now: I wandered lonely as a cloud, that floats on high o'er vales and hills, when all at once I saw a crowd, a host, of little yogurt pots.

But we mustn't snigger. As our Consumer Affairs Minister has pointed out in launching a garden safety campaign, thirty people were killed in gardening accidents last year. I can well believe it, my ninety-five-year-old grandfather having departed this earth after plunging a gardening fork into his foot.

And in the same period 30,000 were injured, one per cent of them by tripping over hosepipes. What percentage sustained bloody noses from treading on garden rakes is not disclosed but it must be a substantial number, as must the number of green-fingered victims of garden rollers, wheelbarrows, lawn-mowers, cucumber frames, pruning shears, sacks of chemical fertiliser, compost heaps and bonfires. Not to mention the time the vicar dropped a prize marrow on his foot at the harvest festival.

And yet you get poets insisting that a garden is a lovesome thing, God wot.

For me, those figures only go to confirm what I have long suspected: that a garden is a very good place to keep out of. Not that I have had much truck with gardens. On the two or three occasions when I have owned one I have had it paved over. A couple of chairs, a table with an umbrella stuck through it, something with ice and lemon in a long glass and a few potted plants are all I require from the space outside the window.

Not only do I not get on with gardens but I do not have a lot of time for gardeners either. I know theirs was the world's first hobby but you might as well make a recreation out of painting the Forth Bridge.

Take lawn-mowing. It is on a par with vacuum-cleaning. Yet millions of householders voluntarily choose to spend their leisure time fighting a never-ending battle with a malevolent stretch of grass. If they have time on their hands what's wrong with collecting stamps or making models of St Paul's Cathedral out of spent matches?

It is not as if they ever do anything with the lawn once it has been mown. They never sit on it – there isn't time. I have a gardeners' calendar in front of me and it lists thirty-four separate tasks for lawn custodians during the course of the year, over and above mowing. To wit: brush off dead leaves. Rake up moss. Weed. Brush off worm casts. Repair worn edges. Apply fertiliser dressing. Apply weedkiller. Apply

216

fungicide. Sow new lawn areas and protect from birds. Rake and scarify. And so on and so on.

And that's only the grass. There is the rest of the garden clamouring for attention. The hardy annuals, the herbaceous perennials, the bush fruits, the evergreens, the late potatoes. The month of April alone demands thirty-one assorted chores. Thin out those shoots. Sow those tomato seeds. Apply that mulch. Move those bedding plants. Tote that bale. Get a little drunk and you land in the cold frame.

And all for what? If you grow fruit and veg, I grant you have the satisfaction of your very own radish and redcurrant glut – provided you've done all the sowing, pruning, spraying and similar stretches of hard labour. The flowers you can sniff at, taking care not to poke yourself in the eye with a bent stick. The lawn you can look at, frowning as you note a molehill that was not there yesterday.

But gardeners pay little attention to the end result, and indeed your average garden is never finished. In gardening manuals and magazines you see pictures of gardens in a glossily completed state but in real life it's never like that. The lawn is disfigured by a snaking hosepipe and a great sack of fertiliser, the vegetable patch is bedecked with wire netting to keep off the birds, and the flower beds are sown with yogurt pots. The typical garden is so littered with tools and equipment and bags of plant food and so disfigured by work in progress that it resembles a flattened-out cement quarry.

A gardener's work, like woman's work, is never done; and when he's not doing it he's reading about it. Why, I wonder, are there no magazines or Saturday newspaper columns devoted to housework, which is gardening's indoor equivalent? Now is the time to make that bed. Wash breakfast things. Plump up all cushions and dust flat surfaces. Prepare vegetables for lunch.

Thomas Edward Brown (any relation to Capability Brown, I wonder?) got it wrong. To the dedicated gardener, it is not a garden which is a lovesome thing, God wot, it is the act of gardening, God help him. Gardeners garden for the sake of having gardened, and if everything happens to come up roses, that's a by-product.

Have a good Easter Monday now. Lift and split those

clumps of snowdrops, space out growing plants, prune early-flowering shrubs and don't get your foot stuck in the watering-can.

Monday, April 1, 1991

The log of The Larches

A London firm of estate agents has launched a log book scheme for home owners, whereby prospective buyers will be enabled to browse through a complete record of any property and its maintenance during its voyage through life.

Good idea – but like most good ideas not entirely a new one. It happens that I have in my possession the Log of the Des Res The Larches, a pleasant semi-detached craft moored in Suburbiton, Nor' Nor' West, which has been meticulously kept by its master, Mr J Scroggs, since he first took command. A few extracts:

October 1, 1988. Easterly winds. Rain. Removal van did not arrive until second dogwatch, men having misread chart and gone wrong way round M25. So begins our long journey on the choppy seas of home ownership. Wardrobe will not fit in master cabin.

October 2. Showers. Found that we can hear every word from radio room of craft next door, the Des Res Dunroamin. Previous skipper should have pointed out that The Larches has wafer-thin walls. Crew complaining about having to squeeze past wardrobe on landing on way to latrines.

218

October 15. Loose slate warnings. Builders having gone aloft, they report that they do not want to give us a botched job, whole roof will have to be replaced. Will think about it. Have taken carpenter on board to build fitted wardrobe – that's enough expense for one month.

October 20. Rain. Taking on water badly. Is streaming through ceiling of master cabin and into new fitted wardrobe, where it has formed puddle in my shirt drawer. Builders say we cannot say they did not warn us, now we will have to take our place in roof repair queue. Council refusing to tow away old wardrobe jettisoned in forard garden.

October 25. Fog. Italian wall tiles in galley coming unstuck one by one. Noticed for first time large piece of linoleum wedged between layers of double-glazing in portside bay window.

October 28. Sleet. Went aboard Des Res Dunroamin to complain about noise from radio room. Found Dunroamin skipper unco-operative and abusive, asking sarcastically if we were proposing to dump any more old furniture in forard garden. Rang local church on semi-to-shore telephone to ask if padre had any use for old wardrobe. Told only if we chop it up for firewood and deliver it ourselves.

October 29. Northerly winds. Called in double-glazing man to see what can be done about piece of lino wedged in portside bay window. Told that whole system will have to be dismantled, and since it's obsolescent anyway why don't we go whole hog and have new double-glazing fitted at advantageous rates. Signed on dotted line.

October 30. Becalmed. Door of new fitted wardrobe stuck. Carpenter insists there's nothing wrong with his workmanship, explanation is that wood has become warped owning to shirt drawer awash like bilges. Planed fitted wardrobe. It now swings open all the time.

November 3. Showers. Builders came aboard to carry out roof repairs. Say they will have to revise previous estimate in upward direction, as roof is now in worse state than it was. Do not see why state of old roof should affect price of new roof but am in no position to argue, as whole craft now leaking.

November 8. Council nailed notice to mast stating that old

wardrobe in forard garden is public nuisance and giving us seven days to get rid of it.

November 11. Rain. Master cabin still taking on water despite new roof. Builders insist dampness is due to condensation caused by new double-glazing. Find dislodged Italian wall tile wedged between new layers of double-glazing in galley.

November 12. Nor' easterly winds. Make bonfire of old wardrobe in forard garden, not realising that Des Res Dunroamin lies to nor' east of The Larches. Sparks set his rose bushes on fire.

November 13. Hail. Letter from Des Res Dunroamin's solicitor demanding compensation. Letter from building society giving notice of stiff increase in mooring fees. Discover that wardrobe fire has badly cracked starboard side double-glazing. Master cabin taking on hailstones the size of golf-balls. Thinking seriously of abandoning craft and putting her up for sale . . .

Thursday, December 15, 1988

Pennies from heaven

L et us be clear about this from the start. By new pennies I do not mean new pence, as those numismatical tiddly-winks were known for a while before we distilled their essential nastiness into the expression new pee, later to become simply pee. No, by new pennies I mean new pennies.

Back in the days when there were threepenny bits in Christmas puddings and jovial uncles doled out half-crowns to favoured nephews, the Royal Mint used to do its bit towards the festive season by distributing fresh supplies of the nation's coinage well in time for Christmas.

Thus, each December, every handful of change became a jackdaw's nest of shiny shillings, sparkling sixpences, flashing florins and bright new pennies, standing out like gems among the dulled and tarnished currency of the common round.

At my end of the money market, we saw little of the glittering silver coins that circulated up there in the rarefied higher reaches of the economy. Copper futures was about our level. And so we applied ourselves to the task of acquiring new pennies as blemishless and sharp in detail as the chocolate pennies on the Christmas tree, and as burnished as tea-shop kettles. We hoarded them. We treasured them. We were new penny Midases.

The magic of possessing coins of the realm dated for a year that was yet to come – for of course, these were technically New Year new pennies – was matched only by our wonderment at the shimmering new pennies themselves. It was like having a cache of doubloons – whatever doubloons might have been.

The getting together of our collection of new pennies occupied a major part of the Christmas preparations. It was a two-stage operation. First, raw wealth had to be accumulated – bent old halfpennies, mildewed Victorian pennies so worn that they were little more than dark copper wafers, the occasional hideously-disfigured threepenny bit that was apparently the victim of a hit and run accident with a steam roller.

This assembly of clapped-out coinage was acquired by singing carols, running errands, delving down the sides of sofas or, in desperation, outright begging. It then, in the hands of our street's sorceress's apprentices, had to be transmuted into gold – swapped, that is to say, for shiny new pennies.

Grown-up relatives and neighbours recognised that they had an obligation to hand over such new pennies as came into their possession. Sometimes, very near to Christmas, they might part with a brand new penny without requiring a battered old one in return, and that was a bonus. Other supplies were procured by bartering with sweetshops, pestering strangers at tram-stops or hanging about outside the Yorkshire Penny Bank accosting its customers, who we firmly believed must traffic entirely in pennies.

Come Christmas week, a collection of new pennies could amount to all of tenpence or elevenpence. There were rare cases where some junior Croesus's hoard would tip the shilling mark – but it was unheard of to trade in your new pennies for a new shilling or two new sixpences. That would have been like possessing an old master and keeping it in a bank vault.

What you did with your new pennies was to look at them, trickle them through your fingers, polish them on your sleeve, build them up in little stacks on the kitchen table, count them, marvel at them. They were brighter and more fascinating than the baubles on the tree.

Occasionally, you would take your new pennies for an outing, securely tied in a handkerchief in case they rolled out of your pocket and down the fever drain. The object of this expedition was to see what ultimately you would buy with them – for from the very outset you knew that like the doomed Christmas turkey, your seasonal fortune had but a limited lifespan.

Would it be spent on a chocolate Santa for your mother, a soap teddy bear for Dad and a marzipan pig for Gran – or a soap Santa, a marzipan teddy bear and a chocolate pig – or a marzipan Santa, a chocolate teddy bear and a soap pig? You stared into the twinkling sweetshop window for tormented hours, fingering your stock of new pennies until they grew hot to your touch. Then you took them home and counted them again in case one really had burned a hole in your pocket and fallen through it.

Among the sure-fire signs that Christmas was nigh, such as the mysterious parcels in the cistern cupboard and the build-up of supplies of tangerines and candied peel in the larder, was the slow discolouration of your new pennies, as they gradually lost their sheen with each succeeding day. You would shine them up, of course, but now they would leave tell-tale greenish marks on the hem of your mother's best Irish linen tablecloth, and by nightfall they would be dull again. That could mean only one thing. It was time to spend them.

You left it until the last possible minute on Christmas Eve and then you hurried off to the sweetshop, heart pounding in case the chocolate Santa or the marzipan pig had gone. You solemnly unwrapped your hanky full of treasure on the shop counter and handed it over, your pangs at losing your new pennies mitigated by the sights and smells of what money could buy. Then it was Christmas; and thereafter, for another year, a penny was but a penny, worth ten aniseed balls and nothing more.

Thursday, December 24, 1987

Awash with apostrophe's

The annual Apostrophe Show in London's Hyde Park, organised by the AAAA (Association for the Annihilation of the Aberrant Apostrophe) had to be abandoned this week when torrential rain flooded the giant marquee and washed thousands of apostrophes down Rotten Row.

Police horses reared, and crocodiles of school-children scattered in terror as the avalanche of apostrophes hurtled towards them. Firemen, many of them in inverted commas, fought steadfastly to divert a torrent of incorrect genitive singulars before they could clog London's drains – or drain's, as they would have become if polluted by aberrant apostrophes.

Commissionaires in protective brackets risked becoming contaminated into commissionaire's by courageously using upturned question marks to rake in hundreds of wrongly-punctuated negative particles as they floated past; while distinguished visitors to the Show, some of them in capital letters, hooked up nearly a tonne of escaped unacceptable informal contractions.

The hero of the calamity was a little boy in italics who caught a cluster of apostrophes with his fishing net just as they were about to be washed into the Serpentine. But for his quick thinking, the famous Hyde Park lake would now be the S'erpentine.

Despite these valiant efforts, the Show's organisers feared last night that enough apostrophes to convert all the bananas in all the greengrocers' shops in Britain into bunch'es of banana's were still unaccounted for. An AAAA spokesperson warned that the runaway apostrophes are likely to limpet themselves to the first piece of printed matter in their path, particularly any containing the letter S.

Already, several notices advising the public to be on the lookout for sodden apostrophes have been vandalised into notice's about s'odden apostrophe's.

The Apostrophe Show had only just been declared open by a royal personage when the skies opened and exhibits were washed from their stands.

Mr K Waterhouse, described as a newspaper columnist, said: 'It was worse than the Blitz. I was admiring a particularly fine specimen submitted by Mr K L of Newark, Notts, from his local army surplus store – EX-MILITARY SUPPLY'S, GOOD'S DISPLAY'D HERE OBTAIN'ABLE FROM BASE CAMP STORE'S – when suddenly I could feel my shoes and socks turning into shoe's and sock's.

'Looking down, I was horrified to see that I was up to my ankles in swirling apostrophes. It was like wading through a bog of misprints. I have never seen anything like it, not even in the *Guardian*.'

The royal guest of honour was studying a *Sunday Telegraph* picture headline sent in by B N of Luton, Beds, PRINCESS MARGARETS' FAIR FACE, when bodyguards dived for a display cabinet of aberrant apostrophes which had been washed off its stand and was bobbing towards him. A bystander said: 'He was within an ace of becoming Prince Charle's.'

As the freak downpour continued, the flooded marquee quickly began to resemble an alphabetical aquarium, with wrongly-punctuated signs, advertisements and even whole sentences sloshing about in the water.

A handbill from Pearl's Fish Restaurant, Buckhurst Hill, Essex, tipped as hot favourite in the Catering Section – WE ARE NOW TAKING BOOKING'S FOR XMAS PARTIE'S, FUNCTIONS, BUSINESS LUNCHE'S ETC – was swept from its owner's hands as he waded towards the judges' table.

A potential winner in the Signwriting Class, THUR'SDAY, submitted by G G C of Ealing, was wrenched from its context and later found bobbing forlornly amid the wreckage. A dazed nun clutching a crumpled ALL SOUL'S JUMBLE SALE handbill was comforted by an ambulance man whose own St Johns apostrophe had been washed away in the deluge.

In a statement from Apostrophe House last night, the Life President of the AAAA said: 'It is a tragedy. We had some magnificent entries this year, including really unusual ones such as the double-apostrophised GIFT'S'S & TOY'S'S shop sign loaned by L N of Swindon.

'They are all gone, as well as many irreplaceable exhibits from our Apostrophe Museum which we always put on display at our annual Show. The apostrophes were not insured. We shall just have to build up our collection again from scratch.

'Fortunately, our Members have always been most generous in donating aberrant apostrophes to the AAAA. Retired green-grocers can often be persuaded to make covenants signing over their accumulation of superfluous apostrophes – cabbage's, potatoe's etc – to the Association, and printers' proof-readers occasionally leave us their private collections in their wills.

'So despite this setback the AAAA's future is assured, especially since – as I had intended to remark, with mixed feelings in my annual address – aberrant apostrophes are now reproducing themselves like nymphomaniac rabbits wherever the printed word is found. I am sorry that this year's show was a wash-out. Now we must gird ourselves for our Winter Exhibition at Alexandra Palace.'

Later, an AAAA official firmly pooh-poohed the rumour that one of the water-logged apostrophes, a refugee from a

BAG'S FREE, BROLLY'S FREE advertisement by the John Myers mail-order firm, had made its way into this column and infiltrated the headline.

Thursday, July 23, 1987

Christmas cautions

I n conjunction with the Health Education Authority, the British Medical Association and the Chief Constables Association, I have been asked to wish you all a cautious Christmas.

While the festive season is the worst period of the year for domestic accidents, outbreaks of fire, assaults on the person, heart attacks, burglaries, drink-driving cases and incidence of food poisoning, there is no reason why we should not all have a moderately happy Christmas provided we take reasonable precautions, behave sensibly, wrap up well and do not overdo it.

Here, then, are some timely warnings for you to cut out and keep (but do for goodness sake be careful with the scissors).

DECORATIONS. Statistics show that twenty per cent of all broken or sprained limbs sustained over the Christmas period are caused by people falling off step-ladders while putting up the decorations. The safest way to put up the decorations is to do it while sober, or better still, pin them at such a height that a step-ladder is not needed. Care should be taken, however, that paper-chains are not strung across the room so tightly as to present a strangulation hazard during games of Visually Impaired Person's Buff. Note: unsterilised drawing-

226

pins can result in blood poisoning if trodden on in stockinged feet.

CRACKERS. These can cause such a nasty fright to children of a nervous disposition that it's amazing they've not been banned under some EC regulation or other (the crackers, that is, not the children – although come to think of it, putting the little perishers to bed during the Christmas party would reduce the risk of spillages and breakages). The solution is carefully to remove the bang from each cracker before use. Wear rubber gloves and do not throw the bangs on the fire. Do not smoke while removing bangs. In fact do not smoke at all.

HOLLY. Nasty, prickly stuff. See Government Health Warning in the carol 'The Holly And The Ivy': 'The holly bears a berry as bitter as any gall.' In extreme cases it can be fatal. As for mistletoe, not only is it a poisonous parasite but as we have already been warned by our American cousins, it is a major source of sexual harassment and is very probably responsible for the spread of AIDS to boot.

CHRISTMAS PUDDING WITH BRANDY BUTTER. Are you mad? Why not go the whole hog and give your guests a half-pound lump of suet each? If you insist on stuffing your loved ones with calories like so many Strasbourg geese, at least use wholemeal flour, bits of carrot instead of candied peel and low alcohol polyunsaturated cholesterol-free spread as a substitute for the brandy butter. Whatever you do, don't set the pudding alight. It may look spectacular, but the same effect can be achieved more safely by wiring it up to an electric light bulb.

TURKEY. I don't have to spell out the dangers attendant upon an undercooked turkey, especially if it's just come out of a microwave oven. Quite frankly, you'd be better off serving a slightly-stunned live sheep. If you must have a turkey, stick to vacuum-packed turkey slices but for God's sake keep an eye on the best-eaten-by date. If this means having your Christmas dinner on Saturday the 23rd, so be it.

NUTS. There is no reason why you should not enjoy the traditional nuts and wine within reason, provided that you are not driving, and so long as you take two elementary precautions. One: make sure the nuts are already shelled, in case a bit of flying Brazil nut flies out of the nutcrackers, lodges in someone's eye and lands you with a bill for compensation. Two: fit up a simple pulley device to the ceiling. In the event of any of your guests choking on a nut, just string them up by the heels and slap them firmly on the back.

CHRISTMAS CARDS. Do you realise how many pulp forests have to be felled each year just so that you can go on exchanging seasonal greetings with a bunch of people you don't see from one year's end to the next? Give Planet Earth a break and restrict your Christmas card list to six (recycled, of course). This will also help Mr Postman clear his backlog of bills, income tax demands, poll tax forms, Health Education Authority leaflets and other essential mail.

THE TREE. And talking of forests, you honestly think that a good way of celebrating the season of goodwill to all humankind is to go out and chop down a tree, do you? On top of which act of vandalism, you are then proposing to create a deliberate fire hazard by leaving the tree draped in defective winking lights while you go off to sing carols – thus exposing yourself, incidentally, to the peril of being mugged. Forget the tree and shove a sprig of privet in a plant-pot instead.

FUN AND GAMES. Tests prove that hide and seek, bobbing for apples, postman's knock, hunt the slipper, grandmother's footsteps and suchlike activities are more hazardous than skateboarding blindfolded round the M25. If you must risk getting everybody over-excited by playing games at Christmas, restrict yourself to a nice quiet round of Old Maid (though don't blame me if you get reported for ageism).

And finally, CHRISTMAS PRESENTS. You do realise, don't you, that the current flu epidemic is being spread entirely by sneezing hordes roaming around department stores and shopping malls in the restless search for oven gloves, aftershave lotion and soap on a rope? Do your health a favour and give book tokens.

Have a safe Christmas. You know it makes sense.

Thursday, December 21, 1989

228

The magic toyshop

I think you should be the first to know that I have decided not to buy Hamleys. I was tempted, to be sure, when I heard that the West End toy superstore was up for sale. I have always wanted a toyshop. But I have been brooding about it while taking a few days off and I have reached the conclusion that this is not the toyshop I want.

Hamleys is Aladdin's Cave crossed with Lilliput. Whatever toys rich adults have to play with, from a Porsche to a home computer, Hamleys have it in miniature for their pampered offspring. The kind of toyshop I have in mind is one where the most expensive item on offer is a Hornby train set.

There is nothing for it: I shall just have to set up on my own. Somewhere small, ideally in one of our sturdy, down-to-earth provincial townships where when a little girl asks for a doll's house she does not expect a Barbie-doll mansion so lavish that Father Christmas would have to take out a mortgage on it.

Perhaps I may look around for suitable premises while I am avoiding the Labour Party conference up in Blackpool this week.

Even more ideally it should be on a shopping parade between the chip shop and the sweet shop and just around the corner from a school. I should require no fewer than a dozen small noses pressed to the window at any given hour of the day.

My policy would be simple. It would be to stock all the toys that should – in a perfect world with that perfect equality that will be preached at the Winter Gardens this week – pass through the hands of every child at least once before childhood recedes into a golden haze.

Thus, for a start, we should do a roaring trade in yo-yos, cap pistols, kites, magnets, toy drums, roller-skates, penknives (including the blade for taking stones out of horses' hooves), and bumper packets of stamps containing at least one Tristan da Cunha triangular and something Slav the size of a perforated cigarette card.

My contention is that no childhood is complete without invisible ink, a device for seeing round corners, a conjuring set, another device that enables one to throw one's voice, a fountain-pen, and a propelling-pencil that writes in three colours. These items would be permanently in stock.

This magic toyshop – for I see it with the aura of a Christmas grotto all year round – would be resolutely sexist in outlook. There would be cowboy outfits and tram conductor sets for the boys, Red Indian squaw and nurses' outfits for the girls. There would be male-orientated Little Carpenter sets with hammer, saw, pincers and ruler secured to a card with rubber bands. There would be female-orientated dolly's tea-sets.

Oh yes, and bumper annuals. I feel strongly about bumper annuals. Today's children's annuals are so unbumper that you could almost roll them up and stuff them in a Christmas stocking. Reps trafficking in this short-weight fare will get short shrift. I want the bumper annuals I knew in my own childhood, as thick as family Bibles. Admittedly the pages were the thickness of plywood but they were good to handle. To be read, of course, under the bedclothes with the aid of a torch purchased from the magic toyshop.

You will have noticed that our catalogue does not extend to pedal cars, bicycles, extravagant rocking-horses, air rifles, cameras and such-like expensive impedimenta. Surely these are the kind of toys for which children yearn? Yes, but I didn't say my policy was to give the little perishers what they want. It is to give them what they ought to have.

My toyshop would be a kind of proficiency test centre for childhood. If you believe, with me, that every child ought to be able to play Monopoly and snakes and ladders before being allowed into adolescence, that every child ought to be able to hit the back of a bald head with a trajectory blown from a peashooter at ten yards, and that every child should gain its mouth-organ and John Bull printing outfit badges just as Cubs and Brownies gain their woodcraft badges, then you will give me your custom.

Monday, October 3, 1988

230

Shar & Tray on English

A s is their custom in the summer months, Sharon and Tracy were doing a spell as temps in the offices of the Eyeglass and General Insurance Company, where the hour of eleven found them enjoying their coffee break. (So, come to that, did the hours of nine, ten and noon.)

'Did you see in the paper where it says the biggest majority of secryties can't spell?' asked Sharon, unwrapping a low-cal chocolate wafer.

'Spell what?' asked Tracy.

Sharon re-checked her source. 'It don't say. But according to this survey what's come out, thirty-one per cent of companies fink their secryties don't know proper English.'

'Serve them right for giving jobs to foreigners,' said Tracy, dunking a macaroon. 'How much is thirty-one per cent, anyway?'

Deep corrugations in Sharon's flawless brow indicated that she was doing some furious mental arithmetic. 'Lemme see now, a per cent is a tenf, so you're talking about free-and-a-bit.'

'That ain't too bad then, if only free-and-a-bit companies fink their secryties can't read nor write proper,' said Tracy.

'Wonder if this dump is one of them?' mused Sharon.

'Shouldn't fink so. Cos when Mr Brize-Norton gave me a letter to do yesterday, I only had to type it four times. Do you know what he had the nerve to say after all that, though? "Oh, forget it, Tracy," he says, "I'll telephone them instead." Why couldn't he of done that in the first place instead of putting me to all that trouble?'

'Some people,' sympathised Sharon.

'I don't agree wiv spelling anyway,' said Tracy. 'Cos don't you remember at school when we had that English lesson once, and Miss Bates said Shakespeare couldn't spell?'

'That just shows all she knows, cos if he couldn't spell, how could he of written all them books? I mean to say, he wouldn't of known when to write thee and when to write thou, would he?'

'What's the difference?' asked Tracy.

'Between thee and thou? I don't fink there is none,' said Sharon.

'There you go, then.'

This avenue of debate having proved to be a cul-de-sac, Sharon attempted to widen the discussion by referring to another bit she had read in the paper, to the effect that there was a learned professor who believed that grammar should be studied through the medium of Kylie Minogue's lyrics.

'That's stupid,' said Tracy, having digested this information. 'That's reely, reely stupid. I mean to say she can't even sing proper. All right, so this professor might have a point – she's a lot better than Dickens, granted. But if they're going to learn kids English froo compact discs, what's wrong wiv Madonna?'

'She's American,' pointed out Sharon.

'Yeh, but it's all the same language, ennit? Cos the Yanks came from England back in history. Wiv Christopher Columbo.'

'All the same, they use a lot of different words from what we do,' insisted Sharon. 'Frinstance, same as where we say neether, they say neither.'

'I don't say neether,' corrected Tracy.

'Neither do I,' said Sharon. 'It must be the other way round.'

'Anyway,' said Tracy, fearing that she was being led into deeper waters than she could keep afloat in, 'what are these free-and-a-bit companies banging on about? What diffrence does it make whether their secryties don't write proper or not?'

'They say it makes a bad wossname wiv the customers.'

'That don't affect us then,' said Tracy decisively. 'Cos being an insurance company, this dump don't have no customers.'

'How do you make that out, Tray?'

'Well,' explained Tracy, by no means confidently. 'They don't sell nothing, do they?'

'They sell insurance,' said Sharon.

'Yeh, but the punters get their money back, don't they,

Shar? I mean to say if your mum takes out an insurance policy and the roof blows off, she don't pay them, they pay her.'

'What if the roof don't blow off, though?'

'I fink she has to wait till she's dead in that case,' said Tracy uncertainly. 'Then they pay it to you, being as how you're the next of skin.'

Feeling that the conversation was taking a morbid turn Sharon decided to sum up. 'Anyway, I just hope Mr Brize-Norton don't start accusing *me* of not knowing proper English, or he'll get a right mouthful.'

At this juncture, Sharon and Tracy found themselves under the basilisk gaze of the typing-pool supervisor. They hunched over their machines and gave a fair imitation of two audio-typists at work.

'Tray?' said Sharon after a perplexed moment.

'Wossat, Shar?'

'How do you spell "Dear Sir"?'

Thursday, June 27, 1991

Out of their class

A s was his inviolable Sunday custom after a visit to the Cross-eyed Ferret, Mr Ackroyd threw his dinner in the fire, belched, scratched, twanged his dangling braces and was about to clout the youngest of the voluminous Ackroyd brood for drinking HP sauce straight from the bottle, when his eye caught a headline on one of the pages of the *Daily Mail* which lined the table.

'By the 'eck!' exclaimed Mr Ackroyd. 'Hast read t'table-cloth, lass? They're doing away wi' t' working class!'

Mrs Ackroyd complacently sipped her saucer of tea. 'Nivver. T'Government wouldn't allow it. Who'd go down t' pit and empty t' middens if there were no working class?'

'It's Government what's doing it, tha gormless bitch!' stormed Mr Ackroyd, thumping the table with a violence which startled the family whippet in the act of stealing a York-shire pudding. 'Here – shift me boots off t' table and read what it says!'

Mrs Ackroyd read slowly, her lips moving. '"Blurred class divisions have forced t' Office of t' Population Census to aban-don its seventy-six year practice of grading people by social class." Well I'll go to t'foot of our stairs!'

'What's to become of us, lass, answer me that?' demanded Mr Ackroyd, wiping a sleeve across his nose.

'It says here,' advised Mrs Ackroyd, tracing her finger over a sauce-stained paragraph, 'that wi' greater affluence and a new generation of t'Yuppies, t'old class distinctions are no longer relevant. Ee, Albert, fancy us being abolished. Does tha think they'll serve an eviction order?'

'I'd like to see 'em try!' said Mr Ackroyd, grimly fingering his broad leather belt. 'As for t' class distinctions being abol-ished, t' first Ackroyd to become a Yuppie will know about it, so think on! Now go get some coal out o' t' bath and chuck it on t' fire.'

Meanwhile, behind the bay windows of Rosedene, a pleas-ant suburban semi, Mr and Mrs Brown were spending a quiet afternoon together in their tastefully-furnished lounge while the twins were out playing tennis.

Mrs Brown knitted a scarf while Mr Brown, contentedly puffing his pipe, read his newspaper.

'Good Lord!' exclaimed Mr Brown, as he turned a page. 'Have you read this, darling? They're scrapping the middle class – official!'

'Privatising it, do you mean, dear?' asked Mrs Brown tran-quilly, turning a row. 'Are you going to buy shares?'

'Not privatising it – abolishing it!' said Mr Brown, tapping his pipe out on the tiled fireplace in some agitation. 'See what it says here – "Middle class, upper class and working class are to be scrapped." It's the grammar schools all over again!'

'Oh dear,' said Mrs Brown, 'Mummy won't like that at all! Isn't there anything to be done about it?'

'There certainly is!' Mr Brown rose with determination.

'Now you're not going to do anything foolish, dear!' cautioned Mrs Brown. 'You're not going to march on the Town Hall like you did when they put up the rates?'

'A middle-class Englishman has to do what a middle-class Englishman has to do!' said Mr Brown. He kissed his wife lightly on the forehead. 'You'd better start supper without me, darling – I may be some time.'

'Oh, Edwin!' cried Mrs Brown, dropping her knitting in alarm as he headed for the study. 'You're not . . . ?'

'I must, my dear. Yes, Angela, I'm going to write to my MP.'

And in the library of Upshot Hall, a Jacobean pile deep in the shires, Lady Upshot decisively crossed unsuitable names off her list of possible guests for the forthcoming hunt ball, while Lord Upshot cleaned his sporting rifle in the gunroom next door. A discreet cough announced the presence of Jorkens, the family retainer.

'Beg pardon, my lady, but there is a person at the door. He says he is from the Office of Population Census.'

'Send him round to the servants' entrance, Jorkens.'

'I did, my lady, but he was most insistent you be informed that the upper class is to be abolished.'

'Nonsense, Jorkens. You have been drinking.'

'I regret to say that the information is correct, my lady. Britain officially becomes a classless society in 1991.'

In the stunned silence that followed, a shot rang out from next door. Her face impassive, Lady Upshot rose, looked into the gunroom at the lifeless figure of her husband stretched out on a tiger-skin rug, and closed the door.

'Very well, Jorkens, that will be all. Oh, and tell Cook we shall only require dinner for one this evening.'

Monday, November 2, 1987

235

Arnold again

I see that British Rail's brother-in-law Arnold has made another killing. He has persuaded BR to progressively phase out its five regions – the original LMS, LNER, GWR, SR and Scottish systems – and replace them by about twenty smaller units, to be called profit centres.

I can just imagine the telephone conversation in which Arnold sold British Rail on the idea.

'Hello, Barry? Arnold this end. How's Elaine? Still on the blue pills, is she?'

'No, she's on the pink ones now, Arnold, her back's been playing her up. How's Moira and the boys?'

'Couldn't be better, Barry, and we're all looking forward to a nice break in the time-share flat. Listen, I'll tell you why I'm ringing. Do you happen to be thinking about reorganising British Rail again in the foreseeable future?'

'Thinking about it, Arnold? We never think about anything else. What's on your mind?'

'Well, you remember that last reorganisation scheme I sold you, Barry, where you started calling all the passengers customers? No complaints, I hope?'

'None at all, Arnold, except from the customers. What about it?'

'I've been thinking, Barry. What are customers for? What is their only purpose?'

'I'm not with you, Arnold.'

'You're a bit slow on the uptake this morning, Barry. Listen. Why does British Rail need customers?'

'I sometimes wonder, Arnold.'

'The same as any other organisation, Barry – to make a profit. That's what business is all about, right?'

'True enough, Arnold. Can't argue with that.'

'Which is why you now call passengers customers, right? But that's only half the story, Barry. Why are you still calling your regions regions?'

'Come again, Arnold?'

'Your regions, your stations, your ticket-offices, Barry, are where your mug punters queue to pour money into British Rail's pocket, am I right or am I right?'

'That's if we can get the staff to turn up, Arnold.'

'So why don't you stop pussyfooting around and call them what they really are, so the customers will know where they stand? Profit centres. Little gold-mines, Barry. Bingo!'

'Bingo, Arnold – I like it.'

'I'll send you all the details with my invoice, Barry. Love to Elaine. Must dash – I've got a golf match fixed up with British Telecom's nephew.'

'Just one thing before you ring off, Arnold. What do we call the regions that aren't making a profit? Loss centres?'

'Listen – don't do anything till you hear from me, Barry. Promise?'

Monday, April 15, 1991

The care free zone

S he was about fourteen, going on thirty. If she ever had a childhood, it must have been as brief as a butterfly's lifespan. Too listless to hold out her hand for alms, she squatted in a wretched huddle on the pavement, a filthy blanket around her shoulders, her eyes dead, her pinched, oval face a mezzotint of misery.

The last time I saw such a sight was in the stews of Cairo. But this was in the Earl's Court Road on a hot afternoon in

May. I believe I was the only one who gave her a second glance.

Child destitution has been slowly creeping up on us in these high-tech years of democratic capitalism, fancy house prices, chrome-and-mirror cocktail bars and Hooray Henries making a shady killing in the City. Don't tell Sid, but there are scenes to behold that could have come straight out of Hogarth.

Prostitutes as young as thirteen are a common sight in some of the inner cities. Teenage winos lie around shop doorways or squabble for territory with the adult dossers who are their peers. Tourists arriving at Victoria from Gatwick or the Channel ports are bemused to find themselves accosted by child beggars, as they would be in Calcutta. In Soho, there are school-leavers sleeping in cardboard boxes.

The obverse of Victorian prosperity was deprivation and the depravity which deprivation brings; and the starkest picture in that tableau of squalor was child poverty. Poverty not only of material possessions but poverty of hope, poverty of opportunity, poverty of education, of health, of moral values.

We are not witnessing the second coming of Victoria but even the most sanguine of observers would have to agree that Charles Dickens, were he around now, would not go short of copy. But we do not have a Dickens – although I see that the lady who has been described by some as his modern successor has produced what one critic called the first SDP novel.

The child hookers and the kids in cardboard boxes blink in the dazzle of the arc lights as another TV documentary is made about their plight; everybody watches, the programme gets some excellent reviews and picks up an award or two, and everybody forgets. They forget because no one is making them remember. Nobody cares.

Perhaps I had better qualify that. Of course this country is packed with compassionate people, and there are legions of dedicated torch-bearers all caring away like billy-ho. But corporately we don't care, or certainly we don't care enough. Every political reign has its own particular, peculiar voice and the voice of the present reign – more of a rasp, really – is not a caring one.

This is not to say that Mrs Thatcher doesn't care or even that her followers don't care (though some of them notoriously don't give a hoot). But the climate of Thatcherism has produced a breed, mainly of Yuppies and Young Fogies, who look on this squalid passing show with something like a sneer.

They are cocky and confident enough to put their – shall we say controversial – views into circulation with wit and cogency. And thus it has come about that it is quite respectable again, as it was in the Thirties, to attack the unemployed for idleness, the poor for fecklessness, and those tribes of lost children for bringing it upon themselves, aided and abetted by striking teachers and stupid parents. And nobody cares.

There is a cause here, aching for political embrace. The nation does have a conscience, but it has to be stirred, for it has long been asleep – lulled by the unrelenting materialism of the governing party and the undiminishing partisanship of the party that no longer governs and looks increasingly as if it never will again.

Caring about others – not about oneself, not about one's tax slice or one's pay rise or one's own job – is in itself a fine cause, and all the more noble when the others we are asked to care about are the young who should be our hope and future. It is a cause particularly suited to the Welsh passion and rhetoric of Neil Kinnock, who is himself a caring person and has it in him, I still believe, to arouse that sleeping conscience.

Yet where is Kinnock's Labour Party? Squabbling about black sections and the inalienable right of every constituency committee to do its bit towards losing the election. Beavering away, at grass-roots level or rather weedroots level, for the brave new cause of a council grant to buy a photocopier for the single-parent lesbian workshop. One Labour candidate I know fought (and lost) last week's council elections on the issue of women's rights and the need for more cycle paths. Tonight Ken Livingstone, the darling of the Left, goes on TV to discuss the burning injustice of Page Three girls. What a party!

It is curious how Labour, the party that cares or used to, has come to be dominated, in so many areas, by utterly selfish people concerned only with their own puny, single-issue bigoted cause. Yet all around them is this panorama of despair with children begging in the streets or reeling in the gutter.

And nobody cares. The political activists were never more active, but they are living in a care free zone.

Monday, May 11, 1987

Parts we couldn't reach

Meccano back, eh? I'll overlook them bringing it out in Yuppie yellow and blue, instead of the traditional Fever Hospital green and red. Maybe now I can complete my working model of the Singapore Floating Dock.

I never got very far with this ambitious project, owing to a shortage of parts. In fact given my Meccano resources I would have been better advised to embark on something a mite simpler, like a miniature perforated table.

You see, I didn't actually own a Meccano set. (Altogether now: Aahh!) Neither did anyone else I knew. Someone around our neighbourhood must have had one though, for there were bits of Meccano in every toy cupboard.

Along with marbles and cigarette cards, Meccano's strips, rods, pinions, flanged plates and double-arm cranks circulated as street currency. While no one ever cornered enough parts through these complex swapping deals to construct anything more elaborate than a crude railway signal, they did have other uses. A single Meccano No 2 strip would afford hours of amusement.

You could lick the paint off it. You could press it to your face so that the perforations raised tiny bubbles of flesh. You could dig a grave for a pet mouse with it, then press it into service as a tombstone. You could clamp it between your teeth and make a sproinging noise with it.

I confess, though, that the principal pleasure I got out of Meccano was a peripheral and vicarious one. A boy I knew called Leonard took the *Meccano Magazine*, a fat lavishly illustrated monthly, price sixpence. Why, when like the rest of us he had but a couple of flanged plates to his name, I've no idea. Perhaps because the mag had little to do with Meccano itself, being filled with articles on How Your Daily Bread Is Made and the Work Of A Railway Goods Yard.

Though Leonard's mother would not allow his *Meccano Mag* on the swaps market – it would have fetched two *Dandy*s and a *Wizard*, minimum – close friends with clean hands were admitted to his house to read it. I made a point of sucking up to Leonard and every month paid him a social call.

I already knew how our daily bread was made – your mother lined up the baking-tins and got on with it. (That reminds me – how long is it since anyone last heard that evocative street taunt, 'Go on home, your mother wants your boots for loaf-tins'?) As for the work of a railway goods yard, I had already seen that at first hand, and been raced off the premises by the watchman. It was not *Meccano Mag*'s editorial contents I craved on my monthly fix, but its advertisements.

There was page after page of them. It was like a Christmas catalogue appearing all year round, a Santa's Workshop in photogravure. There were Hornby trains, Hamley's gliders, Bassett-Lowke's motor-boats, Lott's real stone building bricks, Adana printing machines. There were roller-skates and cameras and bicycles and air pistols – all this and Meccano too.

The little circle of readers centring on Leonard's house had as much hope of owning any of this loot as of going up in a Sunderland flying-boat, but we could look, couldn't we? It was like pressing your nose to a toyshop window without your cold breath steaming up the pane and spoiling the view.

As Christmas approaches, we're hearing once again the familiar puritan plaint that it's very hard on badly-off parents to have to explain to their children that they can't afford the lavish and expensive toys being plugged on the TV commercials. I must say our parents never had the slightest difficulty in that regard.

We realised that there was Meccano for the rich and Meccano for the poor. One lot came in boxes with a picture of a mobile crane on the lid, and the other, slightly bent, was swapped in the street or snatched by some juvenile Burke and Hare from the graves of pet mice. This is not to say we meekly accepted our station in life. We were realists, and what we lacked in No 2 strips and curved flanged plates we made up for in ingenuity and imagination.

It might have looked like a heap of rusty metal and string to you but to me it was the Singapore Floating Dock.

Thursday, November 26, 1987

As Things turn out

Hats off to Professor James Lake of the University of California, who has identified the common ancestor of all living creatures – a sulphur-eating single-cell organism which spent its days basking in boiling hot springs some 3,000 million years ago.

The Professor does not give this thing a name. Let us, for the time being, call it the Thing. And now on to my own researches, which have unearthed a record of what must have been one of the first conversations ever, between two of the earliest Things.

242

'What are you thinking about?' asked the first Thing, breaking a silence of several decades.

'Oh, this and that,' said the second Thing. 'Mostly about evolution, if you must know.'

'What is evolution?' asked the first Thing.

'It is where we turn into animals and fish and that,' said the second Thing.

'What are animals and fish?' asked the first Thing, with his inquiring mind.

'They are, or rather will be when we turn into them, forms of life that hang about on four legs mooing or grunting as the case may be,' said the second Thing. 'Apart from the fish, that is, which will swim around and waggle their tails.'

'I cannot see this happening,' said the first Thing, having digested this information. 'Not in my lifetime, anyway.'

'Of course it won't be in your lifetime, you wet nelly!' exclaimed the second Thing. 'It will take millions of years, if not billions.'

The second Thing snapped off a bit of sulphur and sucked it meditatively. 'We will also,' he continued, 'evolve into birds, flying about and tweeting.'

The first Thing attempted to shake his head in dissent, but then recollected that he did not possess one. 'If God had wanted us to fly,' he said sententiously, 'He would have given us wings.'

'He has every intention of giving us wings, nerd!' said the second Thing testily. 'That's what I'm telling you. And after that He will turn us into people.'

'What are people?' asked the first Thing.

'Human beings,' said the second Thing. 'Creatures that will walk the earth in trousers, shooting one another and that.'

'It does not sound like a barrel of laughs,' said the first Thing.

'Perhaps I am painting too bleak a picture,' conceded the second Thing. 'They will not all be shooting one another, by any manner of means. They will not even all wear trousers. Some of them will wear mini-skirts.'

'I like it,' said the first Thing.

'And they will spend their lives doing all sorts of interesting things,' predicted the second Thing.

'What kind of interesting things?'

'All the interesting things you can think of, mate. Like painting pictures and inventing steam engines and building cathedrals and jogging and washing the car and that. Oh, yes, and propagating the species – that will be activity numero uno. I know we propagate sometimes, but they will propagate like there is no tomorrow.'

'Coo!' said the first Thing. 'What else will they do?'

'It will depend on the personalities involved,' said the second Thing. 'Some will climb mountains, some will become school-teachers, professional golfers, disc-jockeys and so on. A small minority of them will become a bloke named Arthur Scargill. Others will go into politics.'

'What are politics?' asked the first Thing.

'It is too complicated to explain in full,' said the second Thing. 'But there will be these political parties – Labour, Conservative, Liberal and Social Democrat. And the people who run them will wear big rosettes and troll up and down the country making speeches about education and value-added tax and that.'

'Big deal,' said the first Thing.

'Well it can't be any more boring than lolling about in a boiling hot spring day in, day out,' retorted the second Thing, falling into a sulk.

'Have a bit of sulphur,' said the first Thing in conciliatory tones, after a month or two's brooding silence.

'Ta,' said the second Thing, mollified. He nibbled the peace offering thoughtfully. 'Do you believe in reincarnation?'

'What is reincarnation?' asked the first Thing.

'It is when you die and come back as something else,' said the second Thing. 'Like one of these creatures on four legs I was telling you about.'

'Crikey!' said the first Thing.

'Or as people, even. Just think,' said the second Thing dreamily, 'if you and me decided to go into politics, three million years from now we could end up as leaders of the Liberal Party and the Social Democrats.'

The first Thing considered this possibility.

'I do believe,' he said at last, 'that I have more of a future sitting here in this boiling hot spring, eating sulphur.'

Monday, January 18, 1988